# Best Hikes Near
## Philadelphia

## HELP US KEEP THIS GUIDE UP TO DATE

Every effort has been made by the authors and editors to make this guide as accurate and useful as possible. However, many things can change after a guide is published—trails are rerouted, regulations change, techniques evolve, facilities come under new management, and so forth.

We welcome your comments concerning your experiences with this guide and how you feel it could be improved and kept up to date. While we may not be able to respond to all comments and suggestions, we'll take them to heart, and we'll also make certain to share them with the authors. Please send your comments and suggestions to the following address:

FalconGuides
Reader Response / Editorial Department
246 Goose Lane
Guilford, CT 06437

Or you may e-mail us at: editorial@falcon.com

**Thanks for your input, and happy trails!**

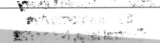

# Best Hikes Near
## Philadelphia

JOHN L. AND DEBRA YOUNG

**FALCON**GUIDES

GUILFORD, CONNECTICUT
HELENA, MONTANA

**For Cameron James Young**

**FALCON**GUIDES®

An imprint of Rowman & Littlefield
Falcon, FalconGuides, and Outfit Your Mind are registered trademarks of Rowman & Littlefield.

Distributed by NATIONAL BOOK NETWORK

Copyright © 2016 by Rowman & Littlefield

Maps by Alena Joy Pearce © Rowman & Littlefield
All interior photos by the authors

British Library Cataloguing-in-Publication Information Available

**Library of Congress Cataloging-in-Publication Data**
Young, John L.
  Best hikes near Philadelphia / John L. and Debra Young.
    pages cm
  "Distributed by NATIONAL BOOK NETWORK"—T.p. verso.
  Includes index.
  ISBN 978-1-4930-0671-7 (paperback) — ISBN 978-1-4930-1836-9 (e-book)  1.  Hiking—Pennsylvania—Philadelphia Region—Guidebooks. 2.  Philadelphia Region (Pa.)—Guidebooks. I. Title.
  GV199.42.P4Y68 2016
  796.5109748'11—dc23
                                                                                    2015028558

∞™ The paper used in this publication meets the minimum requirements of American National Standard for Information Sciences—Permanence of Paper for Printed Library Materials, ANSI / NISO Z39.48-1992.

The authors and Rowman & Littlefield assume no liability for accidents happening to, or injuries sustained by, readers who engage in the activities described in this book.

# Contents

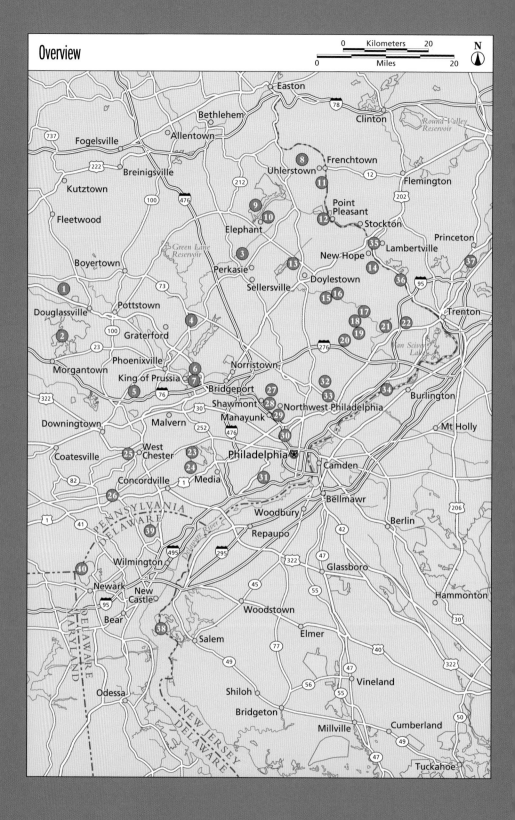

Kilometers

Miles

N

# Acknowledgments

As always, I want to thank my wife and coauthor Debra Young for her support in taking care of all the behind-the-scenes work—such as running the campsite—that doesn't show up on the pages of a hiking book. This time out Debra was also in charge of mapping the hikes. Thanks also to Keith Miller for his technical help in the field and to John Shinaberger for his software support.

Thanks to all our hike mates: Keith and Cindy Miller, John and Pat Shinaberger, Linda and Earl Ross, Jim and Linda Houghtling, Bobbie and Michael Muntz, Charlene James, Jonella Roundtree, and Amy Houghtling.

Many thanks also to Craig Wilhelm, commander of the Nase-Kraft American Legion Post 255 in Sellersville; to Bob Opacki and Michele Buckley of the New Jersey Office of Communications and Visitor Services; Georgia Brous of the Bensalem Visitor Center; Beryl Himmelsback of Nockamixon State Park; and Teri Murphy of Plumstead Township.

Thanks to Devon and Bob Bauman, and John and Sarah Haubert of Ringing Rocks Family Campground in Upper Black Eddy for their outstanding hospitality.

We'd also like to thank our top-notch editors, Imee Curiel and Meredith Dias, for their patience and attention to detail.

# Introduction

As the author of *Hiking Pennsylvania*, I had of course hiked all over the state, including the southeastern tip and the Philadelphia area. In the Poconos I hiked to the top of Mount Minsi to get a once-in-a-lifetime view—and photo—of the Delaware River. For *Hiking the Poconos*, I hiked sections of the McDade Trail from Milford Beach to Hialeah Beach, alongside the Delaware River. In short, I thought I knew what the Delaware River looked like; but, when I dropped south of I-80 on River Road to begin this book, I saw a whole new river and, to my eyes, a whole new world of hiking possibilities.

As with my previous hiking guides, for *Best Hikes Near Philadelphia*, I sought out sights I'd never seen before. And when I found an historical feature or an aspect of the land that affected the waterways, the forests, or hiking trails, I investigated it so that you and I would know just what is underfoot, and how it got to be that way.

• • •

With a population of over 4 million people in the Greater Philadelphia area, you wouldn't think it would be possible to find a peaceful spot where you could be alone. But as you'll find out in this hiking guide, which includes hikes in New Jersey and Delaware, it is indeed possible. Of course, you don't have to be alone to enjoy the beauty of a cascading waterfall or to come upon an old stone boundary wall or to examine the ruins of a dilapidated springhouse: You could bring your significant other, your children, your best canine buddy, or maybe your camera, or all of the above.

The beauty of the hikes in this book is that you won't have to take a personal loan to buy gas for your vehicle, simply because none of the hikes listed here are more than 60 miles from Center City. Also, the majority of the hikes in this guide are rated easy to moderate, so other than a good pair of hiking boots, you won't need any expensive equipment to enjoy these day hikes. In short, there are no hard climbs in this guidebook; on the other hand, there are plenty of easy to moderate hills to climb in southeastern Pennsylvania.

Much of the terrain immediately around Philadelphia is relatively flat, and of course, that's because the city, along with southeastern parts of Bucks and Delaware Counties, sits on the geological region known as the Atlantic Coastal Plain. If you were to travel inland from the Coastal Plain you would come to a point, known as the fall line, where the Coastal Plain meets the Piedmont Plateau. In fact, on one hike you will come to a rare instance where you can hike on one side of the fall line, step over it, and then hike on the other side.

Many of the hikes in the Philadelphia area are centered around or affected by streams and rivers; indeed, most of the hikes in the state of Pennsylvania are centered around water features such as streams, rivers, waterfalls, lakes, and canals. The reason for this is simple: The state of Pennsylvania has more moving water than any other state, including Alaska.

The streams and waterways in this book were once a major part of the life force of the early inhabitants of this area, the Lenni Lenape Indians. Of course the Lenape fished these streams and rivers; they also used fish baskets and fish traps, as well as spears and bows and arrows, to harvest the bounty. Lenape hunters tracked their prey to the streams, and in this way the animals created a path to and alongside the streams, and as the hunters followed them, their footsteps helped create a walking path.

Many of these paths remain today as hiking trails. One such trail, in Point Pleasant Community Park, is named after a Lenape chief called Chief Running Deer and runs alongside Tohickon Creek just a mile or so from where the Tohickon enters the Delaware River.

Another fascinating aspect of hiking in the Philadelphia area is that, seemingly, everywhere you hike, you find history. For example, if you were hiking on the Neshaminy State Park River Walk Trail way back in 1682, you could have been there when 38-year-old William Penn made his first land purchase in the New World. The tract he purchased bordered on the north side of Neshaminy Creek where the Neshaminy enters the Delaware River.

If you were hiking that same trail a year later in 1683, you would have had the chance to see William Penn make his second land purchase, this time of the land that borders the Neshaminy from the south. This second tract included the land that is today Neshaminy State Park.

One of the most picturesque hikes in the book is the Pennypack Park Trail, which runs alongside a section of the 22.6-mile-long Pennypack Creek, as it makes its way southeast through Montgomery and Bucks Counties and the northeast section of the city of Philadelphia before it empties into the Delaware River. In 1697 William Penn ordered the first bridge to be built across Pennypack Creek along the King's Highway, known today as Frankford Avenue. The bridge is still in use today.

The fall line runs across the creek at Frankford Avenue, and while this factor ended navigation on the Pennypack, the rushing water it created downstream provided the water power for a number of flour mills built along the creek. Most of these mills were owned by Swedish colonists who had settled in the area they called Pennypack Valley before William Penn appeared. Nonetheless, the mills thrived for two reasons: There was an almost unlimited source of water power, and the location of the mills, which was closer to the mouth of the creek, gave farmers a place to sell their grain that was closer than the city of Philadelphia.

Business was good in the Pennypack Valley, so good in fact that in 1701 William Penn built his own mill along the creek and called it the Pemmapecka Mill.

A long list of well-known and notable historical figures who helped create the history of this area, and in doing so, wrote the first chapter of American History. Many of the hikes in this book will lead you to the front door of their lives. For example, the first hike in the book will lead you on a tour through the homestead and farm where American icon Daniel Boone was born and spent his youth walking the same forest paths that you will.

John James Audubon's stepmother and stepfather shipped him off from their home in France to southeastern Pennsylvania with the hope that he could take charge of his father's lead mine at a place called Mill Grove. But, as we know, John James had a much different lifestyle in mind when he landed here. He spent his days studying the animals and birds on the 175-acre estate, and in the same woods that remain intact today he conceived the idea of banding birds to see if they returned to the same site year after year.

It is said that the role of the writer is to make old things new and new things familiar. I have set out to do just that; so enjoy my work, and most of all, enjoy the hikes!

## Weather

The Philadelphia area experiences all four seasons. The average annual precipitation in Philadelphia is 41.45 inches, and moisture is fairly evenly distributed over the course of the year. The greatest precipitation totals normally occur in early summer, with a maximum of 4.3 inches in July. The infrequent passage of a tropical storm in late summer may bring exceptionally high rainfall totals in August and September.

Winters are much less severe compared with those in northern and western Pennsylvania. The average January maximum/minimum temperatures are 38°F/23°F and the mean annual snowfall is about 20 inches. Most winter storms are accompanied by a mixture of snow, sleet, and rain due to the modifying effects of mild Atlantic air.

Summers are notoriously hot and humid in the Atlantic Coastal Plain, with minimal breezes to stir the heat and humidity. Summer nights are often warm and sticky, made more uncomfortable by the urban heat island effect of buildings and pavement absorbing and retaining heat. The mean July maximum/minimum temperatures in Philadelphia are 86°F/67°F, and readings of 90°F or higher occur on average about twenty-three days a year.

The Piedmont begins in the northwestern part of Philadelphia and continues westward just beyond Gettysburg to the foothills of the Appalachians. The topography is comprised of rolling hills and extensive farmland, with elevations ranging from 100 to 600 feet above mean sea level.

The climate of southeastern Pennsylvania is beneficial for farming, and fruit trees and vegetables generally enjoy a frost-free season of about 170 to 180 days.

Winters are usually moderate, with few days of subzero temperatures. The average January maximum temperature ranges from 36°F to 39°F; minimum readings vary from 18°F to 22°F. Winter snowfall is relatively light, averaging from 25 to 35 inches; also, the majority of winter storms are accompanied by a mixture of snow and rain.

### Temperature Chart

| Month | Average High (°F) | Average Low (°F) | Precipitation (in.) |
|---|---|---|---|
| January | 38° | 23° | 3.03 |
| February | 41° | 25° | 2.64 |
| March | 51° | 33° | 3.78 |
| April | 62° | 42° | 3.54 |
| May | 73° | 51° | 3.7 |
| June | 81° | 61° | 3.03 |
| July | 86° | 66° | 4.33 |
| August | 84° | 64° | 3.5 |
| September | 76° | 57° | 3.78 |
| October | 64° | 45° | 3.19 |
| November | 53° | 36° | 2.99 |
| December | 42° | 28° | 3.34 |

## Flora and Fauna

The heavily forested areas and scenic rolling hills of the Piedmont Province provide habitat for plants and animals in the urban environment of southeastern Pennsylvania. Hiking the forests you'll see large oak, poplar, hickory, maple, walnut, and beech trees. You will also encounter a sparse understory of mountain laurel, rhododendron, and other bushy plants.

One of the most common animals to be seen in southeastern Pennsylvania is the state mammal, the white-tailed deer; hikers will also see foxes, raccoons, rabbits, and squirrels, as well as songbirds and migratory species, all of which use the woodlands, streams, lakes, and wetlands for food and cover. A number of areas in the Philadelphia region have been designated by the National Audubon Society as Important Bird Area(s) and Important Mammal Area(s).

Hikers will also encounter managed areas, where volunteers and volunteer organizations essentially take over the land and, in one instance, plant fields with native grasses in order to provide a habitat for many animals and hopefully encourage the return of field birds such as the bobolink, grasshopper sparrow, and meadowlark.

There are also a number of preserves located throughout the Delaware River Valley, where land managers and volunteers are attempting to reforest and restore forests and degraded farm fields into young floodplain forests, grassy floodplain areas, cool season grassland, warm season grassland, old field succession, as well as pine and mixed hardwood plantations dominated by mixed oaks and other hardwoods.

There are three hikes in this book that are part of the Natural Lands Trust, which owns and manages 42 nature preserves on 22,000 acres in eastern Pennsylvania and southern New Jersey. One of these is the John Heinz National Wildlife Refuge and when you hike it you will experience what the coastal area looked like before man moved in and changed it; when you hike the Binky Lee and the Stroud Preserves, you will learn how the Europeans came to this area and established farms on the rolling hills of the Piedmont.

As the population of the area grew, the land from many of these early farms was sold to developers to create housing developments. By the twentieth century much of the open land was developed, and that's when the Natural Lands Trust stepped in and began procuring the land and set about returning it to its natural state.

As for the flora of the area, there is no better way to experience local plant life than to hike Bowman's Hill Wildflower Preserve, Tyler Arboretum, or the Five Mile Woods Nature Preserve. In fact when you hike Five Mile Woods, you will be able to experience the plant life on both sides of the fall line, which runs through the preserve and separates the Coastal Plain from the Piedmont Plateau.

## Wilderness Restrictions/Regulations
Hiking in the Greater Philadelphia area is done primarily in city, county, community, and state parks, as well as in privately owned and managed nature preserves and in national parks such as Valley Forge and Washington Crossing. And, of course, there are a number of privately held, nonprofit nature centers that charge an entrance fee to help offset operating expenses. The Philadelphia area also has the privately owned Longwood Gardens and Tyler Arboretum, which charge entrance fees and post schedules as to when the parks are open.

Some of the best hiking in the Philadelphia area is in state parks. Indeed, much of the best hiking in the states of Pennsylvania, Delaware, and New Jersey is in its state parks. There is no fee for day-use state parks in Pennsylvania; some day-use state parks in Delaware charge an entrance fee; and in New Jersey, both residents and nonresidents can buy an annual pass.

## Getting Around
### Area Codes
The area code for Philadelphia is 215. This area code also covers four counties: Bucks, Delaware, Montgomery, and Philadelphia.

The 267 area code covers the same four counties as 215: Bucks, Delaware, Montgomery, and Philadelphia.

The 484 area code covers these counties: Berks, Bucks, Carbon, Chester, Delaware, Lehigh, Montgomery, and Northampton.

The 610 area code covers these counties: Berks, Bucks, Carbon, Chester, Delaware, Lehigh, Monroe, Montgomery, Northampton, and Philadelphia.

## Roads

For the purposes of this guide, the best hikes near Philadelphia are confined to a one-hour drive from Center City in downtown Philadelphia. This stretches west to Elverson; north to Upper Black Eddy; south to Harrisonville, New Jersey; and east to Princeton, New Jersey.

A number of major interstates converge just north of the city of Philadelphia. The following are used extensively throughout the book: I-76, I-276, I-476, and I-95.

The Pennsylvania Department of Transportation offers information on road conditions on its website at www.dot.state.pa.us. From November 1 to April 30 only, condition reports are also available by calling toll-free (888) 783-6783 (in state) and (717) 783-5186 (out of state). You can access information on public transportation, welcome centers, highway maps, pedestrian walkways, and more on the website.

## By Air

Philadelphia International Airport (PHL) is 11.6 miles south of Center City Philadelphia off I-95. 8000 Essington Ave., Philadelphia 19153; (215) 937-6937 (for general information); contactPHL@phl.org.

## By Rail

Southeastern Pennsylvania Transportation Authority, 1234 Market St., Philadelphia 19107; (215) 580-7800; www.septa.org.

## By Bus

Southeastern Pennsylvania Transportation Authority Bus serves Bucks, Chester, Delaware, Montgomery, and Philadelphia Counties. 1234 Market St., 4th Floor, Philadelphia 19107; (215) 580-7800; Twitter: @SEPTA SOCIAL; Facebook: Facebook.com/septaphilly.

## Visitor Information

Visit Philadelphia, 30 S. 17th St., Ste. 2010, Philadelphia 19104; (215) 599-0776; visitphilly.com; questions@visitphilly.com.

# How to Use This Guide

Take a close enough look, and you'll find that this guide contains just about everything you'll ever need to choose, plan for, enjoy, and survive a hike near Philadelphia. Stuffed with useful Philadelphia-area information, *Best Hikes Near Philadelphia* features forty mapped and cued hikes. Here's an outline of the book's major components:

Each section begins with an **introduction to the region,** in which you're given a sweeping look at the lay of the land. Each hike then starts with a short **summary** of the hike's highlights. These quick overviews give you a taste of the hiking adventures to follow. You'll learn about the trail terrain and what surprises each route has to offer.

Following the overview you'll find the **hike specs:** quick, nitty-gritty details of the hike. Most are self-explanatory, but here are some details on others:

**Distance:** The total distance of the recommended route—one-way for loop hikes, the round-trip on an out-and-back or lollipop hike, point-to-point for a shuttle. Options are additional.

**Hiking time:** The average time it will take to cover the route. It is based on the total distance, elevation gain, and condition and difficulty of the trail. Your fitness level will also affect your time.

**Difficulty:** Each hike has been assigned a level of difficulty. The rating system was developed from several sources and personal experience. These levels are meant to be a guideline only and may prove easier or harder for different people depending on ability and physical fitness.

*Easy*—Five miles or less total trip distance in one day, with minimal elevation gain, and paved or smooth-surfaced dirt trail.

*Moderate*—Up to 10 miles total trip distance in one day, with moderate elevation gain and potentially rough terrain.

*Difficult*—More than 10 miles total trip distance in one day, strenuous elevation gains, and rough and/or rocky terrain.

**Trail surface:** General information about what to expect underfoot.

**Seasons:** General information on the best time of year to hike.

**Other trail users:** Such as horseback riders, mountain bikers, inline skaters, and so on.

**Canine compatibility:** Know the trail regulations before you take your dog hiking with you. Dogs are not allowed on several trails in this book.

**Land status:** National forest, county open space, national park wilderness, and so on.

**Fees and permits:** Whether you need to carry any money with you for park entrance fees and permits.

**Maps:** This is a list of other maps to supplement the maps in this book. USGS maps are the best source for accurate topographical information, but the local park map may show more recent trails. Use both.

**Trail contacts:** This is the location, phone number, and website for the local land manager(s) in charge of all the trails within the selected hike. Before you head out, get trail access information, or contact the land manager after your visit if you see problems with trail erosion, damage, or misuse.

**Special considerations:** This section calls your attention to specific trail hazards, like a lack of water or hunting seasons.

The **Finding the trailhead** section gives you dependable driving directions to where you'll want to park. **The Hike** is the meat of the chapter. Detailed and honest, it's a carefully researched impression of the trail. It also often includes lots of area history, both natural and human. Under **Miles and Directions,** mileage cues identify all turns and trail name changes, as well as points of interest. **Options** are also given for many hikes to make your journey shorter or longer depending on the amount of time you have.

Don't feel restricted to the routes and trails that are mapped here. Be adventurous and use this guide as a platform to discover new routes for yourself. One of the simplest ways to begin this is to just turn the map upside down and hike any route in reverse. The change in perspective is often fantastic, and the hike should feel quite different. With this in mind, it'll be like getting two distinctly different hikes on each map. For your own purposes you may wish to copy the route directions onto a small sheet of paper to help you while hiking, or photocopy the map and cue sheet to take with you. Otherwise, just slip the whole book in your backpack and take it all with you. Enjoy your time in the outdoors and remember to pack out what you pack in. As you take advantage of the spectacular scenery offered by the Philadelphia area, remember that our planet is very dear, very special, and very fragile. All of us should do everything we can to keep it clean, beautiful, and healthy, including following the **Green Tips** you'll find throughout this book. And at the end of this guide are helpful tips on hiking in general, should you choose to take your hiking adventures farther afield or to extend some of the trips profiled.

## How to Use the Maps

**Overview map:** This map shows the location of each hike in the area by hike number.

**Route map:** This is your primary guide to each hike. It shows all of the accessible roads and trails, points of interest, water, landmarks, and geographical features. It also distinguishes trails from roads, and paved roads from unpaved roads. The selected route is highlighted, and directional arrows point the way.

# Trail Finder

| Hike No. | Hike Name | Best Hikes for Waterfalls | Best Hikes for Great Views | Best Hikes for Children | Best Hikes for Dogs | Best Hikes for Stream Lovers | Best Hikes for Lake Lovers | Best Hikes for Nature Lovers | Best Hikes for History Lovers |
|---|---|---|---|---|---|---|---|---|---|
| 1 | Daniel Boone Homestead | | | ● | | | | | ● |
| 2 | French Creek State Park | | | ● | | | ● | ● | |
| 3 | Menlo and Lenape Parks to Veterans Memorial | | | ● | ● | ● | | ● | ● |
| 4 | Central Perkiomen Valley Park | | | ● | ● | ● | | ● | |
| 5 | Binky Lee Preserve | | ● | ● | ● | | | ● | |
| 6 | John James Audubon Center at Mill Grove | | | ● | | | | ● | ● |
| 7 | Valley Forge National Historic Park | | | | ● | | | | ● |
| 8 | Ringing Rocks County Park | ● | | ● | | | | ● | |
| 9 | Nockamixon State Park: Old Mill Trail | ● | | ● | | | ● | ● | ● |

| # | Park | 1 | 2 | 3 | 4 | 5 | 6 | 7 | 8 |
|---|------|---|---|---|---|---|---|---|---|
| 10 | Nockamixon State Park: Elephant Trail | | • | • | | | | | |
| 11 | Tinicum County Park to Uhlerstown Covered Bridge | • | | | | • | • | | |
| 12 | Point Pleasant Community Park: Chief Running Deer Trail | | | | • | | | | • |
| 13 | Peace Valley Park | | • | • | | • | • | | |
| 14 | Bowman's Hill Wildflower Preserve | | • | | • | • | • | | |
| 15 | Dark Hollow Park: Eight Arch Bridge | • | • | | • | • | | | |
| 16 | Dark Hollow Park: Power Line Vista | | • | | | • | | • | |
| 17 | Tyler State Park: Covered Bridge Trail | • | • | | • | • | • | | |
| 18 | Tyler State Park: Craftsman's Trail | • | • | | | • | • | | |
| 19 | Churchville Nature Center | • | • | • | | | • | | |
| 20 | Tamanend Park | • | • | | • | • | • | | |

| No. | Site | | | | | | | | |
|---|---|---|---|---|---|---|---|---|---|
| 21 | Core Creek Park | | • | • | | • | • | • | |
| 22 | Five Mile Woods Nature Preserve | | • | | | | • | | |
| 23 | Ridley Creek State Park | • | • | | • | • | | | |
| 24 | Tyler Arboretum | • | • | | • | | • | | |
| 25 | Stroud Preserve | | • | • | • | • | • | • | |
| 26 | Longwood Gardens | • | • | | | | • | | • |
| 27 | Andorra Natural Area | • | • | | | | • | | |
| 28 | Wissahickon Gorge: North Loop | • | • | | • | • | | | • |
| 29 | Manayunk Towpath | • | • | | | • | • | | • |
| 30 | Boxers' Trail | • | | | | • | • | • | |
| 31 | John Heinz National Wildlife Refuge: Impoundment Loop | | • | | | | • | | |

| # | Park | 1 | 2 | 3 | 4 | 5 | 6 | 7 | 8 |
|---|------|---|---|---|---|---|---|---|---|
| 32 | Lorimer Park | | • | | • | • | • | | |
| 33 | Pennypack Park | | • | | • | • | • | | |
| 34 | Neshaminy State Park | | • | | • | • | • | • | |
| 35 | Delaware River Valley: Lambertville to Stockton | • | | | | | | • | |
| 36 | Washington Crossing Historic Park | • | | | | | • | | |
| 37 | The Princeton Woods | • | • | | • | | • | | |
| 38 | Finn's Point | • | | | | | • | • | |
| 39 | Brandywine Creek State Park | | • | | | | • | • | |
| 40 | White Clay Creek State Park | | • | | • | • | • | • | • |

# Map Legend

| | | | |
|---|---|---|---|
| ══40══ | Interstate Highway | ≋ | Boat Ramp/Launch |
| ══45══ | US Highway | ⏝ | Bridge |
| ══144══ | State Highway | ■ | Building/Point of Interest |
| ══4004══ | County Road | ⛺ | Campground |
| ─────── | Local Road | ✹ | Capital |
| ─ ─ ─ ─ ─ | Unpaved Road | ○ | City/Town |
| ┼─┼─┼─┼ | Railroad | ╱ | Dam |
| ▬▬▬▬▬▬ | Featured Trail | ⦚ | Gate |
| ─ ─ ─ ─ ─ | Trail | ▲ | Mountain/Peak |
| ─────── | Paved/Bike Trail | 🅿 | Parking |
| ‖‖‖‖‖‖ | Boardwalk/Steps | 🅰 | Picnic Area |
| ─ ─ ·· ─ ·· ─ | State Border | 🚻 | Restroom |
| 〰 | Small River or Creek | 🗼 | Tower |
| ⬭ | Pond/Lake | ➊ | Trailhead |
| ⋙ | Waterfall | ❓ | Visitor/Information Center |
| ▭ | State Park/Forest | 🔭 | Vista/Viewpoint |
| ⬚ | Preserve | | |

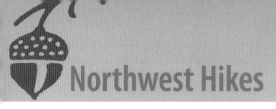

# Northwest Hikes

There were two things that Daniel Boone and John James Audubon had in common: They each lived their formative years in the Philadelphia countryside, and they each liked to spend time in the forests around their homestead, learning, as it were, the skills that would make them famous and part of American folklore.

As you hike the paths on these two vastly different homesteads, it's easy to imagine that you're hiking back in time and just around the next bend you'll meet up with Daniel taking aim at a white-tailed deer or John James setting a twig trap for an elusive specimen.

American history continues to unfold as you hike the grounds of Valley Forge National Historic Park, where, after suffering two crushing defeats in Philadelphia, General George Washington and 11,000 of his patriot soldiers spent the harsh winter of 1777–1778. On this hike you will visit the Washington Memorial Chapel, the Memorial Arch, and the statue of Baron Frederic von Steuben, the Prussian military leader who changed Washington's army from a dissolute band of irregulars to a disciplined fighting machine.

There are 120 state parks in the Pennsylvania State Park system. You will be doing a short, exploratory hike in one of them: French Creek State Park, which is perhaps one of the nicest parks in the system. There are nine hikes of various lengths and skill levels in the park, and it is for that reason I have devised a short, mostly flat beginner's hike so that if you've never hiked on a rugged terrain, this will give you a chance to get acclimated and test your skill level. Essentially, this hike is a loop around Hopewell Lake and just about anybody, including children, can hike it. The east branch of Perkiomen Creek runs through Menlo and Lenape Parks, a popular urban park complex with paved walkways/bike paths, mature shade trees, an historic covered bridge, and a Veterans Memorial. The Perkiomen continues through the Perkiomen Valley and eventually ends at the Schuylkill River; the Perkiomen Trail runs alongside the stream and provides a flat, paved hike/bike trail where you can hike or bike as far as you want, always remembering if you hike 5 miles out you must hike 5 miles back.

There are a number of short, easy hikes on the Binky Lee Preserve in Chester County. The land here is part of the Natural Lands Trust, and it shows: The Binky Lee is not only well maintained, but in the center of it all there is an open field on a grassy knoll that provides excellent views and, if you're there at just the right time, you can experience the breeze that lifts out of the valley to the top of the knoll. Needless to say, Binky Lee is an excellent site for a picnic.

# Daniel Boone Homestead

*It's not often that you can walk in the footsteps of an American icon, but on this hike that is exactly what you will be doing as you hike the same lanes and forest paths where Daniel Boone once tilled the land, trapped and hunted, and learned the skills that would serve him so well as an adult. This easy hike leads you from one building to the next, giving you a feel for how things were back in the mid-1700s. Be sure to bring your children.*

**Start:** At the visitor center parking lot

**Distance:** 1.7 miles

**Hiking time:** 1.5 hours

**Difficulty:** Easy

**Trail surface:** Paved walkways, gravel roads, forest footpath

**Best season:** Year-round

**Other trail users:** Equestrians on the bridle paths, tour groups

**Canine compatibility:** Leashed dogs allowed. However, dogs are not allowed within the white-fenced area around the Daniel Boone House, nor are they permitted in any buildings.

**Land status:** Owned by the Pennsylvania Historical & Museum Commission

**Fees and permits:** Self-guided tour: $3; guided tour: $6

**Schedule:** Tues to Fri, 9 a.m. to 5 p.m., Sat. 10 a.m. to 5 p.m., Sunday 11 a.m. to 5 p.m.; closed Monday; check website for seasonal hours

**Map:** USGS Birdsboro

**Trail contacts:** Daniel Boone Homestead, 400 Daniel Boone Rd., Birdsboro, PA 19508; (610) 582-4900; www.danielboonehomestead.org

**Finding the trailhead:** Pick up US 422 at King of Prussia. Drive west approximately 31.5 miles, passing Pottstown. After Pottstown, look for CJ's Tires on the right, then the brown Daniel Boone Homestead sign on the right. Turn right and take the first right at the light onto Old Daniel Boone Road and drive 0.5 mile to the Daniel Boone Homestead on the left. Enter and drive to the visitor center parking lot. Trailhead GPS: N40 17.846' / W75 47.647'

## THE HIKE

The Daniel Boone Homestead sits on the original 579 acres of rolling hills and farmland that Daniel Boone's father, Squire Boone, purchased when he and his wife Sarah settled here in the Olney Valley in 1730. Squire Boone was a skilled weaver, blacksmith, and farmer; he was also a clever craftsman who built his one-room log cabin over a spring so that the water from the spring flowed through a trough in his basement and kept the family provisions cool.

Daniel Boone was born in that cabin in 1734, and by the time he was twelve Daniel had received his first rifle from his father. As was common in those times for most young men who lived on a farm, he soon learned the hunting, trapping, and fishing skills that would not only put food on the table for his family, but would serve him just as well when he joined Braddock's army in 1755 near Pittsburgh during the French and Indian War. His skills were further tested a few years later in North Carolina defending his family against Cherokee raids and in 1769 when he was captured by the Shawnees and held for two years before he escaped and returned to his family in North Carolina.

Daniel's life and exploits as a frontiersman continued. In 1784 John Filson published Daniel's biography. Soon after, he became the best-known frontier fighter in the land and his life became the stuff of legend—a legend that continues to thrive into the twenty-first century.

The Bertolet House and bakehouse/smokehouse provide an example of eighteenth-century Pennsylvania German log architecture.

To begin this tour through Daniel's birthplace, start from the visitor center and walk downhill on the path to the smokehouse, which, like the Boone House, was built in the eighteenth century, though no one knows exactly when. Back in those days all the family's meats were smoked in order to preserve them. The meat was hung on the ceiling joists, and then a fire made of apple or hickory logs was built on the dirt floor. As the smoke wafted up, it cured the meats. The smoked meat was then stored overhead in the loft.

The next stop is the Blacksmith Shop, which was built in nearby Amityville in 1769 before it was moved and reconstructed here as an example of what Squire Boone's shop would have looked like.

From here the trail is a gravel road that leads uphill to the Bertolet House, which was built in 1737 in the Olney Valley but was reconstructed here on the Boone Homestead in 1968 to serve as an example of eighteenth-century Pennsylvania German log architecture, complete with a centrally located fireplace, steeply pitched roofs, flared eaves, and casement windows.

The hike continues on the gravel road to Daniel Boone Lake, which was created in 1940 on Owatin Creek to provide a nesting place for various waterfowl. Once at the dam you turn right onto a path that runs alongside the lake and eventually the creek. At a small bridge over the creek you turn right and follow the trail through the dense undergrowth for 0.3 mile, when you arrive back at the Bertolet House and Bertolet Smokehouse.

You then walk to the water-powered Bertolet Sawmill, which was built in the late eighteenth or early nineteenth century and continued to operate until the 1940s. The hike crosses Owatin Creek on a wooden bridge and takes you to the 1940s era Wayside Lodge, after which you return across the bridge and walk to the Smokehouse where you started then up the path to the visitor center.

## MILES AND DIRECTIONS

**0.0** Start at the visitor center. Walk on the path to the Smokehouse. Walk past the Blacksmith Shop.

**0.1** Turn left onto the gravel road and walk uphill.

**0.3** Turn right to visit the Bertolet Bakehouse/Smokehouse and the Bertolet House. Return to the gravel road and turn right.

**0.5** Arrive at Daniel Boone Lake and turn right onto the hiking trail that runs alongside the lake.

**0.8** Arrive at a small bridge over Owatin Creek and turn right. Follow the trail back to the Bertolet House and the Bertolet Bakehouse/Smokehouse. Then continue to the gravel road.

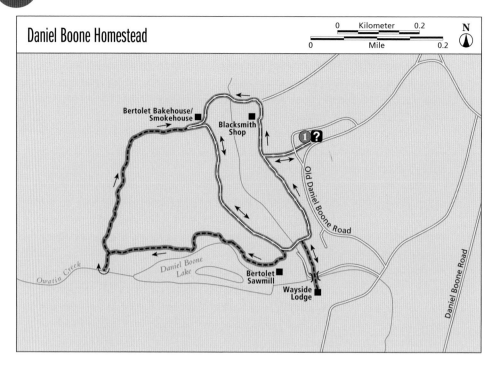

**1.1** Turn right onto the gravel road and walk to Bertolet Sawmill. Cross the bridge over the creek and explore the Wayside Lodge on the other side, return and walk to the Smokehouse, and then turn right onto the path to the visitor center.

**1.7** Arrive back at the visitor center.

**🌿 Green Tip:**
*Donate used gear to a nonprofit kids' organization.*

# French Creek State Park

*After you finish this 2.5-mile loop, you can visit historic Hopewell Furnace, a once-thriving industrial plantation built on the border of Berks and Chester Counties in 1771. See a restored iron maker's village, complete with implements and tools, sheds, furniture, and houses.*

**Start:** The Hopewell Lake Boat Launch

**Distance:** 2.5-mile loop

**Hiking time:** 2 hours

**Difficulty:** Easy

**Trail surface:** Gravel roads, rocky lakeside footpath, paved walkways

**Best seasons:** Spring, summer, fall

**Other trail users:** Hikers only

**Canine compatibility:** Leashed dogs permitted

**Land status:** Pennsylvania State Park

**Fees and permits:** No fees or permits required

**Schedule:** Open daily from 8 a.m. until dark

**Map:** USGS Elverson

**Trail contacts:** French Creek State Park, 843 Park Rd., Elverson, PA 19520; (610) 582-9680; www.dcnr.state.pa.us/stateparks/findapark/frenchcreek

**Finding the trailhead:** From Philadelphia take the I-76 W ramp to Valley Forge. Drive 0.2 mile and keep left at the fork; follow signs for I-76 W/Valley Forge and merge onto I-76 W. Drive 17.9 miles and keep left at the fork; follow signs for I-76 W/Harrisburg and merge onto I-76 W. Drive 28.0 miles and take exit 298 to merge onto I-176 N toward PA 10/Morgantown/Reading. Drive 0.3 mile and take exit 1A for PA 10 N toward Beckersville. Drive 0.1 mile and turn right onto PA 10 N/Morgantown Road. Drive 0.5 mile and take the third right onto Joanna Road. Drive 0.9 mile and turn right onto Elverson Road. Drive 0.6 mile and take a slight left onto Hopewell Road. Drive 2.4 miles and continue onto Park Road. Drive 1.9 miles to the park office. Continue past the park office and turn into the Hopewell Lake parking lot. Trailhead GPS: N40 11.880' / W075 47.427'

French Creek State Park is one of the top state parks in the system. Within its 7,730 acres there are more than 35 miles of well-marked and well-maintained hiking trails. One connector trail will even lead you to the Hopewell Furnace National Historic Site. At Hopewell Furnace you will learn how southeastern Pennsylvania—because of its combined natural resources of water power, iron ore, and abundant timber—played an important role in the fledgling colonies defeating the British in the Revolutionary War.

The iron ore of course was combined with the also-abundant mineral limestone and smelted into iron; the blast furnaces used a bellows system and charcoal to produce heats up to 3,000°F to forge the iron ore into iron. Local timber was harvested and stacked on pads that were then covered with dirt and left to smolder and make charcoal. The furnace at Hopewell used 800 bushels of charcoal a day.

When the war began, Hopewell owner and ironmaster Mark Bird switched from making stove plates to making cannons and shot for the Continental Army and Navy. After the war and throughout its life span, Hopewell suffered one setback after another, as the technology to develop iron and steel shifted away from charcoal furnaces and the labor-intensive processes that accompanied them.

Hopewell did have one heyday from 1816 to 1831, when it concentrated on producing the popular Hopewell cast-iron stoves. But by the 1840s the flame of prosperity was extinguished for the final time.

The 68-acre Hopewell Lake is a perfect site for a float along the tranquil water.

The restoration of Hopewell Furnace reflects that period in the 1840s. Many of the buildings, houses, and barns stand today as they did then, and in summer there are re-enactors to lead visitors through the grounds and explain how the ironworkers' jobs were done and how the families lived on the compound and how other workers did tasks that supported the workers and their families.

There are also ongoing events throughout the year: In May there is Sheep Shearing Day, in August it's Fueling the Furnace Day, in September it's Harvest Time Day, in October it's Family Social Day, and in December it's Iron Plantation Christmas.

Our hike is a shortened section of the Boone Trail. It's an easy loop that was designed to allow novice hikers the chance to see for themselves the highlights of this park, such as the swimming pool, Hopewell Lake and its spillway, and a perennial beaver dam, without doing any strenuous climbing.

## MILES AND DIRECTIONS

**0.0**   Start at Hopewell Lake boat launch parking lot. Facing the forest, start from the far left side of the parking lot. Walk through the opening in the trees and cross a bridge over a feeder stream. Follow the blue blazes through the picnic area and past the swimming pool.

**0.4**   Turn left onto the gravel road that comes out of the parking lot.

**0.5**   Enter the forest.

**0.9**   Get on the gravel road toward the spillway. Within 100 feet the trail leaves the gravel road and cuts right and takes you to the road that leads behind the spillway.

**1.1**   Arrive at a bridge behind the spillway. Continue straight and start uphill on wooden steps. Take the left fork up the wooden steps and arrive at a trail intersection. Follow the blue trail. (The yellow trail overlaps the blue trail here.) Arrive at a Y. The yellow trail goes off to your right. Take the left fork and stay on the blue trail.

**1.3**   Disregard a trail that heads toward the lake.

**1.4**   The blue trail cuts right.

🐾 **Green Tip:**
*Pass it down: The best way to instill good green habits in your children is to set a good example.*

# French Creek State Park

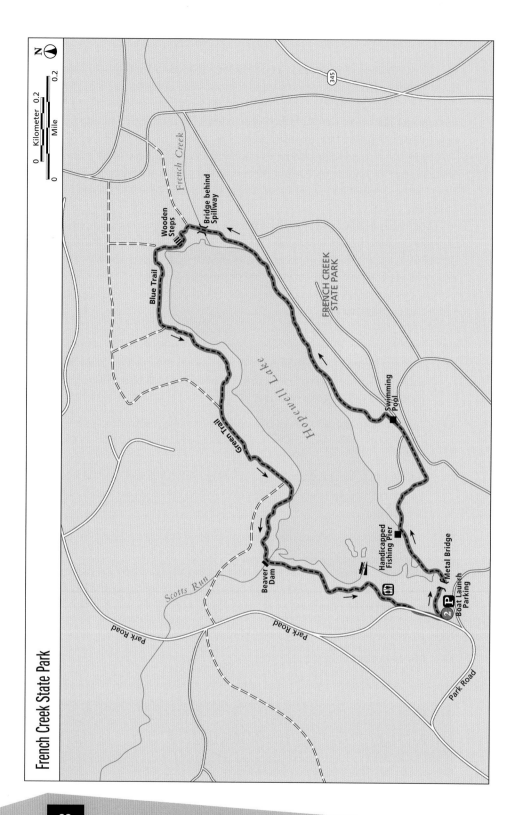

**1.5** The green trail comes in from your right and joins the blue trail.

**1.6** Arrive at a sandy area.

**1.7** Come to a gravel road and turn left toward the lake. Pass the green and yellow trail that goes off to your right. Stay on the service road.

**1.9** When you get 10 feet from the lake, turn right and take the left fork at the Y.

**2.1** Arrive at the beaver dam.

**2.3** Come to a Y. Take the left fork, heading toward the lake. Get on the paved path and follow it past the boat launch to the restrooms and turn right. Walk to the parking lot.

**2.5** Arrive back at your vehicle.

## Hopewell Big Woods

Once you've finished your hike in French Creek State Park—if you have any energy left—you can explore Hopewell Big Woods, 73,000 acres of forest that surrounds French Creek State Park and the Hopewell National Historic Site. There are also 4,000 acres of old-growth forest laced with pristine streams, as well as 116 miles of hiking trails, 18 miles of horseback riding on the Horse-Shoe Trail, 20 miles of (difficult) mountain biking trails, and a 60-foot fixed-pin rock wall for the rock climber in your group. For the paddlers there is Hopewell Lake, Scotts Run Lake, and the nearby Schuylkill River. If you want to extend your visit there is an area for tents and RVs and cabins in French Creek and Warwick Woods.

 **Green Tip:**
*Use phosphate-free detergent—it's less harmful to the environment.*

*If you just want to relax and take time to check out the colorful butterfly bushes or soak up some local history— including an old-time amusement park complete with a carousel and a pair of famous bridges—or visit a veterans' memorial and covered bridge, this easy hike along a peaceful stream is for you. Except for an optional steep climb up a dirt path to take in the Perkasie Carousel, this hike could be considered handicapped accessible.*

**Start:** The parking lot on East Walnut Street

**Distance:** 2.3 miles

**Hiking time:** 1.5 hours

**Difficulty:** Easy

**Trail surface:** Macadam roads, paved walkways, dirt path

**Best seasons:** Spring, summer, fall

**Other trail users:** Bicyclists, dog walkers

**Canine compatibility:** Leashed dogs permitted

**Land status:** Borough Community Park

**Fees and permits:** No fees or permits

**Schedule:** Open daily, dawn to dusk

**Map:** USGS Telford

**Trail contacts:** Borough of Perkasie, 620 W. Chestnut St., Perkasie, PA 18944; (215) 257-5065; admin@perkasieborough.org

**Finding the trailhead:** From Philadelphia head east on South Penn Square toward South Broad Street/Avenue of the Arts. Make a slight left onto John F. Kennedy Boulevard. Take the first right onto North Broad Street. Drive 4.9 miles and take a slight left onto Belfield Avenue. Drive 0.6 mile and take a slight right onto Ogontz Avenue. Drive 2.5 miles and take a slight left to stay on Ogontz Avenue. Drive 1.5 miles and continue onto PA 309 N. Drive 21.1 miles and take the PA 152 exit toward Telford/Sellersville. Drive 0.2 mile and turn right on PA 152 S. Drive 0.7 mile and turn left to stay on PA 152 S. Drive 0.8 mile and continue on North Main Street. Drive 0.2 mile and turn right onto East Walnut Street. Trailhead GPS: N 40 21.798' / W 075 18.338'

## THE HIKE

This hike has a few surprises. At 0.5 mile you come upon a pair of cable suspension bridges—known originally as the Twin Bridges—that were built in 1936 as a project sponsored by the New Deal's Work Project Administration. The bridges were based on the design that noted bridge designer John Roebling used in 1867 when he designed the Brooklyn Bridge in New York City, and although he didn't live to see the bridge completed in 1883, he became one of the most famous bridge designers of his era.

Your next stop at 0.8 mile is the site of one of the oldest covered bridges in Bucks County. It was built of pine and oak in 1832 and originally crossed Pleasant Spring Creek, but by the mid-1950s it was condemned as unsuitable for vehicle traffic. At this point the Perkasie Historical Society rescued the 93-foot-long Town Truss structure and moved it to its present location in 1959, renaming it the South Perkasie Covered Bridge. Today visitors can still read the inscription that warned early travelers to be aware of speeding: "$5 Fine for Any Person Riding or Driving Over This Bridge Faster Than a Walk or Smoking Segars On."

After the covered bridge you loop back to the path and get on the narrow dirt path that leads you uphill to Menlo Park, where a once-thriving amusement park offered carousel rides and toboggan rides, a movie and dance hall, a bowling alley, an ice cream parlor, and a swimming pool. The original Perkasie Carousel, which was built in 1891, has been replaced by a modern version that was installed in 1951; this one has thirty-six wooden horses and two chariots.

In 1983, American Legion Post 255 built a memorial to honor veterans from each branch of the armed services.

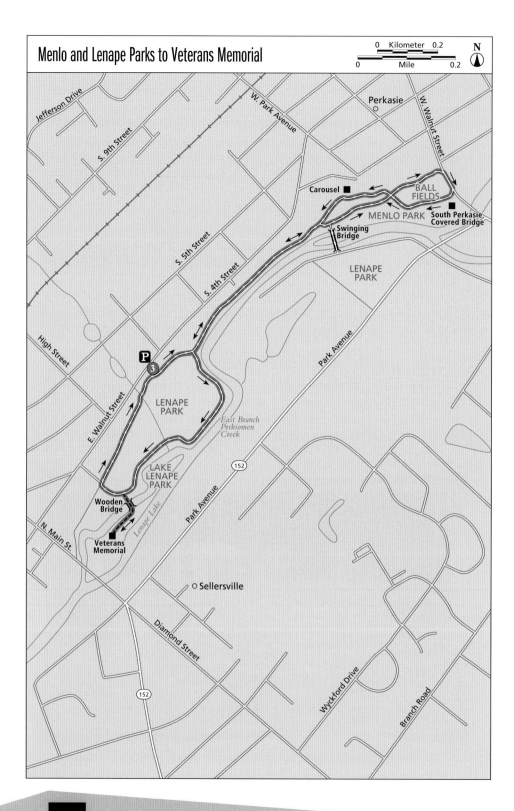

In 1955 Perkasie Borough bought the park, and today there is a modern swimming pool as well as the carousel, which is open for business on a number of weekends and holidays throughout the year.

From the carousel you hike downhill to the path, then retrace your steps toward where you started out, but you turn left and walk to the stream where you get on a wooden bridge that takes you across Perkiomen Creek and your chance to visit a veterans memorial that too has a history: The original memorial was a granite boulder with a plaque commemorating World War I veterans. It was set near the five-points intersection in Sellersville, where every now and then it was damaged when a vehicle ran into it.

In 1983, American Legion Post 255 moved the boulder and made it the centerpiece of a new memorial, which would honor veterans from World War I, World War II, Korea, Vietnam, and Desert Storm. The memorial also displays the flags of the five military branches as well as the American flag and the Sellersville borough flag.

## MILES AND DIRECTIONS

**0.0**  Start at the parking lot on East Walnut Street. Turn left on the macadam road and pass the first baseball field on your right.

**0.2**  Turn left with the stream on your right.

**0.5**  Come to the suspension bridges on your right. Pass a pavilion on your left. Pass the second baseball field on your right then cross over a small stream on a wooden bridge.

**0.7**  Arrive at West Walnut Street and turn right.

**0.8**  Arrive at the South Perkasie Covered Bridge, then continue on the path.

**0.9**  Cross over the original walkway and begin climbing up the hill on a dirt path.

**1.0**  Arrive at the carousel. After your visit, start down the hill and take the path on your right.

**1.1**  Arrive at the paved path and turn right and retrace your steps.

**1.4**  Turn left.

**1.7**  Turn left again.

**1.8**  Turn left again and cross a small steam on a wooden bridge, then walk to the veterans memorial. After your visit, retrace your steps back to the bridge and continue straight.

**2.1**  Turn right.

**2.3**  Arrive back at the parking lot.

# Central Perkiomen Valley Park

As you start this hike, you'll see plenty of young mothers with their young children. One reason for this is that the trailhead shares the parking lot with the park playground; another reason is that this is an easy hike with plenty of trees that provide deep shade. There are bicyclists pedaling along as well, but there is room for everyone on this 10-foot-wide trail, which is mostly paved and well-maintained. You get up-close views of Perkiomen Creek and two creek crossings—one on a modern iron bridge, the other on an old railroad trestle bridge.

**Start:** Plank Road trailhead
**Distance:** 4.2 miles out-and-back
**Hiking time:** 1.5 to 2 hours
**Difficulty:** Easy
**Trail surface:** Asphalt, crushed limestone, gravel
**Best season:** Year-round
**Other trail users:** Bicyclists
**Canine compatibility:** Leashed dogs permitted
**Land status:** Montgomery County Parks and Heritage Services

**Fees and permits:** No fees or permits
**Schedule:** Dawn to dusk daily
**Maps:** USGS Collegeville; Perkiomen Trail map
**Trail contacts:** Central Perkiomen Valley Park, 1 Plank Rd., Schwenksville, PA 19437; (610) 287-6970; Montgomery County Parks and Heritage Services: www.montcopa.org

**Finding the trailhead:** From Philadelphia take the I-76 W ramp to Valley Forge. Drive 0.2 mile and keep left at the fork; follow the signs for I-76 W/Valley Forge and merge onto I-76 W. Drive 16.7 miles and take exit 327-328A-328B for US 202 N toward US 422 W/King of Prussia/W Chester/Pottstown. Take exit 328A on the left to merge onto US 422 W toward Pottstown. Drive 9.5 miles and take the PA 29 N exit toward Collegeville. Drive 0.3 mile and turn right onto PA 29 N/South Collegeville Road. Drive 2.4 miles and turn right onto East Main Street. Drive 318 feet and take the first left onto PA 29 N/1st Ave. Continue to follow PA 29 N for 3.9 miles, then turn right onto Plank Road and go 0.3 mile. Trailhead GPS: N40 14.389' / W075 27.305'

## THE HIKE

The history of the Perkiomen Trail begins in 1868 when the Perkiomen Railway Company began running trains from Oaks to Pennsburg. This new form of transportation was a major factor in the development and growth of the area, and by 1920 the Perkiomen Valley had become a popular vacation spot. In 1944 the railway was purchased by the Reading Railroad Company, but suburban development and the advent of the automobile as the favored form of transportation led to the demise of passenger cars along this line, so by 1955 the passenger trains were discontinued and by the 1970s the Reading Railroad was bankrupt.

Montgomery County purchased much of the railway right-of-ways, and by 2003 it had developed the Perkiomen Trail, which is 19.5 miles long and runs alongside the scenic Perkiomen Creek. The trail begins at Green Lane in the north and continues to Oaks in the south, where it connects with the Schuylkill River Trail.

Perkiomen Creek, which by the way was named after the Lenape Indian term *Pakihm Unk*, which means "cranberry Place," is a 37-mile-long tributary of the Schuylkill River, which begins in Berks County and ends at the Schuylkill River near the community of Audubon.

Our hike begins at the Plank Road trailhead, heading toward Collegeville. At 0.4 mile you cross the creek for the first time. At 1.3 miles you come to an oversize chain-link fence with a sign that informs you that you are passing the property

This trail is not only paved, flat, and shaded, it has pleasant bathrooms.

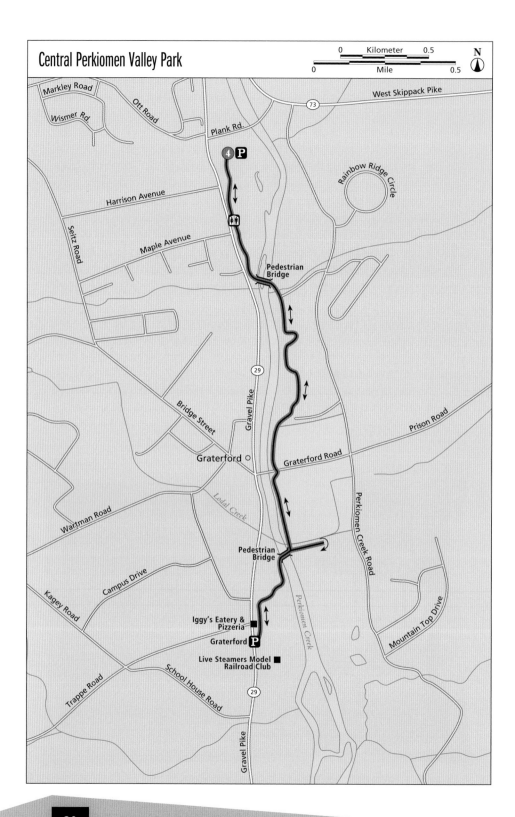

Kilometer

Mile

N

Markley Road

Wismer Rd

Ott Road

73

West Skippack Pike

Plank Rd.

4 P

Rainbow Ridge Circle

Harrison Avenue

Seitz Road

Maple Avenue

Pedestrian
Bridge

29

Bridge Street

Gravel Pike

Graterford

Graterford Road

Prison Road

Lodal Creek

Perkiomen Creek Road

Wartman Road

Pedestrian
Bridge

Campus Drive

Kagey Road

Perkiomen Creek

Mountain Top Drive

Iggy's Eatery &
Pizzeria

Graterford P

Live Steamers Model
Railroad Club

Trappe Road

School House Road

29

Gravel Pike

of the Graterford Prison, which was built here in 1929 to replace the infamous Eastern State Penitentiary.

The entire prison facility sits on 1,730 acres and includes an extensive prison farm as well as a number of garment factories, a shoe factory, and a mail distribution center. The prison compound itself comprises 62 acres surrounded by 30-foot-high walls.

At 1.6 miles you cross the creek on an old railroad bridge that remains intact long after the trains quit running. The bridge has been retrofitted for hikers and bicyclists as part of the nationwide Rails-to-Trails Conservancy initiative.

At 2.0 miles you pass Iggy's Eatery & Pizzeria on your right just before the Graterford trailhead at 2.1 miles, where you turn around and head back the way you came. But as you make the turn-around, you see a small railroad crossing sign on the left that reads, "Pennsylvania Live Steamers."

The Live Steamers is a club of railroad aficionados who build scale model steam engines and other railcars, as well as the railroad tracks on which to run them. The club has been in existence since 1946, and I imagine if you hiked here at the right time on the right day, you would see the miniature railroad in action.

## MILES AND DIRECTIONS

**0.0**    Start at the Plank Road trailhead. Walk from the parking lot to the trail kiosk and turn left onto the rail, heading toward Collegeville.

**0.2**    Pass the restrooms on your left.

**0.4**    Cross over Perkiomen Creek on an iron bridge.

**0.8**    Trail takes a sharp left. Stay on paved trail.

**0.9**    Trail becomes crushed limestone. Pass a private home and parking area for the Hollywood trailhead on your right.

**1.3**    Arrive at Graterford Road.

**1.6**    The trail continues to the right. Do not take that trail. Instead turn left and loop around to the old railroad bridge entrance.

**1.7**    Cross the creek on the old railroad trestle bridge.

**2.0**    Pass Iggy's Eatery & Pizzeria on you right. There are picnic tables and a bathroom here.

**2.1**    Arrive at the Graterford trailhead parking lot. Note the Live Steamers Club. Retrace your steps back to where you started.

**4.2**    Arrive back at the Plank Road trailhead.

*You begin this hike on a mowed pathway that runs between a wind-blown knoll on your left that was once a farmer's field, and a grassy floodplain area on your right. You cut down off the knoll and enter a young floodplain forest that is so well maintained it reminds you of a park. The trail then meanders through a mature hardwood forest, over a few streams, and into a pine plantation as you complete the circle through the period farm buildings and back to where you started.*

**Start:** The kiosk uphill from the parking lot

**Distance:** 1.8-mile loop

**Hiking time:** 1.0 hour

**Difficulty:** Easy, with some short climbs

**Trail surface:** Mowed path, typical forest footpath

**Best season:** Year-round

**Other trail users:** Equestrians, hunters

**Canine compatibility:** Leashed dogs permitted

**Land status:** Natural Lands Trust

**Fees and permits:** None

**Schedule:** Open sunrise to sunset year-round

**Map:** USGS Malvern

**Trail contacts:** Binky Lee Preserve, 1445 Pikeland Rd., Chester Springs, PA 19425; (610) 827-0156; www.natlands.org

**Finding the trailhead:** From Philadelphia take the I-76 W ramp to Valley Forge. Drive 0.2 mile and keep left at the fork, follow signs for I-76 W/Valley Forge and merge onto I-76 W. Go 17.9 miles and keep left at the fork; follow signs for I-76 W/Harrisburg and merge onto I-76 W. Drive 6.7 miles and take the exit toward PA 29 N/Charlestown Road. Drive 0.9 mile and turn right onto PA 29 N/Charlestown Road. Drive 1.1 miles and turn left onto Pikeland Road. Drive 2.5 miles and turn left onto Street Road. Drive 0.6 mile and take the second right onto Pikeland Road. Drive 0.8 mile to your destination. Trailhead GPS: N40 05.815' / W075 36.129'

**Special considerations:** Hunting is permitted on the preserve. Signs are posted when hunting is taking place. Contact the preserve for information about hiking during hunting season.

## THE HIKE

The Binky Lee Preserve consists of 112 acres of former farmland that is being returned to more natural woodlands and meadows. A hike along one of the trails here provides you with a look at what modern-day reforestation actually looks like.

Binky Lee started out as one of the many eighteenth-century farms that dominated much of early Chester County countryside. Although many of those original farm buildings are gone, the barn, which was built in the early 1800s, is still standing. And although it has undergone restorations and renovations over the years, it retains much of the character and features of the original structure.

The Binky Lee Preserve is one of forty-two local preserves in southeastern Pennsylvania and south New Jersey owned and managed by the Natural Lands Trust. In total the Trust owns and manages over 22,000 acres in the Delaware Valley. Its goal is to protect natural areas by helping communities preserve more of their land by providing leadership in managing natural resources and creating opportunities for people to connect with the land.

As you start this hike you realize that the open meadow on your left was once the farmland where crops were planted and harvested. Today the wind blows the wildflowers and tall grasses there, making it a perfect place to be on a lazy summer afternoon. In fact there is a short hike that simply takes you around the perimeter of this knoll so that you can enjoy the fantastic views of the rolling hills that surround the preserve.

This refurbished springhouse has its own cistern for holding water.

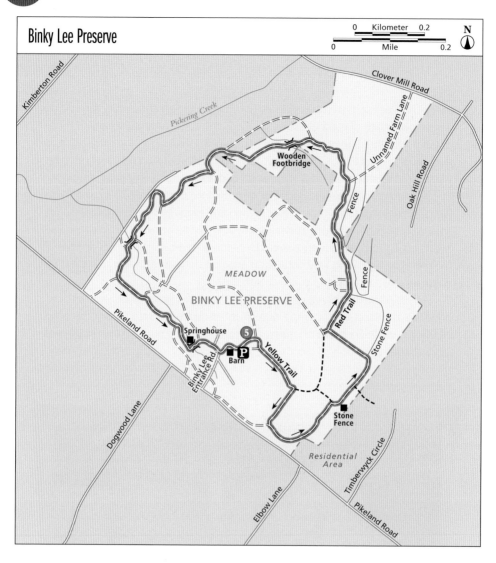

Binky Lee Preserve

There is an added bonus here for hikers who also enjoy bird watching. Because Binky Lee is isolated and there are secluded areas of grasslands, the site is excellent for viewing grassland birds such as the Eastern meadowlark, Eastern bluebird, bobolink, American kestrel, red-tailed hawk, northern harrier, and woodcock.

As you make your way downhill on the trail, you walk along a lane of locust trees that you quickly realize are set apart like fence posts; in other words, these trees were planted by man. In fact, since 1989 when the Trust acquired the land, there have been over 10,000 trees planted.

Once you reach the bottom of the knoll, you walk through a flat area planted with startlingly green grass; it is so green and healthy looking, in fact, that you feel like you're walking in a well-kept city park. But this feeling doesn't last long, as you realize that the trail through the forest leads uphill through a typical Pennsylvania hardwood forest, complete with a rocky footpath, forest duff, and giant boulders scattered along the way.

The climb back up is steep but short, so before you know it, you're back on top, and this time you're facing another direction; it creates an altogether different vista from the one you saw when you started out. From here the trail wends through the forest, crosses two small streams that empty into Pickering Creek, then brings you to a visit with a springhouse. Then you pass the barn and return to the parking lot.

## MILES AND DIRECTIONS

**0.0** Start at the parking lot. Walk uphill past a gate to the trail kiosk. Facing the kiosk turn right onto the yellow trail. At this point the red trail coexists with the yellow. You soon pass a pin oak tree beside the trail.

**0.1** Turn right and go downhill past a row of locust trees.

**0.2** Turn left.

**0.3** The trail enters the forest. You come to a Y. Take the trail to the left. Ignore the trail to the right; it goes to the residential section.

**0.4** You reach the top of the hill. Turn right and walk toward a stone fence. You are now on the equestrian trail that leads you back to the open meadow in the center of this hike.

**0.6** Arrive at an intersection. Turn right and follow the red blazes alongside a fenced area.

**0.9** Cross an unnamed farm lane. Then cut away from the corral and head for the forest.

**1.0** Cross a stream on a wooden footbridge.

**1.4** Turn right on the red trail, which runs alongside the road on your right.

🍂 Green Tip:
*Never let your dog chase wildlife.*

**1.5** Cross a small stream on a wooden bridge. Ignore a trail that cuts across the red trail and leads to the paved road. The trail turns left and you see bluebird boxes. Stay to the right at the Y.

**1.8** Come to another Y. Follow the red blazes and cross the same small stream on a second bridge. Pass a bat house, then walk toward the springhouse with the stream on your right. Walk toward the old barn, turn left on the road, and walk to the parking area and back to your vehicle.

## Pennsylvania's Official State Animal

If you hike in Pennsylvania long enough, sooner or later you're going to see a whitetail deer. In fact, the Pennsylvania Department of Natural Resources (DCNR) estimates that today there are 1.5 million whitetails in the state. That figure works out to be 30 deer per square mile; according to DCNR studies, in the 1700s the population was 10 deer for every square mile.

Whitetail not only provided food for early Pennsylvania settlers, but the hide provided clothing and in some cases shelter. In 1721, the Pennsylvania House of Representatives passed the nation's first game laws to protect the whitetail and other game animals and birds. In 1959 the state of Pennsylvania named the whitetail deer as the Pennsylvania state animal.

Each year more than 1 million deer hunters fan out across the state in hopes of bagging a trophy-size whitetail. But many soon learn that it's not all that easy to bring down an animal that can run 40 miles per hour, swim 13 miles per hour, and jump a 9-foot-high fence. And if that's not enough to give you pause, with a flick of its white tail it can warn others that a hunter is nearby.

# John James Audubon Center at Mill Grove

*There are a number of interesting trails here, and there are a number of ways to connect the various trails to create your own hike. This hike is an easy hike for beginners who like their adventures more or less on level ground; in other words, there's very little climbing. At the start of the hike, you pass the historic Mill Grove home where John James Audubon once lived. From there you walk a forest footpath, then a mowed path through a delightful meadow, and on to make a loop around an ingenious chimney sweep tower.*

**Start:** The kiosk in the parking lot
**Distance:** 2.0-mile double loop
**Hiking time:** 1.5 hours
**Difficulty:** Easy
**Trail surface:** Forest path, meadow path
**Best season:** Year-round
**Other trail users:** Birders
**Canine compatibility:** No dogs allowed
**Land status:** Montgomery County Historic Site
**Fees and permits:** No fees for self-guided hikes. There is a fee for guided hiking tours and tours of the museum, which is open Tues through Sat 10 a.m. to 4 p.m. and Sun 1 p.m. to 4 p.m.
**Schedule:** Dawn to dusk daily
**Maps:** USGS Valley Forge and Collegeville; Audubon Center Trail Map
**Trail contacts:** John James Audubon Center at Mill Grove, 1201 Pawlings Rd., Audubon, PA 19403; (610) 666-5593; johnjames .audubon.org

**Finding the trailhead:** From Philadelphia take the I-76 W ramp to Valley Forge. Drive 0.2 mile and keep left at the fork; follow signs for I-76 W/Valley Forge and merge onto I-76 W. Drive 16.7 miles and take exit 327-328A-328B for US 202 N toward US 422 W/King of Prussia/W Chester/Pottstown. Drive 0.1 mile and take exit 328A on the left to merge onto US 422 W toward Pottstown. Drive 3.6 miles and exit onto PA 363 N/South Trooper Road. Drive 0.3 mile and turn left onto Audubon Road. Drive 1.2 miles and turn left onto Pawlings Road and the parking lot. Trailhead GPS: N40 07.398' / W075 26.549'

## THE HIKE

John James Audubon was born in 1785 in Les Cayes, Santo Domingo (now Haiti), the illegitimate son of a Creole chambermaid, who died months after his birth, and a French sea captain, who was a plantation owner and slave trader. When his father died, Audubon was raised by his stepmother and stepfather in France. In 1803 his stepfather sent him to America to take charge of his 175-acre estate known as Mill Grove, where he hoped to establish a profitable lead mine.

During the three years that he lived at Mill Grove, Audubon spent most of his time hunting, studying, and drawing birds. His interest in birds led him to conduct the first known bird-banding experiment in North America: By tying strings to the legs of eastern phoebes, he learned that the birds returned to the very same nesting site each year. He also devised a way to insert wire into the dead birds he shot to pose them realistically so he could sketch them.

After leaving Mill Grove, Audubon worked at a series of jobs in Kentucky and elsewhere while pursuing his dream of painting every bird that could be found in America. In 1826 he went to Britain to hire the skilled engravers and copper-plate etchers needed to print the "double elephant" folios—which measured 39.5 inches tall by 28.5 inches wide—he needed to present the birds he drew in full-size, life-like sketches. These etchings were sold as *Birds of America*, Audubon's masterwork.

Built in 1762 and listed on the National Register of Historic Places, Mill Grove was the first American home of artist, author, and naturalist John James Audubon.

When you visit the museum, you will see an early copy of *Birds of America*, as well as original Audubon prints, oil paintings, and Audubon memorabilia, including stuffed models of hawks and owls, along with squirrels, frogs, and raccoons. There is also a painting of the great egret, which was hunted almost to extinction in the late nineteenth century to provide plumes for women's hats. But the Audubon Model Law of 1901 outlawed this practice, and the great egret became the symbol of the Audubon Society when it was formed in 1905.

After you descend from the museum area, the trail takes you into a forest of deep shade and solitude. As you hike the forests and meadows at Mill Grove—perhaps in Audubon's footsteps—you can do your own bird watching of the 190 species of birds that have been observed here since 1953, when the count was begun. However, there is a caveat: Several species have been seen here only once and may never appear again. On the other hand, some of the most-often spotted birds are the blue jay, the northern cardinal, woodpeckers and the northern flicker, the Carolina wren, and eastern phoebes.

At 0.8 mile you come to a site where two logs have been placed beside the trail to let you know you can go no farther in that direction. At this point the trail continues to the left and leads you to a meadow where you walk with the forest on your left and the meadow on your right. You then pass through a tree line and into a second meadow, where at 1.1 miles you cut left into the forest and retrace your steps to Wildlife Sanctuary Road.

The first thing you come to after you cross the road is the chimney sweep tower, which was constructed, quite simply, so that chimney sweeps would spend their time here in the tower and not in the nearby chimneys. From here the trail makes a loop that takes you uphill almost to the entrance driveway before it brings you back down and returns you to Wildlife Sanctuary Road, then uphill again to the museum.

## MILES AND DIRECTIONS

**0.0**   Start at the kiosk in the parking lot. Turn right and walk downhill toward the Audubon homestead, which is now the museum and office. Just before you get to the office, take the sharp left turn and walk downhill. There will be a wooden rail fence on your right and a stone wall on your left.

**0.2**   Cross Wildlife Sanctuary Road, then turn right and go up a set of steps. Cross a pipeline and you are in the forest.

**0.4**   Turn right at the trail intersection and stay in the forest. Follow the blue blazes.

**0.6**   A trail comes in from your left; ignore it.

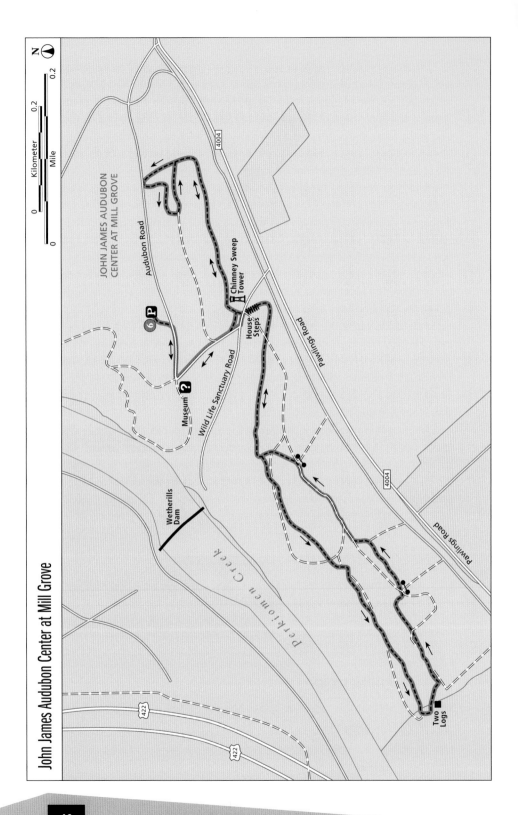

# John James Audubon Center at Mill Grove

JOHN JAMES AUDUBON
CENTER AT MILL GROVE

Audubon Road

Chimney Sweep
Tower

House
Steps

Museum

Wild Life Sanctuary Road

Wetherills
Dam

Perkiomen Creek

Pawlings Road

Pawlings Road

Two
Logs

4004

4004

422

422

N

Kilometer

Mile

0.2

0.2

0

0

**0.8** Turn right at the trail junction, then turn left and walk between the "two-logs barrier," and then left again at the edge of the meadow. There are trails coming in from the right; ignore them and bear left and go straight ahead.

**0.9** Pass through a tree line, then enter a second meadow.

**1.1** Turn left and reenter the forest. Come to a T in the trail (you've been here before). Turn right and retrace your steps back to the wooden steps, cross Wildlife Sanctuary Road, and continue straight.

**1.3** Come to the chimney sweep tower and kiosk. Continue straight up the hill beside the tree line on your left.

**1.5** The trails turns left up the hill.

**1.6** Make a loop and return between two trees. Arrive back at Wildlife Sanctuary Road and turn right to retrace your steps back to the kiosk.

**2.0** Arrive back at the kiosk.

🌿 **Green Tip:**
*Wash dishes or clothes at least 200 feet from a river or lake. Bring the water to a spot with good drainage, and use only biodegradable soap in the smallest amount.*

*Visit one of the most important sites in American history. Walk through the encampment where General George Washington and 11,000 of his patriot soldiers spent the harsh winter of 1777–1778 after suffering two crushing defeats in Philadelphia. Highlights are the reconstructed soldiers' huts, the Washington Memorial Chapel, the Memorial Arch, and the statue of Baron Frederic von Steuben, the Prussian military leader who volunteered to change Washington's army from a dissolute band of irregulars into a disciplined fighting machine.*

**Start:** The beginning of the hike/bike trail on Rte. 23 near the stoplight.

**Distance:** 7.0-mile loop

**Hiking time:** 3 to 4 hours

**Difficulty:** Moderate, due to length

**Trail surface:** Asphalt path through rolling hills

**Best seasons:** Spring, summer, fall

**Other trail users:** Tourists and cyclists

**Canine compatibility:** Leashed dogs permitted

**Land status:** National Park

**Fees and permits:** No fees or permits required

**Schedule:** 7 a.m. to dark daily

**Maps:** USGS Valley Forge, PA; Valley Forge National Historical Park Map

**Trail Contact:** Valley Forge National Historical Park, 1400 North Outer Line Dr., King of Prussia, PA 19406; (610) 783-1077; www.nps.gov/vafo

**Finding the trailhead:** From Philadelphia take the I-76 W ramp to Valley Forge. Drive 0.2 mile and keep left at the fork, then follow signs for I-76 W/Valley Forge and merge onto I-76 W. Drive 16.7 miles and take exit 327-328A-328B for US 202 N toward US 422 W/King of Prussia/W Chester/Pottstown. Drive 0.1 mile and take exit 328A on the left to merge onto US 422 W toward Pottstown. Drive 2.7 miles and take PA 23 W exit toward Valley Forge. Drive 0.3 mile and turn left onto PA 23 W/West Valley Forge Road. Drive past the visitor center and continue 2.4 miles on PA 23 to the Washington's Headquarters parking area on the right. Trailhead GPS: N40 06.140' / W075 27.459'

The chain of events that led to the Revolutionary War actually began with the French and Indian War (1754–1763) between France and Great Britain, which was fought mostly throughout the northern colonies. Although Britain won the war, it had accumulated a large debt in the process, which it hoped to pay off by imposing taxes on its American colonies. The first of these taxes came in 1765 with the Stamp Act, which set a levy on legal documents, pamphlets, newspapers, deeds, and even playing cards. The second tax was the Tea Act, which eliminated the customs duty on tea purchased from the East India Company, a British company, while maintaining the duty on teas imported from other countries. Frustrated to the point of revolt, the colonists were motivated by the Tea Act to hold the famous Boston Tea Party in December 1773.

It was nearly two years, however, before the revolution proper began: April 19, 1775. British troops were ordered to close the Massachusetts Assembly and capture a stockpile of colonial arms. The colonial militia opened fire on the Loyalists, first at Lexington, then at Concord, where the British had retreated. The skirmish was a strong American victory, with the British suffering nearly three times the American losses. Then, in June of 1775, the Continental Congress commissioned George Washington to organize and lead a Continental Army.

General Washington's Valley Forge encampment began when Sir William Howe loaded 20,000 British troops onto 250 ships and landed in the upper end of

Washington set up his Valley Forge Headquarters in what was the home of Isacc Potts.

the Chesapeake Bay. His objective was to capture Philadelphia, home of the Continental Congress. Although Congress had fled the city, Washington had little choice but to meet Howe and defend the city. Washington's 11,000 soldiers, outnumbered and poorly prepared, lost the Battle of Brandywine on September 11 and the Battle of Germantown on October 4. Howe and his troops occupied Philadelphia.

With winter setting in, the prospects for more campaigning diminished. Washington withdrew his forces 18 miles northwest of Philadelphia to set up camp at Valley Forge, where one of their first tasks was to build 1,000 huts to fight off the bitter winds and snow. But the huts did little to stave off the hunger and disease the men faced with the onset of winter. The troops' shoes and garments were so tattered that at one point more than 4,000 men were declared unfit for duty. More than 2,000 men died that winter from typhus, typhoid, dysentery, and pneumonia; about half of the surviving men deserted.

But as weeks wore on and supplies and equipment and fresh troops trickled in, morale began to lift. Skilled Prussian drillmaster Baron Frederic von Steuben volunteered to drill and train the troops in military tactics. Von Steuben's training resulted in better discipline among the ranks and a renewed sense of ability and confidence in the men.

With spring came the news that the French had signed an alliance with the colonists. Then word came that British troops had pulled out of Philadelphia and were heading to New York. But they would not make it in time. Because of Washington and his ragtag troops' efforts to save Philadelphia, Howe could not move his men north quickly enough. This, in turn, led to the defeat of the British at Saratoga, New York, considered by many scholars as a turning point for the American Revolution.

Hiking this trail is much more than making a simple loop over rolling fields; it will take you back in time, where you can walk through the encampment and immerse yourself in the history and drama of an American landmark. If you were to walk this trail at a normal pace, it might take less than two hours. But it's more than likely you'll want to stop, read the educational plaques, and linger at the displays; you may even want to stop for lunch in the picnic area, or take a short break on the grass. For these reasons, it would be best to set aside three to four hours to complete this journey into American history.

## MILES AND DIRECTIONS

**0.0**  Start at the Washington's Headquarters parking lot. Walk past the restrooms and down the steps to visit the train station, Washington's Headquarters, the guard huts, the barn, the stables, and the Potts House. Afterward, walk to Rte. 23 near the stoplight. Turn left onto the hike/bike path and begin a gentle climb past several monuments and soldier huts on Rte. 23.

# Valley Forge National Historical Park

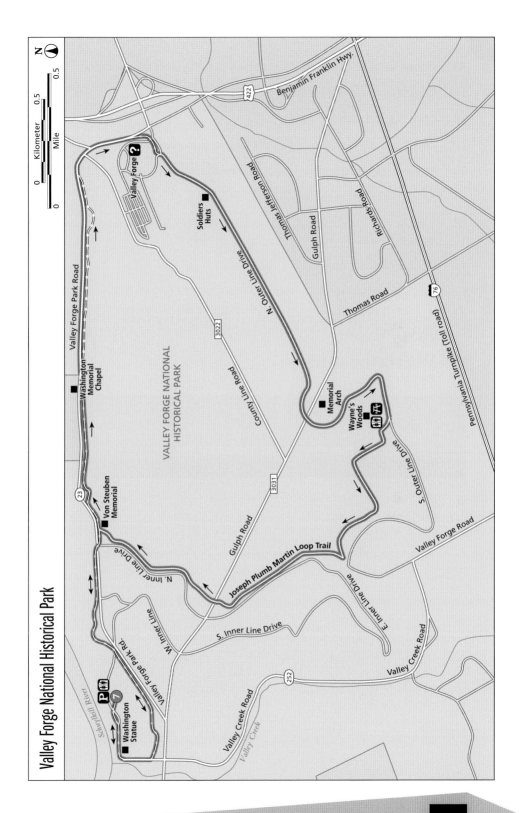

**1.2** Cross Rte. 23. Veer left onto the path and pass the von Steuben statue.

**1.7** Come to the Washington Memorial Chapel on your left.

**1.8** Cross a paved road.

**2.6** Cross a second road and make a short climb to the visitor center.

**2.9** The trail veers left past the visitor center and enters an open field.

**3.3** Arrive at a cluster of soldiers huts.

**3.9** Pass the National Memorial Arch on your left. The trail turns right toward Wayne's Woods.

**4.6** Arrive at Wayne's Woods and a picnic area.

**5.2** Turn right at the fork in the trail.

**6.2** Arrive back at the von Steuben statue. Retrace your steps back to the parking area.

**7.0** Arrive back at your vehicle.

**Green Tip:**
*Especially for day hikes, use a camp stove for cooking so there's no need to make a fire.*

# Northeast Hikes

There are fifteen hikes in this quadrant. The reason for this is that the geology and geography of much of Bucks County created gorges and ravines and fast-moving streams that stretch from one end of the county in the north to the southeastern border, where both streams—the Neshaminy and the Tohickon— end at the mouth of the Delaware River.

When a flood-control dam was built on Tohickon Creek, this became the genesis of Nockamixon State Park and Lake Nockamixon. I chose two hikes of the many hikes in the park. As you might expect, the Old Mill Trail takes you to the ruins of an old mill; the Elephant Trail leads you alongside the lake. Tohickon Creek continues to the next hike at Point Pleasant Community Park just before it empties into the Delaware River.

Lake Galena and Peace Valley Park were created when a flood-control dam was built across the northern branch of Neshaminy Creek, 3 miles north of Doylestown. From there the Neshaminy runs under historic Eight Arch Bridge as it enters Dark Hollow Park; then it continues to a second hike in Dark Hollow. From there the stream wends its way into Tyler State Park and under an historic covered bridge before it passes through the heart of the park, then on to Neshaminy State Park at the Delaware River.

Hiking in this quadrant is not all about the streams, lakes, and Delaware River, however. Drive up Bowman's Hill to the Bowman's Hill Wildflower Preserve and you can hike among the colorful wildflowers and walk the Penn's Woods Tree Trail, which showcases forty-six different native trees of Pennsylvania. For an added bonus, look for the beautifully painted trail signs, which are, in my opinion, the most beautiful trail signs in the state.

And how do you explain the ringing rocks at Ringing Rocks County Park? You don't. Let the experts cast their opinions of this phenomenon; all you need to do is gather up your children and a few hammers and come here and enjoy the crazy sounds as the hammer heads meet the different-sounding boulders.

You can round out your hiking in this section with a visit to a few small nature centers, where you can immerse yourself in learning about the natural world of plants, animals, and trees. In one center, you can brush up on your knowledge of the Lenni Lenape.

# Ringing Rocks County Park

*This is a very short, easy hike; but if you like to explore the mysteries of Mother Nature, it's well worth your time. The Ringing Rocks boulder field is 7 acres of boulders that, when you strike a boulder with a hammer or a piece of lead pipe, it rings out. This hike also takes you to High Falls, the tallest waterfall in Bucks County. Be sure to bring your children and your hammer.*

**Start:** The trailhead at the north side of the parking lot
**Distance:** 1.0-mile out-and-back
**Hiking time:** 1 hour
**Difficulty:** Easy
**Trail surface:** Rocky forest path
**Best seasons:** Spring, summer, fall
**Other trail users:** Tourists
**Canine compatibility:** Leashed dogs permitted
**Land status:** Bucks County Park

**Fees and permits:** No fees or permits
**Schedule:** Dawn to dusk daily
**Map:** USGS Rieglesville
**Trail contacts:** Ringing Rocks Park, Ringing Rocks Rd., Upper Black Eddy, PA 18972; (215) 757-0571; www.buckscounty.org/government/ParksandRecreation/Parks/RingingRocks

**Finding the trailhead:** From Philadelphia take the I-76 W ramp to Valley Forge. Drive 0.2 mile and keep left at the fork, follow signs for 1-76 W/Valley Forge, and merge onto I-76 W. Drive 12.5 miles and take exit 331B to merge onto I-476 N toward Plymouth Meeting. Drive 4.3 miles and take the exit onto I-276 E toward New Jersey; continue 9.1 miles and take exit 343 to merge onto PA 611 N toward Doylestown. Drive 14.5 miles to where PA 611 N turns slightly right and becomes PA 611 N. Drive 12.4 miles and continue straight onto Beaver Road. Drive 0.3 mile and turn left onto Marienstein Road; continue 2.7 miles onto Bridgeton Hill Road. Drive 1.1 miles, then turn left onto Ringing Rocks Road and continue 0.6 mile to the park on the right. Trailhead GPS: N40 21.798' / W075 07.717'

**THE HIKE**

Ringing Rocks is a boulder field that is 7 acres in size and 10 feet deep. It is made up of boulders of every shape and size imaginable. The county park, which surrounds the field, is comprised of 128 acres of forest; there are some boulders—regular boulders, strewn about the forest and along the rocky footpaths. What draws people to the boulder fields is that when some of them are struck with a hard object, such as a hammer, they give out a ringing sound.

The mystery of the Ringing Rocks boulder field has held a fascination for the curious and studious since the days when William Penn still owned the whole state. One early rumor held that witches and practitioners of the Pennsylvania Deutsch healing art known as *powwow* congregated in the area.

In 1965 a geologist from nearby Lafayette College took a few rocks to his lab for testing. He found that when the rocks were struck, they created a series of tones at frequencies lower than the human ear can hear. But when these tones interact with each other, it creates a sound loud enough for humans to hear.

One theory put forth is that while the boulders have gone through ages of the freeze-thaw cycle, some may have cracked inside. When these particular rocks are struck, the blow releases a tension between the cracks.

And there are those who disdain scientific study and simply want to enjoy the mystery. In 1890 Dr. J. J. Ott collected a number of the boulders that rang at

There are boulders of every shape and size strewn about this flat expanse of land that is 10 feet deep and surrounded by an ordinary forest. Aside from the mystery of the pinging, another question is, how did the field come to be located here?

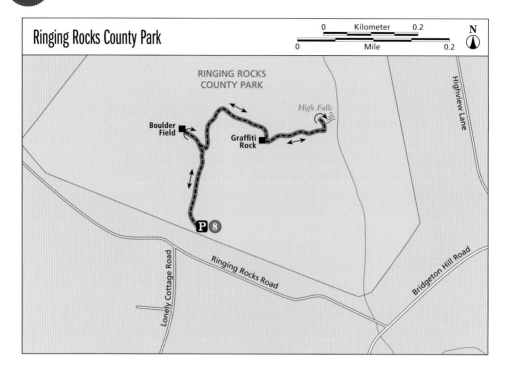

different pitches. Then, with the assistance of a brass band, he played a number of musical selections for the local Buckwampum Historical Society meeting.

The hike begins with a short walk to the boulder field, where you get off the trail and enter the field at one of the different entrances that have been made prominent by years of boots trampling the earth to get to the field.

After the field you return to the trail and continue past a huge square boulder on your right that has been spray painted from stem to stern with colorful graffiti. From there it's on to High Falls, the tallest waterfall in Bucks County with a 20-foot drop off the cliff edge to the base. If you are a waterfall junkie, or if you want to see a lot of water streaming off the cliffs, be sure to come in the rainy season or after a hard rain.

After the falls you simply retrace your steps back to the parking lot.

**MILES AND DIRECTIONS**

**0.0**   Start at the parking area and walk to the trailhead.

**0.1**   Arrive at the edge of the boulder field and walk into it to explore.

**0.2**  Walk out of the boulder field the way you came into it and turn left on the trail.

**0.3**  Arrive at Graffiti Rock.

**0.5**  Arrive at High Falls. Then turnaround and retrace your steps.

**1.0**  Arrive back at the parking lot.

## American Shad

The American shad, which does its spring spawning up the Delaware River from the Atlantic Ocean, is the largest fish of the herring family. This silver fish, with a greenish or bluish sheen on its back, can grow to a length of 30 inches, and the largest will weigh in at 12 pounds. It's a bony fish, but its meat is tasty, and the roe, or eggs, are considered a delicacy.

Native Americans survived on the shad's annual migration, and when European settlers arrived, the Indians taught them how to use fishnets to corral the fish. In fact, the fish caught during the spring shad run on the Delaware River is credited with saving General George Washington's troops from starvation during their time at Valley Forge during the Revolutionary War.

The shad migration continued to thrive in Pennsylvania, supporting commercial fisheries on the Susquehanna and Delaware Rivers. But by the early 1900s the runs stopped on the Susquehanna after hydroelectric dams were constructed across the river and the shad could no longer swim upstream. This left the Delaware River as the only major waterway in Pennsylvania completely accessible to the natural shad migration.

# Nockamixon State Park: Old Mill Trail

*This is an easy hike that starts out in the forest, then passes through a pleasant meadow before leading you to the site of an early nineteenth-century gristmill with its own rock dam. The dam was built to create a holding pond so that if the rushing waters of the stream ran low, water from the pond could be released to keep the gristmill up and running. You will also see artifacts, such as the original millstone, at this site.*

**Start:** The trailhead in the upper parking lot on Deerwood Lane
**Distance:** 1.4-mile loop
**Hiking time:** 1.5 hours
**Difficulty:** Easy
**Trail surface:** Forest footpath, meadow path, paved bike path
**Best seasons:** Spring, summer, fall
**Other trail users:** Tourists, dog walkers, bicyclists
**Canine compatibility:** Leashed dogs permitted

**Land status:** Pennsylvania State Park
**Fees and permits:** No fees or permits
**Schedule:** Dawn to dusk daily
**Maps:** USGS Bedminster; park maps available at park office
**Trail contacts:** Nockamixon State Park, 1542 Mountain View Dr., Quakertown, PA 18951; (215) 529-7300; www.dcnr.state.pa.us/stateparks/findapark/nockamixon

**Finding the trailhead:** Get on I-476 N and take exit 44 for PA 663 N toward Quakertown. Drive 0.5 mile and turn left onto PA 663 N. Drive 3.4 miles and continue on PA 313 E/West Broad Street. Drive 4.8 miles and turn left onto PA 563 N. Drive 3.3 miles and turn right onto Deerwood Lane. Drive 0.1 mile and turn right into the first parking lot. Trailhead GPS: N40 27.599' / W075 14.551'

## THE HIKE

It's hard to imagine now, but there was once a thriving community that sat alongside Tohickon Creek before Lake Nockamixon was created. The history of the village dates back to the 1730s, when the first Scotch-Irish and German settlers arrived in the valley. The first of these settlers was Henry Stover and his wife Barbara, who, along with three other family members, soon owned a sawmill and a number of gristmills.

They named their town Stoverville, but in 1872 when Abram Stover became the town's first postmaster, they renamed it Tohickon Village. By the mid-1800s the village was thriving. Farmers came to town to deliver their milk, visit the country store, pick up feed at the gristmill and lumber from the sawmill, or visit the creamery, blacksmith, or post office.

One mill—the Tohickon Valley Mills—was doing very well. The products from their stone-ground mill were so popular that people came from all over to buy their flour directly from the mill, while other customers, from all over the United States, received their goods by mail order.

Timber was the major local industry, but by the early 1900s the forests were depleted. Other businesses had slowed down as well, so by the time of the Great Depression of 1930, many of the Tohickon businesses had shut their doors. By the mid-1960s there was one business left—a used-goods shop—and only four families still lived in Tohickon.

This stone dam created a holding pond to supply water to the mills if the stream ran low.

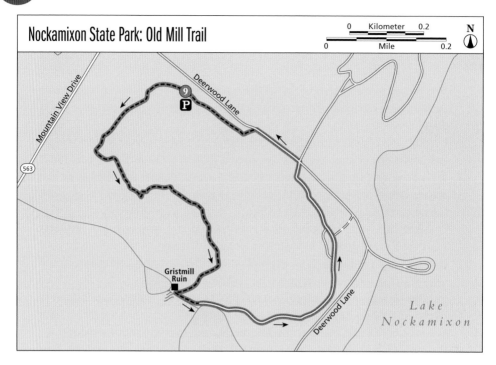

**Nockamixon State Park: Old Mill Trail**

In 1958, the secretary of the Department of Forests and Waters, Dr. Maurice K. Goddard, proposed building a state park and a dam across the fast-flowing waters of Tohickon Creek as a part of the US Army Corps of Engineers plan for the Delaware River Basin. Two other streams, Haycock Run and Three Mile Creek, provided more water, as they emptied into Tohickon Creek at the site chosen for the dam.

The park was originally called Tohickon State Park, but by 1965 the name of the lake was changed to Lake "Nockamixon," from the Lenni Lenape phrase meaning "at the place of soft soil." The park was officially opened as Nockamixon State Park in 1973.

The Old Mill Trail is well maintained and well marked with red blazes. There are other trails in the area, mostly horse trails, that cross the hiking trails, but obviously you should ignore them. Besides, if you stop and look at these intersecting trails, you'll see that the surface of a horse trail is rougher than a hiking trail.

At 0.6 mile you arrive at the mill pond and a tableau constructed to show the various aspects of operating a water-powered mill. As is pointed out on the educational plaque at the site, the mill was located downstream on Tohickon Creek. The discharge water from the pond, and two more ponds upstream, was held and released to keep the paddlewheel running when the normal water flow from the stream was down.

From the dam you connect with the paved bike path, then turn left onto Deerwood Lane to make your way back to the parking lot for the conclusion of a very pleasant hike.

## MILES AND DIRECTIONS

**0.0** Start at the upper end of the parking lot at the sign for The Old Mill Trail.

**0.2** Pass through a rocky section, then the trail turns right. Follow the red blazes.

**0.3** Come to an open meadow and turn left following the red blazes. At 50 feet you come to a Y. Take the path on the right to hike into the forest.

**0.6** Arrive at the waterfall and the ruins of the gristmill and an educational plaque. Continue on the trail.

**0.7** Get on the paved bike path and walk to the right side of the cul-de-sac.

**1.1** Turn left onto the Deerwood Lane and walk uphill.

**1.3** Turn left into the south end of the parking lot.

**1.4** Arrive back at your vehicle.

🍃 **Green Tip:**
*Consider citronella as an effective natural mosquito repellent.*

# Nockamixon State Park: Elephant Trail

*The Elephant Trail runs along the south side of Lake Nockamixon, from the western end of the lake near Elephant Road to the eastern end at the dam. This hike runs from the western end of the lake to the park cabins, where you turn around and take a second section of the trail that runs parallel with the first section. At points along the way you will get an unobstructed view of the lake, with its colorful sailboats, fishing boats, kayaks, and canoes; and, if you're in the right place at the right time of the year, you'll also see migratory waterfowl and raptors that use Lake Nockamixon as a stopover.*

**Start:** The Elephant Trail parking lot on Elephant Road
**Distance:** 3.7-mile figure-eight
**Hiking time:** 2 hours
**Difficulty:** Easy
**Trail surface:** Horse trails, dirt roads, gravel roads, forest footpaths
**Best seasons:** Summer, fall
**Other trail users:** Equestrians, tourists
**Canine compatibility:** Leashed dogs permitted

**Land status:** Pennsylvania State Park
**Fees and permits:** No fees or permits
**Schedule:** Dawn to dusk daily
**Maps:** USGS Bedminster; park maps available at park office
**Trail contacts:** Nockamixon State Park, 1542 Mountain View Dr., Quakertown, PA 18951; (215) 529-7300; www.dcnr.state.pa.us/stateparks/findapark/nockamixon

**Finding the trailhead:** From Philadelphia get on I-476 N and take exit 31 for PA 63 toward Landsdale. Drive 0.6 mile and turn right onto PA 63 W/Sumneytown Pike. Drive 0.9 mile and take the first right onto Wambold Road. Drive 1.8 miles and turn left onto Pennsylvania 1001/Allentown Road. Drive 0.5 mile and take the second right onto Elroy Road. Drive 0.3 mile and continue onto Beck Road. Drive 0.8 mile and continue onto Leidy Road. Drive 0.6 mile to where Leidy Road turns slightly right and becomes West Cherry Lane. Drive 1.4 miles and turn left onto Bethlehem Pike. Drive 0.5 mile and turn right onto PA 113 N/East Main Street/Souderton Road. Drive 5.1 miles and turn left onto Minsi Trail; continue 1.5 miles and take a slight left onto PA 313 W. Drive 0.3 mile and take a slight right onto Old Bethlehem Road. Drive 2.0 miles and turn right onto Creek Road. Drive 0.1 mile and take a slight right onto Elephant Road and into the parking lot on your left. Trailhead GPS: N/40 25.695' / W075 15.123'

## THE HIKE

If you were to look at old maps of the area that is now Nockamixon State Park, you would see that there were many roads that led to the businesses and homes that were located along both sides of Tohickon Creek. In 1965, when construction on the park began, over 290 properties in five surrounding townships were demolished to prepare the area.

If you think that "The Elephant Trail" is a curious name for a hiking trail in rural Bucks County, you're right. There are probably those hikers who, upon hearing the name, picture an overturned circus train where the elephants ran away and were found drinking the waters of Tohickon Creek. But that story is a myth.

The truth is that the trail is named after the tiny hamlet of Elephant, which includes a few houses and a hotel at the intersection of Ridge Road and Elephant Road, less than a mile from the Elephant Trail parking area.

The hamlet got its peculiar name back in 1848 when the Elephant Hotel was opened at that same intersection. The owners hung a large round sign with a picture of a white elephant in the center and the name of the hotel encircling it. Ever since, that intersection became Elephant Hamlet.

On the old map of the area, the Elephant Trail runs alongside Tohickon Creek, then connects with what is now Elephant Road. For those interested, the original Elephant Hotel sign can be seen at the Mercer Museum in Doylestown.

These two man-made walls set here in the middle of the forest must have been built for some purpose, but it's hard to imagine just what they were going to be.

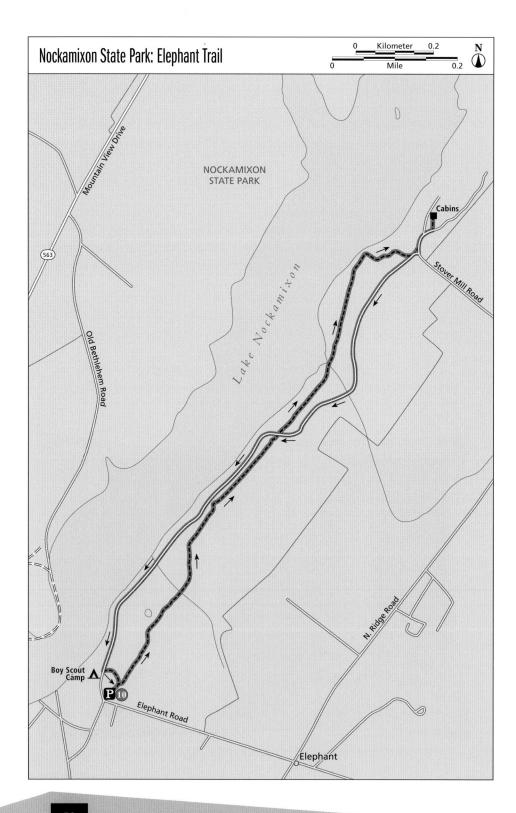

0     Kilometer     0.2

0           Mile           0.2

N

NOCKAMIXON
STATE PARK

Cabins

Mountain View Drive

563

Old Bethlehem Road

Lake Nockamixon

Stover Mill Road

N. Ridge Road

Boy Scout
Camp

P 10

Elephant Road

Elephant

This hike is pretty straightforward. At 0.5 mile you turn right and get on the southernmost trail and continue to the Stover Mill Road trailhead, which is also the access point to walk a short distance to see Cabin No. 1. When you leave Cabin No. 1 and return to the trailhead, facing the trailhead, take the trail that goes off to the left; then at 2.7 miles you cross the trail you came in on, and in effect you have made a flattened figure-eight.

After this, look for the Boy Scout camp on your left, then turn left to reenter the Elephant Trail parking area.

If you do this hike after a hard rain, the trail can be muddy, but if you take the high ground on either side of the trail, you can for the most part keep your boots from getting soaked. It's a short, easy hike, so a little mud won't ruin your hike.

## MILES AND DIRECTIONS

**0.0**  Start at lower end of the parking area by the exit sign. Follow the red blazes.

**0.5**  Cross a small stream. Come to a major trail intersection and turn right.

**1.2**  Cross a stream on a man-made bridge.

**1.3**  The trail takes you very close to the edge of the lake, then cuts inland.

**1.6**  The trail takes you very close to the edge of the lake a second time.

**1.8**  Arrive at an access point parking area. Walk on the road to the cabins. Retrace your steps across Stover Mill Road and take the trail to the left.

**2.7**  Cross over the trail you came in on and continue on the trail closest to the lake.

**3.6**  Pass by the Boy Scout camp. Then turn left to get to the parking lot.

**3.7**  Arrive back at the parking lot and your vehicle.

### Nockamixon State Park Whitewater Release

There are a number of ways to get from Nockamixon State Park to the Delaware River at Point Pleasant Pike. But the quickest and most exciting way to actually get *into* the Delaware River near Point Pleasant is to launch your kayak into Tohickon Creek below the dam at Lake Nockamixon or at Ralph Stover State Park on the first full weekend of November or the third weekend in March and wait for the whitewater rerelease, as the water from the lake is let loose, causing at some points, Class IV rapids to send you on your way.

# Tinicum County Park to Uhlerstown Covered Bridge

*This is an easy, flat hike that anyone can do. You begin on the towpath, where you just might see a great blue heron or a huge turtle floating just below the surface of the water. Once in Uhlerstown you can check out the covered bridge and Lock No. 18. Then it's back to the park, where you can visit the historic Erwin-Stover House, and after that you're free to explore the rest of the park, where there are shaded picnic areas and a playground.*

**Start:** The trailhead bulletin board on the Delaware Canal Towpath
**Distance:** 3.2-mile lollipop
**Hiking time:** 2 hours
**Difficulty:** Easy
**Trail surface:** Gravel, macadam roads, grassy field
**Best seasons:** Spring, summer, fall
**Other trail users:** Bicyclists, baby strollers, joggers, dog walkers
**Canine compatibility:** Leashed dogs permitted

**Land status:** Bucks County Park
**Fees and permits:** No fees or permit
**Schedule:** Open daily, 8 a.m. to sunset
**Map:** USGS Frenchtown
**Trail contacts:** Tinicum County Park, 963 River Rd., Erwinna, PA 18972; (215) 757-0571; www .buckscounty.org/government/ parksandrecreation/parks/Tinicum

**Finding the trailhead:** From Philadelphia take I-95 N and take exit 51 toward New Hope. Drive 0.3 mile and turn left onto Taylorsville Road. Continue 5.1 miles and turn left onto PA 32 N/River Road. Drive 8.0 miles and turn left onto PA 32 N; continue 5.2 miles and turn right to stay on PA 32 N. Drive 5.9 miles and turn left into the park. Continue to the parking lot near the playground. Trailhead GPS: N40 30.359' / W75 04.408'

## THE HIKE

This hike begins at the trailhead bulletin board on the canal towpath. Facing the bulletin board, turn right and walk with the canal on your left. At 0.5 mile you pass a giant locust tree on your right. When you return from Uhlerstown, you will come once again to this tree at 2.3 miles on your left; it is here that you will turn left and enter the park proper.

As you hike from the trailhead to Uhlerstown, you can examine a wooden feeder canal that feeds water under the towpath and into the canal.

At 1.4 miles you arrive at the Uhlerstown Covered Bridge, which, like most covered bridges, is painted red, with a white portal, and one window on each side. The single-span bridge was erected in 1832 using the Town Truss system, and it is the only bridge in the canal system that crosses the Delaware Canal.

When you get to the road that runs through the bridge—Uhlerstown Hill Road—you come to a Pennsylvania Museum Commission plaque that informs you that Uhlerstown was originally called "Mexico" and that its name was changed to Uhlerstown after Michael Uhler, the town's first postmaster. He also owned a line of canal boats, limekilns, coal yards, and a country store at this location.

Just upstream from the bridge you come to Lock No. 18, where you can see the original stone sidewalls and how the lock operates.

After you have explored the lock and bridge, you head back in the direction you came until, at 2.3 miles, you turn left at the giant locust tree and walk

Life along the Delaware Canal can be peaceful and secluded.

through the grassy field onto the gravel road that takes you past the polo field. At this point, if you look on your left, you can see the historic Erwin-Stover House, which has a history that stretches from the Revolutionary War to the twentieth century.

The land for the house was purchased by Colonel Arthur Irwin, a local Revolutionary War hero who had the town of Erwinna named after him. Irwin's son William inherited the land and built the Federal-style house on 126 acres in the early 1800s. When William died, his daughter inherited the property, and at her death in 1846, the home was acquired at auction by Henry Stover, a successful miller. The land and the home, with its giant red barn, remained in the Stover family until 1955, when the family donated the house and barn and the 126 acres of land to Bucks County, which in turn took the property and turned it into the county's first park: Tinicum County Park.

Obviously you can interrupt your hike to tour the house (it's open for tours from noon to 4 p.m. Saturday and Sunday from May 1 through October 31), or you can finish your hike and then return to the house for a tour. Either way, it's a great way to cap off a great hike.

## MILES AND DIRECTIONS

**0.0** Start at the trailhead bulletin board on the Delaware Canal towpath. Facing the bulletin board, turn right and walk north with the canal on your left.

**0.5** Note the huge locust tree on your right.

**1.4** Arrive at Uhlerstown Covered Bridge and Lock No. 18. After you explore Uhlerstown, return the way you came.

**2.3** Arrive back at the giant locust tree. Turn left onto a mowed path and go down the bank. Walk across the field to a copse of trees and hook left around the trees.

**2.4** Arrive at the gravel road and turn left.

**2.5** Turn right and walk past the polo field.

**2.7** Pass the maintenance buildings on your left. Ignore a gravel road going off to your right. At this point you can see the Erwin-Stover House.

**3.0** Turn right on the paved road and walk toward the playground.

**3.2** Arrive back at your vehicle.

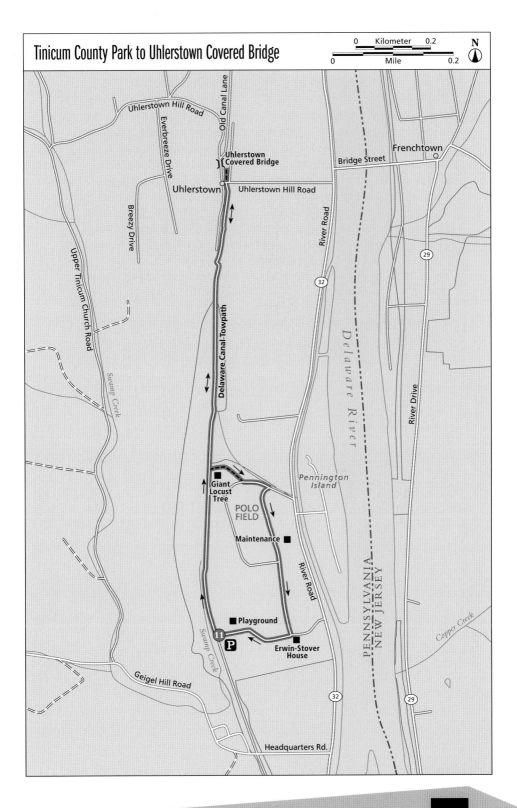

# Tinicum County Park to Uhlerstown Covered Bridge

Uhlerstown Hill Road

Everbreeze Drive

Old Canal Lane

Uhlerstown Covered Bridge

Frenchtown

Bridge Street

Uhlerstown

Uhlerstown Hill Road

Breezy Drive

River Road

Upper Tinicum Church Road

29

32

*Swamp Creek*

Delaware Canal-Towpath

*Delaware River*

River Drive

Giant Locust Tree

*Pennington Island*

POLO FIELD

Maintenance

PENNSYLVANIA
NEW JERSEY

River Road

*Copper Creek*

Playground

11

P

Erwin-Stover House

*Swamp Creek*

Geigel Hill Road

32

29

Headquarters Rd.

0   Kilometer   0.2
0        Mile        0.2

N

## Disc Golf at Tinicum County Park

There are plenty of things to do and see in Tinicum County Park. Actually, the first thing you see when you drive into the park and make your way to the playground parking lot is a metal pole about 4 feet high embedded upright in the ground. This pole has a circular band around its top with evenly spaced chains dangling from the band to a bottom basket. The basket is there to catch the Frisbee-like discs that players (sooner or later) fling into the chains, thus causing the disc to flop into the basket.

Welcome to disc golf. Just like golfers, players in Tinicum Park take their shots then follow-up shots until they are able to land their discs into the basket. The chains are there to slow down and actually stop the discs without causing any major damage. The course at Tinicum has a series of tees where players start out, as well as fairways of different lengths with various obstacles, such as pine trees, to test players' skills.

For more information call Tinicum County Park at (215) 757-0571 or visit the Professional Disc Golf Association at www.pdga.com.

# Point Pleasant Community Park: Chief Running Deer Trail

*Chief Running Deer Trail is a rugged hike: The terrain is rocky, and there are trees down across the trail. However, this hike is suitable for beginners, because, first of all, it's a short hike and, second, there are no long, steep climbs. Plus, if you're interested in seeing one of the most powerful waterfalls on Tohickon Creek, this hike will lead you safely to the water's edge for a world-class view and photo opportunity.*

**Start:** The trail parking lot

**Distance:** 2.0 miles out-and-back

**Hiking time:** 1.5 hours

**Difficulty:** Moderate

**Trail surface:** Rocky forest path, boulders, fallen trees

**Best season:** Fall for foliage

**Other trail users:** Fishermen, dog walkers, kayakers

**Canine compatibility:** Leashed dogs permitted

**Land status:** Bucks County Park

**Fees and permits:** No fees or permits

**Schedule:** Open daily, 8 a.m. to sunset

**Map:** USGS Lumberville

**Trail contacts:** C/O Tohickon Valley Park, Cafferty Road, Point Pleasant, PA 18950; (215) 297-5625; www.buckscounty.org/government/parks/Tohickon

**Finding the trailhead:** From Philadelphia head east on South Penn Square toward Avenue of the Arts/South Broad Street. Go 0.2 mile to where South Penn Square turns slightly left and becomes John F. Kennedy Boulevard. Go 259 feet and turn right onto North Broad Street. Go 0.3 mile and turn right onto the I-676 E/US 30 E ramp to I-95. Go 0.2 mile and merge onto I-676/US 30 E. Go 0.3 mile and take the exit on the left toward Trenton. Go 0.9 mile and merge onto I-95 N. Drive 28.3 miles and take exit 51 toward New Hope. Drive 0.3 mile and turn left onto Taylorsville Road (watch for signs for New Hope.). Continue 5.1 miles and turn left onto PA 32 N/River Road. Drive 8.0 miles and turn left onto PA 32 N. Drive 5.2 miles and continue straight onto Tohickon Hill Road. Go 197 feet to the trail parking area. Trailhead GPS: N40 25.374' / W075 04.023'

### THE HIKE

Tohickon Creek begins in the northwestern corner of Bucks County and runs in a southeasterly direction for 30.0 miles until it empties into the Delaware River at Point Pleasant. Along the way, at about the 19.0-mile mark, it is dammed to create Lake Nockamixon. At 26.0 miles it runs through Ralph Stover State Park and the last 4.0-mile stretch passes through Point Pleasant Community Park, where your hike begins.

The first thing you come to as soon as you turn left on the path from the parking lot is a small veterans memorial area that includes a picnic table; a squared-off boulder with a circular concavity in its center; a stone carving of Chief Running Deer, a prominent Lenni Lenape chief; and a plaque dedicated to an inveterate hiker of this trail.

The word *Tohickon* is a Lenni Lenape word meaning "Deer Bone Creek," which suggests that the land in the creek valley were, in Chief Running Deer's era, prime hunting ground.

If you are interested in looking for wildflowers or other flora, keep your eyes open for trillium, Christmas fern, woodland phlox, mayapples, toothwort, bloodroot, bishop's cap, and wild ginger. You may also see and smell the powerful fragrance of multiflora rose, a white flower that is not a native plant and one most people try to eliminate.

The waters of Tohickon Creek swirl around the creek-bottom boulders, creating a tricky water trail for kayakers to maneuver, while others are content to take in the beauty of nature.

# Point Pleasant Community Park: Chief Running Deer Trail

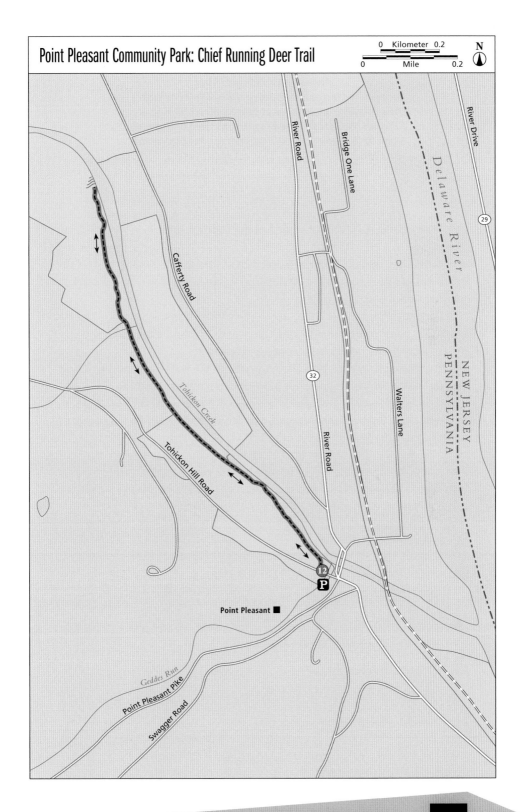

> **Pennsylvania's Brook Trout**
> **Each year over a million Pennsylvania fishermen cast**
> **their lines into 4,000 miles of cold-water streams in**
> **hopes of reeling in a brook trout, the state's only native**
> **trout. In 1970 the "Brookie" was named Pennsylvania's**
> **state fish.**

Tohickon Creek is considered one of the cleanest streams in Pennsylvania. The evidence of this high water quality is that several rare species, such as the riverweed, river sponge, and freshwater mussels are able to flourish in the fast-moving water. Also, the creek is identified as a cold-water fishery and is stocked with trout each year.

Looking at the creek you may notice the difference in the coloring of its riverbed. This happens because the creek basin in this section is lined with alternating bands of Triassic shales, sandstones, and argillites.

The hike is pretty straightforward: You walk a mile on the trail that has its ups and downs, as well as a number of blow-downs scattered here and there, and end at the site of a major waterfall. When you get to the waterfall area, there are flat rocks along the creek where you can walk out, essentially, into the stream to get the best vantage point for a photo.

After the waterfall, retrace your steps back to the parking area. After your hike, consider visiting the Point Pleasant downtown area, which aside from its history as a canal-side village and stagecoach stop, is best known these days as a quaint village with antiques shops, inns, and restaurants.

## MILES AND DIRECTIONS

**0.0**   Start at the parking area. Turn left and enter the memorial area. Turn left onto the trail and walk upstream with the creek on your right.

**0.3**   The trail gets rocky as you begin an uphill ascent.

**0.5**   Pass a small waterfall in the creek.

**0.9**   Come to a rocky washout.

**1.0**   Arrive at the waterfall. Retrace your steps back to the parking area.

**2.0**   Arrive back at the parking area.

# Peace Valley Park

*Although this hike is 6.1 miles, it's an easy hike suitable for just about anyone. If you want to hike and your younger children want to ride their bikes, no problem. The entire trail is paved and in excellent condition, so there are just about as many bike riders as hikers. Also, if anyone needs a break, there are bathrooms and pine-shaded picnic tables on both sides of Lake Galena.*

**Start:** The North Chapman Road parking lot
**Distance:** 6.1-mile loop
**Hiking time:** 2.5 to 3 hours
**Difficulty:** Easy
**Trail surface:** Paved path, forest footpath
**Best seasons:** Spring, summer, fall
**Other trail users:** Bicyclists, baby strollers, dog walkers
**Canine compatibility:** Leashed dogs permitted

**Land status:** Bucks County Park
**Fees and permits:** No fees or permits
**Schedule:** Dawn to dusk daily
**Map:** USGS Doylestown
**Trail contacts:** Peace Valley Park, 230 Creek Rd., Doylestown, PA 18901; (215) 822-8608; www .buckscounty.org/government/ parks/Peacevalley

**Finding the trailhead:** From Philadelphia head east on South Penn Square toward Avenue of the Arts/South Broad Street. Drive 0.2 mile to where South Penn turns slightly left and becomes John F. Kennedy Boulevard. Continue and turn right onto North Broad Street. Drive 7.7 miles and turn left onto PA 309 N/West Cheltenham Avenue; continue 1.3 miles to take a slight right onto PA 309 N. Drive 12.7 miles and take the ramp onto US 202. Continue 3.3 miles and turn left onto PA 152 N/ South Limekiln Pike. Drive 1.4 miles and turn right onto West Butler Avenue. Drive 0.2 mile and turn left onto North Main Street; continue 0.2 mile and take the second right onto Park Avenue. Drive 1.4 miles and turn right onto Ferry Road, then drive 2.9 miles and turn left on to North Chapman Road; continue 0.5 mile to the parking area. Trailhead GPS: N40 20.240' / W075 10.013'

## 13

### THE HIKE

The area that is now Peace Valley Park came into existence when the Lenni Lenape Indians began mining the valley for the large deposits of lead found there. They used the lead to make kitchen and cooking utensils, as well as hunting and hand tools.

After the Lenni Lenape, the land came into the possession of the Free Society of Traders, who discovered galena ore in 1856. Galena is the main ore in lead, and because it has a lower melting point, it is easily separated from lead and was considered a valuable commodity in mining operations. In some instances galena may consist of 1 to 2 percent silver, in which case the silver that is removed is far more valuable than the galena.

The discovery of galena prompted a feverish mining operation, which included zinc, copper, and gold. But the excitement slowly waned until in 1932, when operations ceased and the area was renamed as the village of New Galena.

Construction began on Lake Galena in the early 1970s with an earthen dam built across the North Branch of Neshaminy Creek in the area that is now Peace Valley Park. The purpose of the dam was to provide flood control and to supply water and for recreation. In 1974 the project was completed and 365-acre Lake Galena became the centerpiece of Peace Valley Park.

The 365-acre Lake Galena was created in 1974 for flood control. Today it is the centerpiece of Peace Valley Park, where visitors can fish, kayak, and sail.

This hike, for the most part, circles the lake on a paved hike and bike trail. At 4.3 miles the hike leaves the paved trail and enters into the forest, where hikers get a firsthand look at wildlife and to see if any of the 287 bird species that have been spotted here since 1979 are hanging around.

If you are a serious birder, or an interested beginner, be sure to stop at the Peace Valley Nature Center at the beginning of the hike to get one of their bird checklists. The pamphlet lists all the species of birds that have been seen in the park; it also explains, to the novice, that you have a better chance of seeing certain species of birds during the spring and fall migration. The most common birds in the park are cardinals, woodpeckers, finches, titmice, and sparrows.

If you've finished the hike and are looking for more to do, you could rent a boat and try your hand with a rowboat, canoe, paddleboat, Aqua Finn (a small sailboat), 14-foot sailboat, or kayak single or double. You can rent these craft by the hour or by the day.

## The Nockamixon Cliffs

At 500 feet above sea level, the Nockamixon Cliffs in Delaware Canal State Park are something to see—and, perhaps, climb. Remnants from the Jurassic Period, the cliffs were formed by a weather-resistant, super-hard rock called hornfel. During its creation, the hornfel rock held fast while the surrounding sandstone and shale were eroded by wind and water, giving the cliffs the appearance that they rose up from the surrounding terrain.

You can hike the trails on the cliffs during spring, summer, or fall. But if you want to scale the 500-foot face in the dead of winter, it will be an ice climb. As it turns out, there's a lot of wet ground in the area above the cliffs, and that water seeps through into gullies and forms ice on the face. And because the cliffs face northeast, they receive winter sunlight only from 10 a.m. to 1 p.m., making them ideal for serious ice climbers.

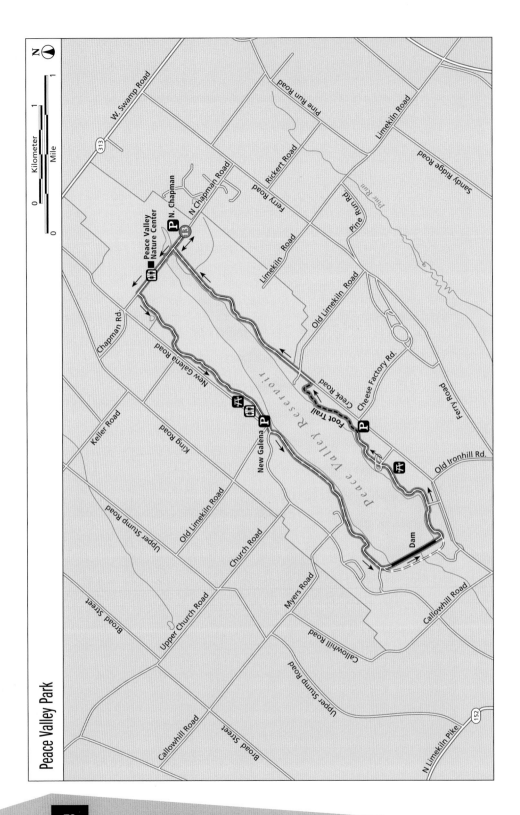

Peace Valley Park

## MILES AND DIRECTIONS

**0.0**   Start at the North Chapman Road parking lot. Leave the parking lot and turn left onto the paved trail.

**0.3**   Pass the visitor and nature center and bathrooms on your left.

**0.5**   Turn left onto the paved path.

**1.6**   Pass the north park entrance and parking area.

**2.9**   Turn left and cross the dam.

**3.3**   Turn left on the trail.

**4.0**   Pass the picnic area.

**4.3**   Leave the paved path and enter into the woods on a footpath.

**4.7**   Turn right at the Y to leave the forest. Then turn left onto the paved path.

**6.0**   Turn right onto North Chapman Road.

**6.1**   Arrive back at the parking lot and your vehicle.

# Bowman's Hill Wildflower Preserve

*You begin this easy hike by walking downhill to a pristine stream where you can explore an authentic millrace dam, then visit a log cabin before you cross the stream on an historic three-arched stone bridge. Next, it's on to the Audubon Trail and a visit to the bird-viewing platform; then it's a short hike to the Pond Trail, where you can explore the aquatic plants and wildlife. From here you take the mowed Meadow Path and pass an historic pavilion on your way back to the parking area.*

**Start:** The Parry Trail trailhead near the parking lot

**Distance:** 1.8-mile loop

**Hiking time:** 1.5 hours

**Difficulty:** Easy

**Trail surface:** Forest footpath, gravel paths, paved roads, and mowed grass

**Best season:** Summer

**Other trail users:** Birders, horticulturists

**Canine compatibility:** No pets allowed inside the fenced portion of the preserve

**Land status:** Owned by the preserve, which is a nonprofit organization

**Fees and permits:** Adults: $5; seniors: $3; children 4–14: $2; children under 4: free

**Schedule:** Preserve is open 8:30 a.m. to sunset daily; visitor center is open 9 a.m. to 5 p.m., Tues–Sun

**Maps:** USGS Lambertville; preserve maps

**Trail contacts:** Bowman's Hill Wildflower Preserve, PO Box 685, 1635 River Rd., New Hope, PA 18938; (215) 862-2924; www .bhwp@bhwp.org

**Finding the trailhead:** From Philadelphia take I-95 N. Take exit 51 toward New Hope. Drive 0.3 mile and turn left onto Taylorsville Road (look for signs for New Hope). Drive 5.1 miles and turn left onto PA 32 N. Drive 2.3 miles and turn left onto Bowman's Hill Tower Road. Take the first left to stay on Bowman's Hill Tower Road. Drive 0.4 mile into the preserve and the parking lot. Trailhead GPS: N40 19.715' / W074 56.606'

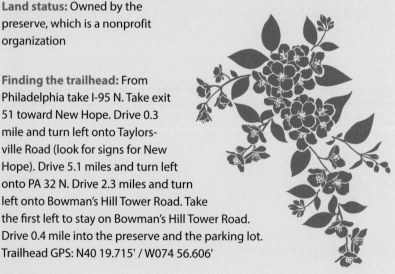

## THE HIKE

No matter where you may have hiked in Pennsylvania, it's unlikely you have hiked anywhere as extraordinary as this 134-acre preserve. To start with, of the approximately 2,000 species of plants native to Pennsylvania, Bowman's is home to nearly 800 of them; and more than 80 of these species are rare, threatened, or endangered native plants designated as Plants of Special Concern in Pennsylvania.

As for trees, between 1890 and 1930 most of the forested lands in Pennsylvania were clear-cut, leaving behind a barren landscape that was devastated by erosion and wildfires. During the 1930s the Pennsylvania Forestry Department began a massive project of reforesting the land, employing mostly young men from the Works Progress Administration and the Civilian Conservation Corps.

In 1944 Bowman's began its own reforesting project. Its objective was to establish a collection of Pennsylvania's native trees. Today that collection is complete and visitors can walk through the preserve's 9-acre arboretum known as Penn's Woods and explore Pennsylvania's forty-six different native trees.

If you want to visit the arboretum after your hike, get the brochure titled "Penn's Woods Tree Trail: A Self-Guided Tour from the Visitor Center." This brochure is also a map that lists each species of tree along its 1-mile route.

Your hike begins at the Parry Trail trailhead near the visitor center and parking lot. You walk downhill to the banks of Pidcock Creek, which is a tributary

Visitors to the pond can explore its aquatic plants and wildlife such as turtles, frogs, and dragonflies.

of the Delaware River. Like many streams across the state, the waters from this stream were used to power mills. And in most cases a dam was built upstream from the mill so that if the creek water got low, water from the dam would be let out to keep the mill operating.

At 0.4 mile you arrive at a log cabin that was built in 1935 as a park ranger station. Made from American chestnut logs by workers from the Works Progress Administration, this was the first structure built in the preserve.

You leave the cabin on a set of steps that lead you to the Azalea Trail and across a historic three-arch stone bridge. Then you're on the Azalea at the Bridge Trail, and here you can look for, naturally, azaleas, plus gentian plants, ferns, and violets. You may also recognize some of the more well-known species of trees, such as the paper birch, American beech, sycamore, white pine, and eastern hemlock.

You are then back at the paved road, which you cross and enter the forest on the Audubon Trail, where you first pass a shelter then a bird-watching platform and blind. Then it's back on the road again until you take the Marsh Marigold Trail, where, because Pidcock Creek overflows and creates a marshy swamp on this side of the road, you are likely to see a yellow plant called a marsh marigold.

Once again you're back on the road and heading for higher ground when at 0.9 mile you turn left onto the Pond Trail, which leads you to a pond where you can observe aquatic plants and pond wildlife such as turtles, frogs, and dragonflies.

On the road yet again you leave the fenced part of the preserve through the gate and turn right onto the Meadow Path, which leads you past the Moore Pavilion before you re-enter the preserve and walk to the parking lot and your vehicle.

## MILES AND DIRECTIONS

**0.0**    Start at parking lot. Walk toward the visitor center and turn right into an open area. Walk 90 feet and turn left onto the Parry Trail.

**0.1**    Turn right on the Millrace Trail.

**0.2**    Come to Pidcock Creek and explore the viewing area with a picket fence, bench, and slate patio.

**0.3**    Arrive at the intersection of the Azalea Trail and the Bucks Trail. Turn left on the Azalea Trail.

**0.4**    Arrive at the log cabin. Turn left on the Azalea Trail and go down the steps. Then turn left again onto the paved road and cross Pidcock Creek on a stone bridge. After crossing the bridge, turn left on the Azaleas at the Bridge Trail.

# Bowman's Hill Wildflower Preserve

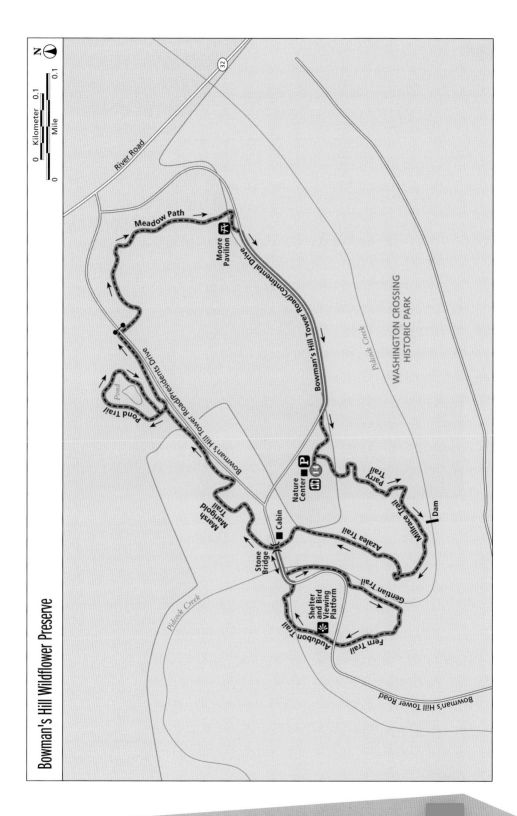

**14**

**0.5**   Turn left on the Gentian Trail. Then turn right on the Gentian Trail.

**0.6**   Turn left onto the Fern Trail. Then turn right onto the Wayside Trail and cross the road and get on the Audubon Trail. Pass a shelter and a bird-viewing platform.

**0.7**   Cross the stone bridge a second time. Then turn left onto the Marsh Marigold Trail.

**0.8**   Turn left onto Presidents Drive.

**0.9**   Turn left at the Pond Trail. Explore the pond, then complete the loop and walk to the road and turn left onto Presidents Drive.

**1.2**   Walk out of the compound through the gate. Then turn right on the Meadow Path and walk to the right of the picnic pavilion.

**1.4**   Turn right on Bowman's Hill Tower Road/Continental Drive and reenter the preserve.

**1.8**   Arrive back at parking lot and your vehicle.

🦆 **Green Tip:**
*Never feed wild animals under any circumstances.*
*You may endanger their health and expose yourself*
*(and them) to danger.*

# Dark Hollow Park: Eight Arch Bridge

*This hike is a double whammy: First, it's a short, easy hike alongside one of the pretti- est streams in Bucks County, where you might see fishermen in waders casting about for native trout or a pair of kayakers floating along as the tree-shaded stream spo- radically reflects the sun. And second, the trail leads you to an historically significant eight-arch bridge, where the only thing you'll need is a camera.*

**Start:** The trailhead on the north side of the parking lot
**Distance:** 1.6-mile out-and-back
**Hiking time:** 1.5 hours
**Difficulty:** Easy
**Trail surface:** Forest footpath
**Best seasons:** Spring, summer, fall
**Other trail users:** Fishermen
**Canine compatibility:** Leashed dogs permitted

**Land status:** Bucks County Park
**Fees and permits:** No fees or permit
**Schedule:** Dawn to dusk daily
**Map:** USGS Buckingham
**Trail contacts:** Bucks County Parks, 901 E. Bridgetown Pike, Langhorne, PA 19047; (215) 348-6114; www.buckscounty.org/government/parks/Dark Hollow

**Finding the trailhead:** From Philadelphia get on the I-676/US 30 E ramp to I-95. Drive 0.2 mile and merge onto I-676/US 30 E; continue 0.3 mile and take the exit on the left toward Trenton. Drive 0.9 mile and merge onto I-95 N, then drive 12.2 miles and take exit 35 for PA 63 W/Woodhaven Road. Drive 0.6 mile and continue on PA 63 W/Woodhaven Road. Drive 2.9 miles and take the exit toward US 1 N/Morrisville. Drive 0.3 mile and merge onto Roosevelt Boulevard. Drive 1.1 miles and continue on US 1 N. Drive 0.2 mile and take the slight left onto Old Lincoln Highway. Drive 0.7 mile and turn left onto PA 132 W/East Street Road; continue for 8.4 miles and turn right on PA 263 N. Drive 3.8 miles and turn right onto Mill Road; continue 0.9 mile to the parking lot on your left. Trailhead GPS: N40 16.144' / W075 04.505'

As you begin this hike, it may be hard to imagine that you are walking into the cradle of American history, but you are.

The original bridge that crossed Neshaminy Creek at the site of the Eight Arch Bridge was built in 1710 to convey travelers on the Old York Road across the creek and on to points north to New York City or south to Philadelphia, as well as all the important cities and villages along the way.

On the evening of August 10, 1777, General George Washington, along with 11,000 soldiers of the Continental Army, marched across that same bridge over Neshaminy Creek on the Old York Road known today as Route 263. Washington's plan was to pass through the village of Cross Roads, known today as Hartsville, on the way to Coryell's Ferry, now New Hope, to cross the Delaware River, then encamp 4 miles beyond the river in New Jersey.

But a dispatch from John Hancock, president of the Second Continental Congress, warned him that a 260-vessel British fleet carrying 17,000 British troops was waiting for him 50 miles south of the Delaware Capes, today Cape May and Cape Henlopen.

After receiving Hancock's warning, Washington decided he needed to meet with his war council before he could continue into battle. He ordered his troops to set up camp in the area around the bridge over the Little Neshaminy Creek while he set up his temporary headquarters and war council in the nearby stone

This eight-arch bridge was built in 1803 to replace the original bridge that was built in 1710. It is the last eight-arch bridge in Pennsylvania.

# Dark Hollow Park: Eight Arch Bridge

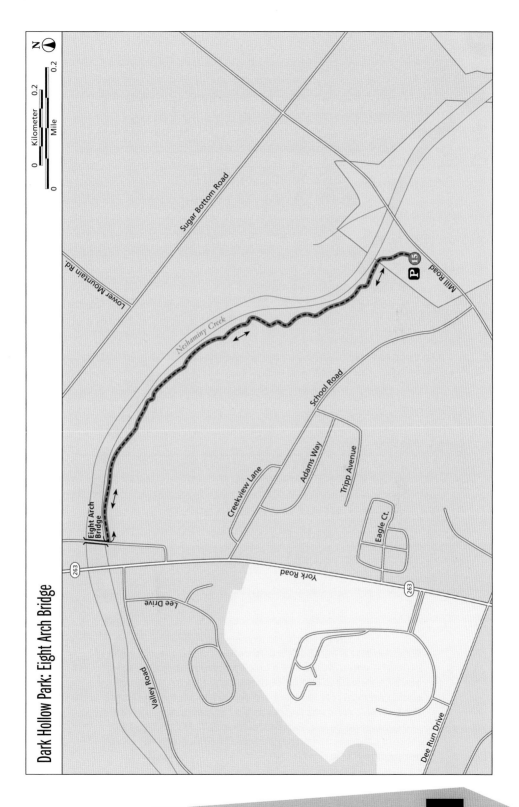

house known as the Moland House, which was the home of John and Catherine Moland. John Moland was a prominent Bucks County attorney who passed away shortly before Washington and his troops arrived, leaving his widow Catherine to take care of the estate.

It was here at Moland House that Marquis de Lafayette and Count Casimir Pulaski, soon to distinguish themselves at the Battle of Brandywine, joined the American Revolution.

History moved on, and in 1803 the Eight Arch Bridge, originally named the Bridge Valley Bridge, after the village of Bridge Valley that existed on both sides of Neshaminy Creek, was built.

The bridge, known today as the Eight Arch Bridge, consists of eight Roman arches, each with a span of 27 feet. The overall span of the bridge itself is 218 feet. It was constructed of field and quarried stone, with rough ashlar, which is polished and squared stone, on its surface.

The trail on this hike goes from shady to sunny as you walk on the hard-packed dark earth alongside the creek, and if it has rained, this trail will be muddy and spotted with mud puddles.

Once you arrive at the bridge, you can walk under it to an area that includes a canoe/kayak put-in, as well as a grassy area just right for a creek-side picnic and an opportunity to photograph the last remaining eight-arch bridge in Pennsylvania.

## MILES AND DIRECTIONS

**0.0**  The trail starts at the trailhead on the north side of the parking lot. Walk into the forest and immediately cross a small stream. At about 350 feet you arrive at Neshaminy Creek, where you turn left.

**0.3**  Cross two deep washout gullies.

**0.8**  Arrive at the Eight Arch Bridge. Retrace your steps back to the parking lot.

**1.6**  Arrive back at the trailhead parking lot.

> ### The Photuris Pennsylvanica De Geer
> *What do these things have in common: a Great Dane and a glass of milk? A ruffed grouse and a brook trout? An eastern hemlock and a black-winged beetle? Nothing. Except each is a Pennsylvania symbol. As for the black-winged beetle, many, if not most, Pennsylvania residents call this bug a "lightning bug," instead of its proper name the "Pennsylvania firefly." And of course for those in academia who study insects, the Latin name is* **Photuris pennsylvanica De Geer.**

# Dark Hollow Park: Power Line Vista

*If you've ever wanted to get away from it all, take this moderate hike. You start out walking where the fishermen walk, alongside Neshaminy Creek, where you will see the "fishermen's paths" that lead to their favorite spots along the bank to start casting. Then it's off for a short climb to a flat area of agricultural fields surrounded by a mixed-hardwood and evergreen forest. It is here, on this wind-blown plateau, that you will find the solitude you seek.*

**Start:** The parking lot

**Distance:** 3.5-mile lollipop

**Hiking time:** 2 hours

**Difficulty:** Moderate

**Trail surface:** Typical forest footpath, dirt road, farm fields

**Best season:** Year-round, dawn to dusk

**Other trail users:** Fishermen

**Canine compatibility:** Leashed dogs permitted

**Land status:** Bucks County Park

**Fees and permits:** No fees or permits

**Schedule:** Dawn to dusk daily

**Map:** USGS Buckingham

**Trail contacts:** Bucks County Parks, 901 E. Bridgetown Pike, Langhorne, PA 19047; (215) 348-6114; www.buckscounty.org/government/parks/Dark Hollow

**Finding the trailhead:** From Philadelphia get on the I-676/US 30 E ramp to I-95. Drive 0.2 mile and merge onto I-676/US 30 E; continue 0.3 mile and take the exit on the left toward Trenton. Drive 0.9 mile and merge onto I-95 N, then drive 12.2 miles and take exit 35 for PA 63 W/Woodhaven Road. Drive 0.6 mile and continue on PA 63 W/Woodhaven Road. Drive 2.9 miles and take the exit toward US 1 N/Morrisville. Drive 0.3 mile and merge onto Roosevelt Boulevard. Drive 1.1 miles and continue on US 1 N. Drive 0.2 mile and take the slight left onto Old Lincoln Highway. Drive 0.7 mile and turn left onto PA 132 W/East Street Road; continue for 8.4 miles and turn right on PA 263 N. Drive 3.8 miles and turn right onto Mill Road; continue 0.9 mile to the parking lot on your left. Trailhead GPS: N40 16.144' / W075 04.505'

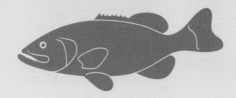

## THE HIKE

Dark Hollow Park is a 650-acre lineal park that runs alongside Neshaminy Creek beginning near Route 263 and the Eight Arch Bridge and ending near Dark Hollow Road. The land that is now the Dark Hollow Park was originally part of a large flood-control project that was comprised of ten sites where impoundment dams were to be built. Eight of the proposed dams were built; the two sites that were not chosen as dam sites were on the Little Neshaminy in Montgomery County near PA 610 and of course the Dark Hollow Dam on Neshaminy Creek near PA 614.

In 1988 the Neshaminy Water Resources Authority designated the Dark Hollow site as a Bucks County Park. The park's main feature is Neshaminy Creek, which is 40.7 miles long and runs through the entirety of Bucks County, as it snakes its way southeast to its confluence with the Delaware River. Along the way it passes through two state parks: Tyler State Park and Neshaminy State Park, which is right at the Delaware River.

For tree enthusiasts there is much to see on this hike as you make your way through a typical lowland and upland hardwood forest. See how many of these you can find: oak, maple, ash, bitternut and shagbark hickory, beech, sycamore, black walnut, tulip, elm, box elder, and wild black cherry mixed with the ever-greens—hemlock, white pine, and red cedar.

Or, for the plant aficionado, see how many of these you can spot: Neshaminy bluebells, common and rare ferns, partridge berry, and native wildflowers including goldenrod, evening primrose, the butterfly flower, native snapdragon, and wood asters.

The view from the top of the power line path on a bright, sunny day.

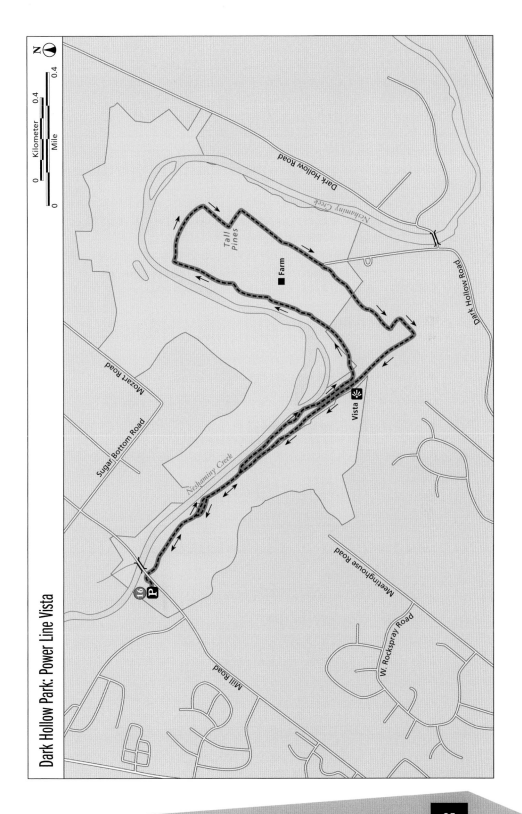

Dark Hollow Park: Power Line Vista

For the fishermen, Neshaminy Creek, which is stocked with native trout in the spring, is classified as a warm-water fishery. You will also find catfish, carp, sunfish, and bass.

The word *Neshaminy* originated with the Lenni Lenape First Nation, and is thought to mean "the place where we drink twice." This phenomenon refers to a section of the creek known as the Neshaminy Palisades, where the course of the water slows and changes direction at almost a right angle, nearly forcing the water back upon itself.

Once you are on the plateau, the trail is essentially flat, although there are a few washout gullies you must cross, and there are farm fields that could be considered uphill, though these climbs are very short.

At 0.9 mile you arrive at the top of the knoll on the power line access road. You reach this same point again at 2.7 miles. It is from this apex that you get the best view of the valley to the east and to the rolling hills to the west.

## MILES AND DIRECTIONS

**0.0** Start at the parking lot. Walk out the vehicle entrance and turn left onto Mill Road. Walk 400 feet and turn right onto the trail.

**0.3** Leave the forest and turn right onto the power line access road.

**0.6** Begin a short climb up the access road.

**0.9** Arrive at the top of your climb. Turn left and walk alongside the farmer's field.

**1.5** Turn right.

**1.7** Turn right and head toward a stand of tall pines.

**1.8** Arrive at the pines and turn left, then turn right heading toward a road and houses.

**2.1** Cross the gravel road and enter a field.

**2.3** Cut through a tree line and jog left.

**2.4** Make a left turn. Pass through a second tree line and cross a washout ditch. Walk 200 feet up the field and turn right at a tree line toward the power line.

**2.5** Arrive at the power line access road and turn right.

**2.7** Arrive at the Power Line Vista. Retrace your steps down the knoll.

**3.5** Arrive back at the parking lot and your vehicle.

# Tyler State Park: Covered Bridge Trail

*Tyler State Park is not only one of the nicest state parks in Pennsylvania, in 2009 and 2011 it was voted the number one state park in the nation. There are so many activities to choose from here that it may be difficult for some park visitors to make a choice. You won't have that problem, because this relatively short, moderate hike to a famous 1870s covered bridge is all laid out for you.*

**Start:** The kiosk at the boathouse parking lot

**Distance:** 2.9-mile lollipop

**Hiking time:** 1.5 to 2 hours

**Difficulty:** Moderate

**Trail surface:** Paved trail, dirt paths

**Best seasons:** Spring, summer, fall, winter

**Other trail users:** Bicyclists, equestrians, cross-country skiers

**Canine compatibility:** Leashed dogs permitted

**Land status:** Pennsylvania State Park

**Fees and permits:** No fees or permits

**Schedule:** Open daily, 8 a.m. to dusk

**Maps:** USGS Langhorne; park map

**Trail contacts:** Tyler State Park, 101 Swamp Road, Newton, PA 18940; (215) 968-2021; www.dcnr.state.pa.us/stateparks/findapark/tyler

**Finding the trailhead:** From Philadelphia get on the I-676/US 30 E ramp to I-95. Drive 0.2 mile and merge onto I-676/US 30 E; continue 0.3 mile and take the exit on the left toward Trenton. Drive 0.9 mile and merge onto I-95 N. Drive 20.9 miles and take exit 44 for US 1 Business/PA 413 toward Penndel/Levittown. Continue 0.3 mile and turn right onto PA 413 S/US 1 Business N, then take the first left onto South Flowers Mill Road. Drive 0.9 mile and turn left onto PA 213 S/East Maple Avenue. Drive 0.7 mile and turn right onto PA 413 N/North Pine Street. Drive 3.0 miles and turn left onto PA 332 W/PA 413 N/SR 532. Continue 1.2 miles and turn left onto PA 332 W. Drive 0.3 mile and turn right toward Main Park Road. Continue 0.2 mile and turn right toward Main Park Road. Drive 0.2 mile onto Main Park Road and continue 1.2 miles to the parking lot on your right. Trailhead GPS: N40 13.971' / W074 58.381'

**THE HIKE**

The land that is now Tyler State Park was originally known as Indian Council Rock, because it was here on a rocky cliff overlooking the valley that Native American tribal leaders held counsel for their members. In time the land changed ownership to small farmers.

Although George Frederick Tyler (1883–1947) was a shrewd businessman, he was also a man-about-town and a world-class sportsman whose interests included mountain climbing, going on safaris, and sailing his yacht. He was the son of *Mayflower* descendant and prominent Philadelphia banker Sidney F. Tyler, who left him a considerable fortune that he used to purchase a number of small farms in the Newton area until he eventually owned the 2,000 acres where he built the Tyler Mansion and operated a progressive dairy farm. After Tyler and his immediate descendants passed away, the land became Tyler State Park, and a portion of it became the setting for Bucks County Community College.

The Schofield Ford Covered Bridge was included in the purchase. The bridge, 164 feet long and 15 feet wide, crosses Neshaminy Creek and was originally constructed in 1873.

According to the "Visit the Historic Covered Bridges of Bucks County" brochure, the original bridge was destroyed by arson in 1991. But through a community effort of more than 800 volunteers it was rebuilt on its original abutments and piers using white oak and Pennsylvania hemlock. And as a result of

There are equestrian trails on both sides of Neshaminy Creek. The Schofield Ford Covered Bridge is designated as the "Equestrian Stream Crossing."

the reconstruction, says the brochure, the Schofield Ford is the only bridge in Pennsylvania that has a queen post truss system supporting a town truss system. The queen post is attached everywhere it makes contact with a diagonal of the Town Truss with a trunnel, which is an oak peg, originally used to construct bridges in the 1800s.

There is no traffic on the bridge; it is instead used by hikers and bicyclists, and it's also part of the equestrian trail.

No matter where you hike in Tyler State Park, you're going to encounter ups and downs in the terrain. The best advice for new hikers is to take it slow as you climb these knolls; and stop every so often and rest. These climbs are short, and once you have made it to the top, you are rewarded with striking views of the valleys, and in most cases the hike on the top is longer and relatively flat.

There is a user-friendly area at the very top of a steep knoll, the covered bridge area, where there are benches and a water fountain nearby. Aside from the bridge itself, the view from this spot is the high point of your hike. Plus, from the rest area the hike is all downhill as you make your way back to the parking lot and your vehicle.

## MILES AND DIRECTIONS

**0.0** Walk out of the boathouse parking lot to the kiosk. The hike starts at the kiosk. Walk toward the stream.

**0.1** Cross the stream on the causeway and turn right on the paved trail.

**0.4** Pass the Thompson Dairy House on your right.

**0.6** Come to a sign for the Dairy Hill Trail. Cross Twining Ford Road and take the dirt equestrian trail. An uphill climb begins.

**0.7** A narrow dirt trail goes off to your right.

**0.8** A second dirt trail comes in from the right and connects with the trail you are on. You then cross the paved Dairy Hill Trail.

**1.0** Turn right.

**1.1** Connect with the Covered Bridge Trail, which is dirt and gravel.

> 🍃 **Green Tip:**
> *Be green and stylish too—wear clothing made of organic cotton and other recycled products.*

# Tyler State Park: Covered Bridge Trail

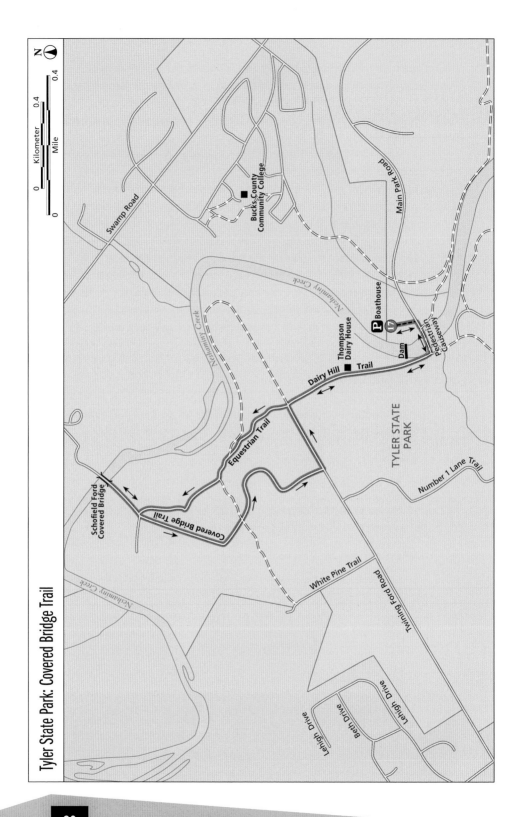

**1.3** Arrive at the Schofield Ford covered bridge. After your visit retrace your steps uphill and get on the Covered Bridge Trail, which is paved.

**1.7** The trail turns left and you arrive at the top of the hill where there are benches to enjoy the view.

**1.8** You pass through sycamore trees on both sides of the road.

**2.1** Turn left onto the Dairy Hill Trail.

**2.3** Turn right onto the paved bike trail and retrace your steps toward the causeway.

**2.7** Turn left and cross the causeway.

**2.9** Arrive back at the parking lot and your vehicle.

## Six Reasons for Covering a Bridge

According to noted Pennsylvania historian George Wise in his book *All in Pennsylvania*, there are six reasons for covering a bridge:

1. To keep water out of the joints, where it might freeze during the winter, or cause rotting in the summer.
2. To keep the roadway dry, for the inner floor was often oiled and became slippery when wet.
3. To strengthen the structure: The added weight was made up for by the increased solidity of the bridge.
4. To give the bridge a barn appearance: Farm animals did not like crossing a rushing river and were liable to run away.
5. To keep the bridge from drying out in very hot weather when it would have loosened, creaked, and sagged.
6. To keep snow off. However, it was often necessary for the bridge keeper to "snow-pave" the bridge so that sleds could cross.

# Tyler State Park: Craftsman's Trail

*Simply put, the Craftsman's Trail is one of the most picturesque hikes in the area. On your way to the stable-turned-workshop and craft center, you hike rolling hills lined with mature trees, cross pristine streams on period stone bridges, and stop and check out the original eighteenth-century stone dwellings, barns, and outbuildings, one with a date stone etched with 1775. And once you get to the Craftsmen's Center, you can stop for a tour or walk through the outdoor works that are on display in the side yard.*

**Start:** The kiosk at the boathouse parking lot

**Distance:** 3.9-mile loop

**Hiking time:** 1.5 to 2 hours

**Difficulty:** Moderate

**Trail surface:** Paved macadam, dirt equestrian trails

**Best seasons:** Spring, summer, fall, winter

**Other trail users:** Bicyclists, cross-country skiers

**Canine compatibility:** Leashed dogs permitted

**Land status:** Pennsylvania State Park

**Fees and permits:** No fees or permits

**Schedule:** Open daily, 8 a.m. to dusk

**Maps:** USGS Langhorne; park map

**Trail contacts:** Tyler State Park, 101 Swamp Rd., Newton, PA 18940; (215) 968-2021; www.dcnr .state.pa.us/stateparks/findapark/ tyler

**Finding the trailhead:** From Philadelphia get on I-676/US 30 E ramp to I-95. Drive 0.2 mile and merge onto I-676/US 30 E; continue 0.3 mile and take the exit on the left toward Trenton. Drive 0.9 mile and merge onto I-95 N. Drive 20.9 miles and take exit 44 for US 1 Business/PA 413 toward Penndel/Levittown. Continue 0.3 and turn right onto PA 413 S/US 1 Business N, then take the first left onto South Flowers Mill Road. Drive 0.9 mile and turn left onto PA 213 S/East Maple Avenue. Drive 0.7 mile and turn right onto PA 413 N/ North Pine Street. Drive 3.0 miles and turn left onto PA 332 W/PA 413 N/SR 532. Continue 1.2 and turn left onto PA-332 W. Drive 0.3 mile and turn right toward Main Park Road. Continue 0.2 mile and turn right toward Main Park Road. Drive 0.2 mile onto Main Park Road and continue 1.2 miles to the parking lot on your right. Trailhead GPS: N40 13.971' / W074 58.381'

## THE HIKE

Aside from being extremely wealthy, George Frederick Tyler knew what he wanted and what he was going to do when he purchased the nearly 2,000 acres that is now the site of Tyler State Park and Bucks County Community College. He wanted a country retreat where he could get away from his home on Philadelphia's Main Line at Georgian Terrace in Chestnut Hill. He also wanted a working farm and a stable of riding horses.

Beginning in 1919 Tyler and his wife Stella Elkins Tyler began buying the land and farms that would become the site of their country retreat. By 1928 they had all the land they needed and work on their country mansion began in 1930. One of their first purchases was the Solly Farm, which became their country estate until they moved into their mansion in 1932.

The mansion, which many consider the finest home ever built in Bucks County, was built in the French Norman revival style. It is 300 feet long with sixty rooms, several towers, and a castellated balcony. It also has twenty fireplaces, gold fixtures in every bathroom, and a ten-car turntable garage, enabling each car to be cranked to its own spot.

In 1932 the Tylers permanently moved to Indian Rock Council, and George Tyler established a stable of twenty-five fine riding horses and restarted a dairy that had been abandoned in 1925. The new dairy was in operation for the next forty years, and the Tylers had one of the leading Ayrshire herds in the country. The Tylers also raised grain, poultry, sheep, and pigs.

The Pennsylvania Guild of Craftsmen has its workshop and showroom in the Tyler family's refurbished stables beside the trail. The guild hosts two major craft events each year.

# Tyler State Park: Craftsman's Trail

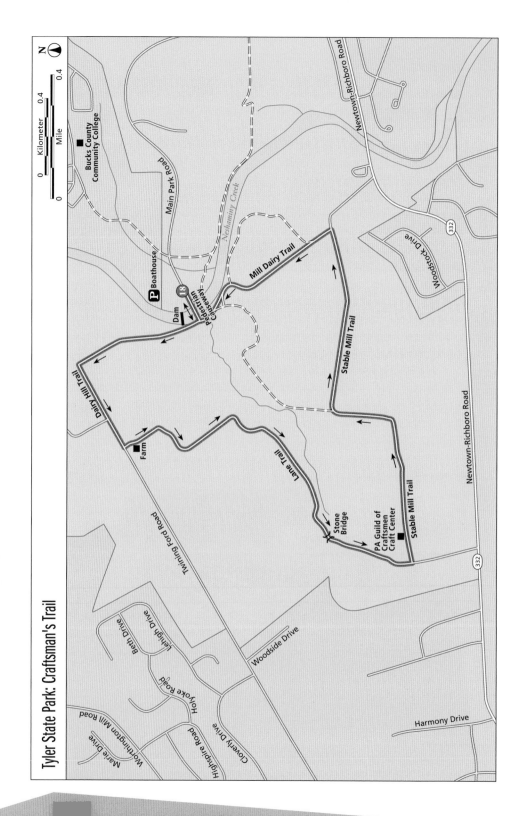

After the Tylers' deaths, approximately 200 acres and the mansion became Bucks County Community College, which was opened in 1965. The remaining 1,771 acres were purchased by the state to create Tyler State Park, which was opened in 1974.

As you cross the causeway and begin this hike, you now have an idea of what all the buildings were used for. You soon pass the Thompson Dairy, which is dated at 1775 and is now a National Historic Site. From there the hike is much like walking through a park spread across the rolling hills that were once part of a working farm.

You may also see horses and riders as you pass the corral and the large parking lot set up for the horse trailers to park. And of course there is the repurposed horse stable that serves as the workshop and display building for the members of the Pennsylvania Guild of Craftsman. And even if you don't visit the craftsman's shop, you will see the extraordinary outdoor works that are placed here and there in the side yard.

All in all, this is a fascinating place to hike.

## MILES AND DIRECTIONS

**0.0**    Walk out of the boathouse parking lot to the kiosk. The hike starts at the kiosk. Walk toward the stream.

**0.1**    Cross Neshaminy Creek, the stream on the causeway, and turn right on the paved trail.

**0.5**    Turn left on the Dairy Hill Trail.

**0.8**    Turn left on the Lane Trail heading toward an old barn.

**1.1**    Cross a small stream on a bridge and arrive at a picnic area with a water fountain on your left.

**1.6**    The Hay Barn Grass Trail cuts across your trail. Disregard it.

**1.8**    College Park Trail comes in from your right. Bear left and cross the stone bridge.

**2.0**    Turn left onto Stable Mill Trail. Pass the Pennsylvania Guild of Craftsmen Craft Center.

**2.5**    The trail turns left.

**2.7**    Turn right onto the Stable Mill Trail.

**3.2**    Turn left onto the Mill Dairy Trail.

**3.8**    Turn right onto the causeway and retrace your steps to the parking lot.

**3.9**    Arrive back at the parking lot and your vehicle.

# Churchville Nature Center

*This easy hike leads you through a forest where you will see a beaker hazelnut, a grandfather beech, sour gum trees, aspens, sassafras, and a white oak, without ever leaving the trail. In other words, somebody laid out this trail, the first loop, with a purpose. The second loop, starting with a stop at the old-time springhouse, leads you past a stand of white pine, then red pine, as you take the trail alongside the Churchville Reservoir.*

**Start:** The Nature Center
**Distance:** 1.6-mile double loop
**Hiking time:** 1 to 1.5 hours
**Difficulty:** Easy
**Trail surface:** Forest footpath, boardwalks; some trails are blind and handicapped accessible with wheelchairs available
**Best seasons:** Spring, summer, fall
**Other trail users:** Birders, educational tours, visiting school groups
**Canine compatibility:** No dogs allowed

**Land status:** Bucks County Park
**Fees and permits:** None
**Schedule:** Dawn to dusk daily
**Maps:** USGS Langhorne; center maps
**Trail contacts:** Churchville Nature Center, 501 Churchville Ln., Churchville, PA 18966; (215) 357-4005; www.churchvillenature center.org

**Finding the trailhead:** Get on I-95 N and take exit 35 for PA 63 W/Wood-haven Road. Drive 0.6 mile to continue onto PA 63 W/Woodhaven Road. Drive 2.9 miles and take the exit toward US 1 N/Morrisvale, then merge onto Roosevelt Boulevard. Drive 1.1 miles and continue onto US 1 N, then take a slight left onto Old Lincoln Highway. Continue 0.7 mile and turn left onto PA 132 W/East Street Road. Drive 2.0 miles and turn right onto Bustleton Pike. Drive 0.2 mile and take a slight left to stay on Bustleton Pike. Drive 1.8 miles to where Bustleton Pike turns slightly right and becomes Churchville Lane. Continue 1.1 miles to the nature center parking lot. Trailhead GPS: N40 11.180' / W074 59.565'

## THE HIKE

Is it possible to learn about the natural world while you're hiking? Here at the Churchville Nature Center, the answer is yes. Their mission is to instill an awareness and appreciation of the natural world in all people through education and to encourage responsible environmental stewardship with a commitment to the preservation of resources and wildlife habitat.

Have you ever wondered how butterflies can fly in large migratory groups and avoid bumping into one another? Stop for a visit to the center's Butterfly House and you'll learn the answer. You'll also learn that there are about 725 different species of butterflies in the United States alone; butterflies taste through their feet and smell with their antenna; and once a butterfly becomes an adult, it has a life span of a few weeks. You can also learn how to encourage butterflies into your garden and what plants they like to eat.

If you were ever curious about how the Lenni Lenape Indians lived and went about their daily lives in the 1500s, you can learn that here at the center's Lenape Village. There are a series of tours, each focusing on a different subject, such as how they made medicines, how they cooked and stored food, and how they made fires using only natural materials.

This hike is short, but it may take you longer than you expected. There is simply so much to see and experience that you may want to stop and explore the various habitats. For example, either before you start the hike or after you've

Sometimes, in order to save a particular tree or bush, you have to curve your boardwalk left then right then left again.

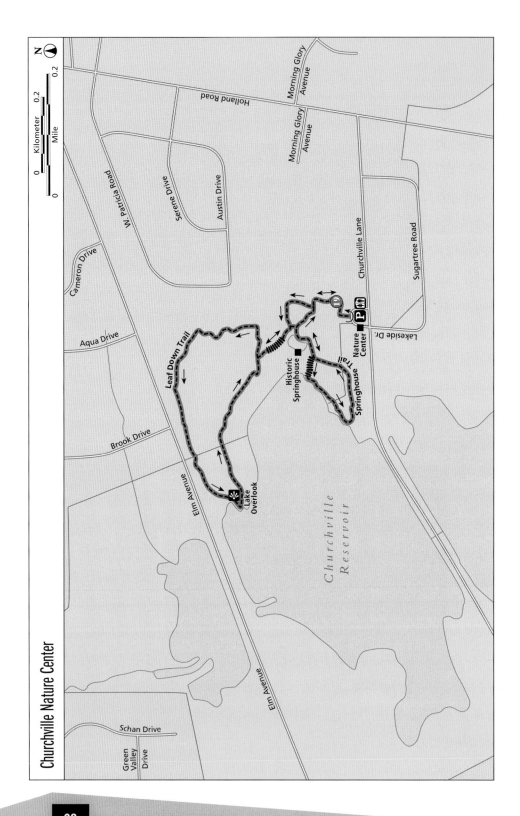

# Churchville Nature Center

finished you can explore the Wildlife Gardens. This area has been landscaped with plants that are beneficial to wildlife and provide a peaceful setting where visitors can discover a butterfly garden, hummingbird garden, and water garden.

Once you're on the trail, you pass through areas of native plants like the bloodroot, with its white petals and yellow reproductive parts, and spring beauties with their pale purple or white petals.

At 0.4 mile you will see a grandfather beech tree just before you begin a loop through a meadow that leads you to the Lake Overlook. From there you hike alongside a swamp and end this loop exactly where you started. From this point, you circle a pond on your way to an old-time springhouse. Then you hike alongside the Churchville Reservoir and pass a stand of red pine, then white pine; then you pass the springhouse a second time as you make your way to the end of the hike.

## MILES AND DIRECTIONS

**0.0**   Leave the parking lot and walk toward the building. Walk along the right side of the building, then walk to the left of the bird blind.

**0.1**   Turn right onto the Yellow Trail.

**0.2**   You arrive at the boardwalk. Turn right at the green arrow.

**0.3**   Turn right onto the green-blazed Leaf Down Trail.

**0.4**   Disregard the Red Trail that goes off to your left. Pass a grandfather beech and an area with benches.

**0.6**   Pass the Blue Trail on your left.

**0.7**   Arrive at the Lake Overlook.

**0.9**   Pass an intersection with the Red Trail.

**1.0**   Arrive back at the beginning of the loop. Turn right to get on the boardwalk. Then turn right onto the Yellow Trail.

**1.1**   Arrive at the springhouse. Pass the springhouse and get on the boardwalk, where you begin on the orange-blazed Springhouse Trail. Walk to the edge of the Churchville Reservoir. Then turn left.

**1.3**   Pass a stand of red pine on your right, then turn left onto the Red Trail. Then get on the Yellow Trail and pass the springhouse again. Arrive at a major intersection and turn right on the Yellow Trail. Stay on the Yellow Trail back to where you started.

**1.6**   Arrive back at the Nature Center where you started out.

# Tamanend Park

*This easy hike leads you alongside and through rows of overgrown shrubs and trees that create dark tunnels for you to walk through. These rows of sometimes-exotic plants were planted here in the 1950s by self-taught botanist William Long to intro-duce new species of trees and shrubs to the Philadelphia area. On this hike you'll also have a chance to explore a stone springhouse and a Colonial-era farmhouse and barn that are listed on the National Register of Historic Places.*

**Start:** The Richard Leedom Trail trailhead beside the park office

**Distance:** 1.2-mile loop

**Hiking time:** 1 hour

**Difficulty:** Easy

**Trail surface:** Wood chips, grass path, typical forest dirt path

**Best seasons:** Spring and summer for wildflowers

**Other trail users:** Birders, dog walkers

**Canine compatibility:** Leashed dogs permitted

**Land status:** Upper Southampton Township Park

**Fees and permits:** None

**Schedule:** Dawn to dusk daily

**Map:** USGS Hatboro

**Trail contacts:** Upper Southamp-ton Township Parks & Recreation, 1255 Second St. Pike, Southamp-ton, PA 18964; (215) 355-9781; www.friendsoftamanend.org

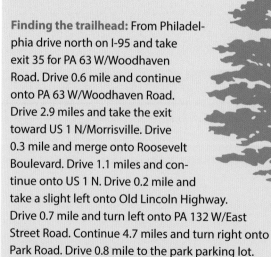

**Finding the trailhead:** From Philadel-phia drive north on I-95 and take exit 35 for PA 63 W/Woodhaven Road. Drive 0.6 mile and continue onto PA 63 W/Woodhaven Road. Drive 2.9 miles and take the exit toward US 1 N/Morrisville. Drive 0.3 mile and merge onto Roosevelt Boulevard. Drive 1.1 miles and con-tinue onto US 1 N. Drive 0.2 mile and take a slight left onto Old Lincoln Highway. Drive 0.7 mile and turn left onto PA 132 W/East Street Road. Continue 4.7 miles and turn right onto Park Road. Drive 0.8 mile to the park parking lot. Trailhead GPS: N40 10.796' / W075 01.922'

## THE HIKE

Even before King Charles II made William Penn the absolute owner of the entire province that would be named Pennsylvania, Penn had his own ideas about how to establish friendly relations with the Indians that King Charles referred to as "savages."

When Penn arrived in America in 1682, he promptly learned the Lenape language and made it his business to get to know the Indians. As a result, he entered into cordial relations with more than twenty *sachems*, the Lenni Lenape word for tribe spokesmen, and one of these, perhaps the most respected *sachem*, was Chief Tamanend.

By 1683, Penn had taken Tamanend as his partner as the two, along with the other chiefs, conceived a treaty between the Europeans and the Indians, which declared that "Europeans and Indians would live in peace as long as the creeks and rivers run and while the sun, moon, and stars endure."

At their meeting in Perkasie in May 1683, Penn began by winning the trust of the Indians for the purpose of "establishing a league of peace and amity." He wanted to make sure that all the Indian claims to land were settled before he began surveying the land and dividing it into tracts that he could then sell to European immigrants.

This eighteenth-century carriage house has been restored and repurposed. The carriage house, barn, and house are listed on the National Registry of Historic Places.

The peace that existed between the Lenape and Europeans lasted until 1737, when Penn's descendants conceived of a fraudulent land purchase known as "The Walking Purchase," which led to the end of the friendship between the Lenape and the white man so that by 1753 the Lenape Indians had vanished from their homeland in what would become known as Bucks County.

Though it is believed that Tamanend died in 1701, his legacy as a gentle man of peace lived on. During the American Revolution, patriots gave the name St. Tamany to a festival celebrating the common man. American writer James Fennimore Cooper made him a character in his most popular novel, *The Last of the Mohicans*, and Tamanend was the hero of the first American opera, *Tamany*. The American warship the *Delaware* bore as its figurehead the bust of Tamanend. The figurehead can still be seen at the Naval Academy at Annapolis. In later years a political organization took the name Tamany Hall.

In 1975, when Southampton purchased land for a park, a "Name the Park Contest" was held, and Tamanend Park was the winning entry.

The land that is now Tamanend Park was part of a 500-acre tract that was owned by William Penn, who divided the land into smaller parcels. The 107-acre parcel that is now the park started out as a tenement farm; the house and the barn were built in the 1740s. The farm changed hands until after World War I, when William and Mary Long made the house their residence.

In the 1930s the Longs turned the farm into an orchard and laid out the rows of trees on parallel contour lines that remain today as the shaded lanes on this hike. In 1938 the Longs deeded the farm to their son William, who turned the orchard into a nursery. By the 1950s he was experimenting with growing rare shrubs and trees.

This hike starts at the trailhead for the Richard Leedom Trail, which is beside the park office. From there it leads to the groves of trees and bushes that form a living portico over the trail, then on to the railroad line before descending a small hill. Next the hike returns to the pond and springhouse beside a sparkling stream and then back to the park office.

---

**🌱 Green Tip:**
*Carry a reusable water container that you fill at the tap. Bottled water is expensive; lots of petroleum is used to make plastic bottles; and the bottles are a disposal nightmare.*

# The Original People: The Lenni Lenape Indians

The Lenni Lenape Indians were the original race of people who lived in the area that was to become known as the Delaware Valley. According to the oral traditions of the Algonquin Indian tribes, of which the Lenape were part, the words *Lenni Lenape* mean the "original people," because the Lenape homeland was the birthplace of the Algonquins.

But the Lenape traditions were altered dramatically when the Europeans—namely the English colonists—landed in the New World in a place that would be called the Delaware Valley. Captain Samuel Argall is recognized as the first European to discover a large bay of water in 1610, which he named the Delaware Bay in honor of Sir Thomas West, Third Lord de la Warr, who was at that time governor of Virginia.

The name *Delaware* was then given to the river that fed the bay and given also to the Lenni Lenape Indians who lived in the newly named Delaware Valley.

Historians have estimated that in the year 1600 there could have been as many as 20,000 Lenni Lenape Indians living in their native homeland. However, during the seventeenth century, their numbers decreased due to tribal wars and several epidemics brought about by the arrival of the Europeans. By the time William Penn arrived with his treaty in hand in 1682, the Lenni Lenape population had been reduced to roughly 4,000.

The Lenape were divided into three groups based on geography and what dialect they spoke. The Munsee lived in the north, the Unami tribe lived in the middle, and the Nanticokes lived in the southern region. These three groups were divided into another three matrilineal groups: the Turtle, Wolf, and Turkey clans. The Turtle clan was most important, and it was from this clan that Tamanend, the chief of the tribal council, made the peace treaty with William Penn.

The Lenape's diet consisted of fish, from the Delaware and its tributaries; wild game such as white tailed deer, rabbits, and fowl; and vegetables such as corn, beans, sweet potatoes, and squash. The women took care of the farming, and the men did the hunting and fishing. They used dugout canoes for transportation and fishing.

Their villages usually consisted of a council house, where tribal councils led by the chief or the king made decisions about how life in the village should be run. The villages were all self-sufficient and generally consisted of several hundred in the warmer months and fewer in the winter, when the men set out for the interior to hunt. Members of the tribes also traded with the Europeans.

But apparently no one, from the chief on down, was happy with the way their existence was going, and these villages had a tendency to blame their troubles on other tribes. So from the 1600s forward, there were escalating hostilities between tribes until two tribes—the Minquas and the Susquehannock—on two different occasions tried to eliminate the Lenape and take over their trading with the Europeans.

With these two brutal skirmishes plus the diseases the Europeans brought, the Lenape lost half or their population and were forced to abandon their land on the west side of the Delaware River. As the colonization of the New World continued the Lenape travelled westward and mostly settled on reservations in the State of Oklahoma and the province of Ontario in Canada.

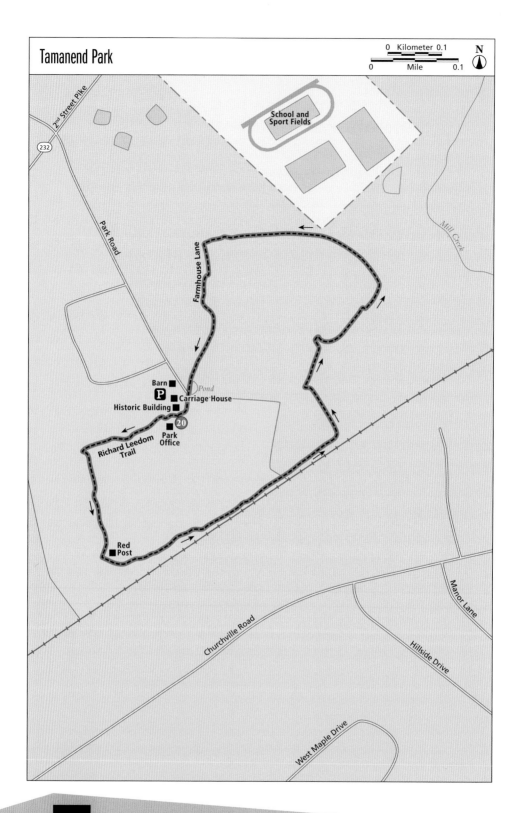

Tamanend Park

0 Kilometer 0.1
0 Mile 0.1

N

2nd Street Pike
232
Park Road
Farmhouse Lane
School and Sport Fields
Mill Creek
Pond
Barn
P
Carriage House
Historic Building
20
Park Office
Richard Leedom Trail
Red Post
Churchville Road
Manor Lane
Hillside Drive
West Maple Drive

## MILES AND DIRECTIONS

**0.0**   Start at the Richard Leedom trailhead beside the park office.

**0.1**   Turn left on a dirt road.

**0.2**   Turn left at the red post and walk beside the old railroad grade on your right.

**0.5**   Turn left.

**0.6**   Turn right, pass three lanes on your left, and turn left onto fourth lane.

**0.7**   Turn left and walk down hill on a mowed path.

**0.9**   Turn left onto Farmhouse Lane.

**1.1**   Arrive at the pond.

**1.2**   Arrive back at the parking lot.

### Pennsbury Manor:
### The Seventeenth-Century Country Estate of William Penn

Even though William Penn lived in Pennsylvania for a total of four years—from 1682 to 1684 and from 1699 to 1701—his ideas and influence regarding religious tolerance and individual rights, to name but two issues, influenced the creation of American democracy. Along the way Penn built his Manor House on 43 acres alongside the Delaware River and called it Pennsbury Manor. The house was rebuilt in 1930 and is now used as a living history museum featuring guided tours, hands-on workshops, and demonstrations of Colonial crafts. (215) 946-0400; www.pennsburymanor.org

*This easy hike is long enough to give you a good workout as you explore the many facilities and activities the park has to offer. For example, if you're a mountain biker, the park has a wooded section that has over 8 miles of single-track over mostly flat terrain with plenty of stream crossings. You can rent a kayak, play tennis, or spread your blanket under a tree and have an old-fashioned picnic. There are also modern bathrooms and pavilions with grills for families or large groups.*

**Start:** The Duchess Lane Picnic Area parking lot

**Distance:** 3.0-mile figure-eight

**Hiking time:** 1.5 hours

**Difficulty:** Easy

**Trail surface:** Paved trail, grass path, park road

**Best seasons:** Spring, summer, fall

**Other trail users:** Dog walkers, bicyclists

**Canine compatibility:** Leashed dogs permitted

**Land status:** Bucks County Park

**Fees and permits:** None

**Schedule:** Dawn to dusk daily

**Map:** USGS Langhorne

**Trail contacts:** Bucks County Parks, 901 E. Bridgetown Pike, Langhorne, PA 19047; (215) 348-6114; www.buckscounty.org/government/parks/CoreCreek

**Finding the trailhead:** Drive north on I-95 N and take exit 44 for US 1 Business/PA 413 toward Penndel/Levittown. Drive 0.3 mile and turn right onto PA 413 S/US 1 Business N. Follow signs for PA 413 S/US 1 Business N. Take the first left onto South Flowers Mill Road. Drive 0.9 mile and turn left onto PA 213 S. Continue 0.2 mile and turn right onto North Flowers Mill Road. Drive 0.5 mile and turn right onto Langhorne Yardley Road. Drive 0.6 and take the second left onto Bridgetown Pike. Drive 0.2 mile and take the first right onto Park Road. Continue 0.4 mile and take the first right onto Duchess Lane and the parking lot. Trailhead GPS: N40 11.777' / W074 55.000'

## THE HIKE

In 1976 Bucks County constructed a dam across Core Creek to provide a multi-purpose reservoir for local communities. A year later, in the summer of 1977, the 174-acre reservoir was named Lake Luxembourg and soon became the center-piece of the 1,185-acre Core Creek Park.

Like all the other creeks in the Delaware River Watershed, the waters of Core Creek eventually end their journey in the Delaware River. Core Creek ends its journey when it empties into Neshaminy Creek, just about a mile below the Lake Luxembourg dam. From there the Neshaminy continues 13.5 miles to the Delaware River to meet its end.

Lake Luxembourg is considered a cold-water fishery and as such anglers can expect to catch trout, which are stocked here annually, as well as bass, walleye, catfish, bluegill, and carp. Fishermen can cast from the shoreline or rent a fishing boat with an electric motor, or they can try their luck fishing from a kayak or canoe.

For the landlubbers, there are, of course, the hiking/biking trail, mountain-biking trails, baseball fields, tennis courts, and, if you've got your own trusty steed, the woodland equestrian trails. And, when the warm weather is gone, don't let that keep you away from the park; instead dress warm and try ice-fishing on the lake, or, if you need a little more action, try ice-skating on a section of the lake set aside for that purpose.

Construction of the dam was finished in 1976, and in 1977 the 174-acre reservoir was named Lake Luxembourg, an extremely popular spot for trout fishing in the spring and fall.

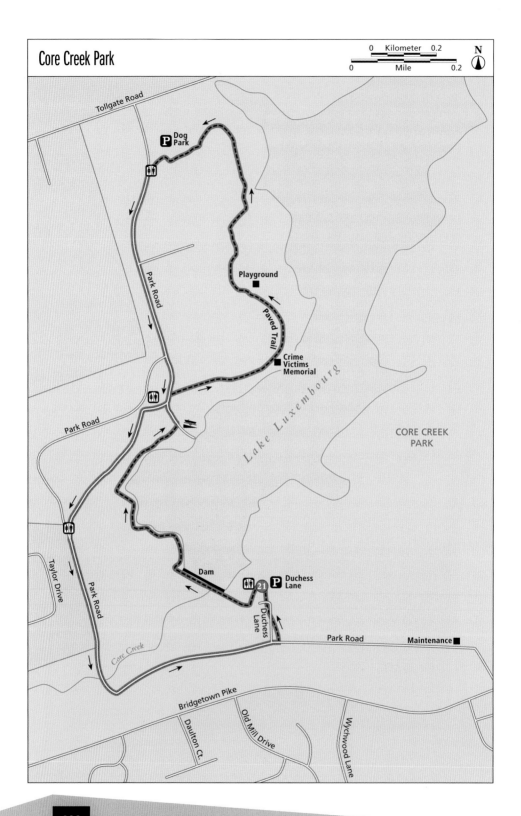

Core Creek Park

0 Kilometer 0.2
0 Mile 0.2
N

Tollgate Road

Dog Park

Park Road

Playground

Paved Trail

Crime Victims Memorial

Lake Luxembourg

CORE CREEK PARK

Park Road

Taylor Drive

Park Road

Dam

Duchess Lane

21

Duchess Lane

Core Creek

Park Road

Maintenance

Bridgetown Pike

Daulton Ct.

Old Mill Drive

Wychwood Lane

Meanwhile, back on land, this hike takes you across the dam and leads you to a classical-style gazebo set on a knoll overlooking Lake Luxembourg. This 5-acre site is the Bucks County Crime Victims Commemorative Arbor.

It was established on this site in 1998 by the Network of Victim Assistance, along with Bucks County commissioners, Bucks County Department of Parks and Recreation officials, area police chiefs, and other law enforcement personnel. In 2004 Mothers Against Drunk Driving of Bucks County added the slate entryway that leads to the gazebo plaza. There are three stone benches around the gazebo to offer visitors a chance to rest or meditate and enjoy the view of Lake Luxembourg.

The hike continues from the memorial through a section of mature trees before leading to the parking lot and the park's next surprise: the Core Creek Off-Leash Dog Park, a landscaped membership park with separate facilities for large and small dogs. The park, which is recognized as one of the top dog parks in the East, has sally ports (secure entrances) for each section and running water for people and spigots for dogs.

Leave the dog park and finish your hike by walking alongside Park Road until you turn left onto Duchess Lane and continue to the parking lot and your vehicle.

## MILES AND DIRECTIONS

**0.0** Start at the Duchess Lane Picnic Area parking lot. Walk past the playground toward the dam then walk across the dam.

**0.2** Turn right and follow the banks of Lake Luxembourg.

**0.4** Bear left up the hill toward boat rental area.

**0.6** Turn left onto the paved boat launch road.

**0.7** Turn right onto the paved path and walk under the mulberry trees.

**0.9** Arrive at the walkway to the Crime Victims Memorial. Leave the memorial and turn right on the paved path.

**1.3** Pass through a section of trees, then enter a parking lot and pass the dog park on your right.

**1.5** Turn left onto Park Road.

**1.9** Turn right onto the paved path.

**2.3** Turn left onto Park Road.

**2.6** Park Road turns left.

**2.9** Turn left into the Duchess Lane parking lot.

**3.0** Arrive back at your vehicle.

# Five Mile Woods Nature Preserve

*Even though this easy hike is only two miles long, you'll experience two completely different ecosystems as you cross over the fall line that separates the coastal plain from the Piedmont Plateau. Along the way you'll see plants such as the high bush blueberry that thrive in the coastal plain, and you will spot honeysuckle and sphagnum moss on the Piedmont Plateau side.*

**Start:** The kiosk behind the preserve office

**Distance:** 2.0-mile loop

**Hiking time:** 1.5 hours

**Difficulty:** Easy

**Trail surface:** Forest footpath, boardwalks, gravel path

**Best seasons:** Spring, summer, fall

**Other trail users:** Birders, nature enthusiasts

**Canine compatibility:** No dogs allowed

**Land status:** Lower Wakefield Township Park

**Fees and permits:** None

**Schedule:** Dawn to dusk daily

**Maps:** USGS Trenton West; preserve map

**Trail contacts:** Five Mile Woods Nature Preserve, 1305 Big Oak Rd., Yardley, PA 19067; (215) 493-6652; www.lmt.org/park-fivemilewoods .php

**Finding the trailhead:** Drive north on I-95 and take exit 46A to merge onto US 1 N toward Morrisville. Drive 0.6 mile and take the exit toward Oxford Valley. Continue 0.2 mile and turn left onto Oxford Valley Road. Drive 0.5 mile and turn right onto Big Oak Road. Continue 0.9 mile to the parking lot on your right. Trailhead GPS: N40 12.269' / W074 50.982'

## THE HIKE

Most of the land on the fall line in the Philadelphia area has been highly developed with housing tracts, malls, and commercial endeavors of all sizes and shapes. But when residents in Lower Wakefield Township were faced with the decision of what to do with the last 300 acres of forest and bogs in their community that encompassed the fall line, they voted to turn the unique slice of land into a nature preserve.

In 1981 a grassroots group of nature enthusiasts began to lay out and create the trails. This group of volunteers, the Friends of the Five Mile Woods, maintains the trail surfaces and trims back trailside growth and overhanging tree branches. They have also built a series of boardwalks that carry hikers over the muddy areas that would otherwise be impassable during the rainy seasons.

The first section of this hike, the Sphagnum Trail, is a boardwalk that carries you over a bog covered in sphagnum moss. The reason that the sphagnum thrives in the bog is because the bog produces the highly acidic environment that the moss requires. There are of course other plants, like honeysuckle, native orchids, pink lady slippers, and cranberry, that also thrive in acidic environments.

Once you're through the bog, you get on the yellow-blazed 5 Mile Trail, which leads you over Queen Anne Creek, then on past the Fall Line Trail, which

The crystal clear water of Queen Anne Creek snakes around the preserve, crossing a number of trails, including the Fall Line Trail.

acts as a dividing line between the two ecosystems. You are now in the coastal plain area, where you will see different plants, such as American holly, high bush blueberry, and sweet pepper bush.

You continue on the 5 Mile Trail to its southern end, where you then turn left on the Creek Trail and cross over Queen Anne Creek a second time. From here it's on to the Heath Trail, which leads you to the giant sweet gum tree and the outdoor classroom, where volunteers from the Roving Nature Center conduct half-day programs with titles like "Dancing with Turtles" for children ages 4 to 10.

Here in the outdoor classroom, the limbs of the giant sweet gum arc over the benches like an open umbrella. And it is here that you learn that the sweet gum tree, that is cultivated, ranges in height from 33 to 50 feet. But in the wild state,

## The Fall Line

The city of Philadelphia, as well as much of the land around it, is situated on the landform known as the Atlantic Coastal Plain, which is 5 miles wide and varies in elevation from sea level to 60 feet above sea level. The Continental Shelf is a broad belt that slants away from land's end and continues to a depth of 600 feet under the Atlantic Ocean. The land that runs inland from the ocean and encompasses the area where Philadelphia, south New Jersey, and Delaware are located is known as the Coastal Province.

If you were to travel inland from Philadelphia, you would arrive at a point where the Coastal Plain meets the Piedmont Plateau, a broad area of rolling hills that continues westward to the Appalachian Mountains in central Pennsylvania. These two landforms meet at the Fall Line, a geological boundary created thanks to the diverse topography in this area.

As streams and rivers flow from the slightly higher, harder Piedmont rock onto the softer Coastal Plain terrain, they create rapids and sometimes waterfalls. As simplistic as it seems, this impact on the waterways was to have a profound effect on how and where towns and cities came to be. For example, when a boat came upriver from the ocean, its journey was over when it got to the rapids or waterfalls; consequently, the towns where the boats stopped became important stopovers for businessmen to bring their wagons to pick up their goods.

The Fall Line also dictated where mills would be built. If you built your mill below the Fall Line, where the rapids were forcefully propelling the water in your direction, the chances of keeping your mill up and running were far greater than if you placed it alongside just any stream or river.

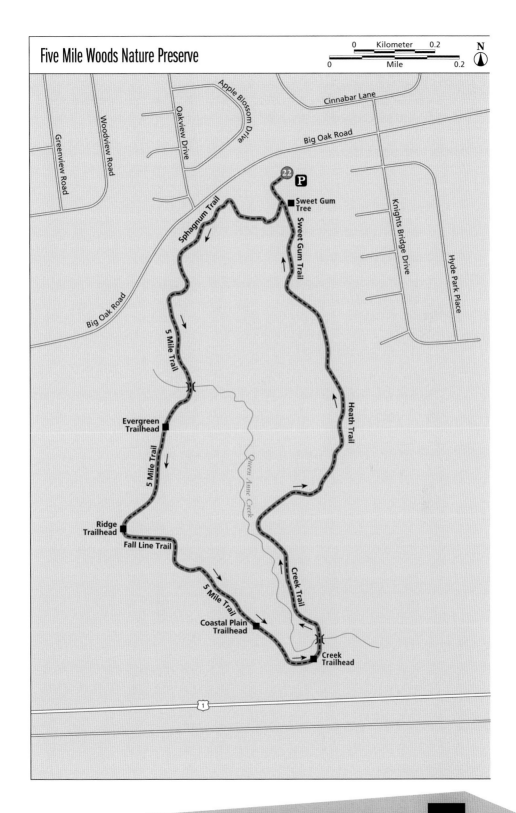

Five Mile Woods Nature Preserve

such as here on the preserve, it can grow up to 150 feet in height, with a trunk up to 2 to 3 feet in diameter, and it may also live to 400 years.

From the outdoor classroom you continue on the Sweet Gum Trail and follow it back to the beginning of the hike.

## MILES AND DIRECTIONS

**0.0** Start at the kiosk behind the park headquarters. Walk 300 feet and turn right onto the Sphagnum Trail.

**0.4** Turn right and get on the yellow-blazed 5 Mile Trail.

**0.5** Cross over Queen Anne Creek.

**1.2** Turn left onto the green-blazed Creek Trail and cross over Queen Anne Creek a second time.

**1.4** Turn right onto the red-blazed Heath Trail.

**1.9** Turn right onto the blue-blazed Sweet Gum Trail.

**2.0** Arrive at a trail intersection and turn right onto the Sphagnum Trail and back to where you started.

# Southwest Hikes

There are only four hikes in this section, but these four are among the most picturesque hikes in the Philadelphia area. In fact, I would rate these hikes among the top five hikes in Pennsylvania. Of course it matters which time of year you hike these spots. For example, when we hiked the Stroud Preserve, which is part of the Natural Lands Trust, it was a sunny day in July, and when we came upon a field of yellow coneflowers with a wide walking path cut through the middle of the field, it was a bright yellow-and-green example of how Mother Nature thinks things should be.

Two of the hikes—Ridley Creek State Park and Tyler Arboretum—are right beside each other, but because the way these two hikes are laid out, it would be difficult to try to hike them both in the same day. First off, Ridley Creek has a series of small hills to climb as well as a half-mile climb on a multiuse trail, making it the most difficult hike in this book.

For hikers there are two sections at Tyler Arboretum. The first section, the main section, has a flat paved trail that leads visitors through its world-class arboretum. This section is fenced in to keep varmints from coming in and eating all the plants and shrubs and so forth. The hiking section is outside the fenced area, and once you're on the trail the forest is much like the forest at Ridley Creek, and like the Ridley Creek hike, the Tyler hike leads you alongside a pristine stream.

Compared to all the other hikes in this guide, hiking in Longwood Gardens is tame. The walkways are flat and paved; nevertheless, no outdoors enthusiast would come to hike in southeastern Pennsylvania without visiting Longwood Gardens. Be aware, however: Hiking the grounds here and seeing all there is to see, is an all-day affair. Enjoy.

# 23

## Ridley Creek State Park

*This moderate hike takes you on a tour of the park's man-made and natural resources. You start at the Hunting Hill Mansion and make your way, sometimes uphill, to the park's namesake, Ridley Creek, which is stocked with trout. From the creek you get on the paved multiuse trail and hike to visit a small eighteenth-century village that grew up around a mill on Ridley Creek. The dam is still there, and after your visit it's uphill to a paved park road that takes you back to where you started.*

**Start:** The kiosk in the parking lot at the park office
**Distance:** 5.4-mile loop
**Hiking time:** 2.5 to 3 hours
**Difficulty:** Moderate
**Trail surface:** Forest footpath, paved bike trail, paved park roads
**Best seasons:** Spring, summer, fall, winter
**Other trail users:** Bicyclists, birders, campers, fishermen, cross-country skiers
**Canine compatibility:** Leashed dogs permitted

**Land status:** Pennsylvania State Park
**Fees and permits:** None for the park; fee to visit Colonial Pennsylvania Plantation, open weekends Apr through Nov; (610) 566-1725
**Schedule:** Sunrise to sunset daily
**Map:** USGS Media
**Trail contacts:** Ridley Creek State Park, 1023 Sycamore Mills Rd., Media, PA 19063; (610) 892-3900; www.dcnr.state.pa.us/stateparks/findapark/ridleycreek

**Finding the trailhead:** From Philadelphia take I-95 S, then take exit 7 for I-476 N. Drive 0.6 mile and continue on I-476 N for 4.5 miles. Take exit 5 to merge onto US 1 S/Media Bypass toward Lima. Drive 1.7 miles and take PA 252 exit toward Media/Newton Square. Drive 0.2 mile and turn right onto PA 252 N/North Providence Road (signs for Pennsylvania 252 N). Drive 0.5 mile. Turn left onto North Providence Road, then turn right to stay on North Providence Road. Drive 2.4 miles, then turn left onto Gradyville Road and continue 1.1 miles to a slight left onto Sandy Flash Drive South. Drive 0.6 mile to the parking area behind the park office. Trailhead GPS: N39 57.051' / W75 27.109'

## THE HIKE

If you visit Ridley Creek State Park, you'll be pleased to learn that aside from everything else you'd expect to find in a state park, this one has a fully restored eighteenth-century farm. Actually the farm, which is called the Colonial Pennsylvania Plantation, has been in existence since before the Revolutionary War, and on weekends from April to November you can tour the farm and watch volunteer reenactors work the farm and keep up with their household chores.

Back in the Colonial days, a small village was built around the mill that operated on Ridley Creek. The village buildings are gone now, or used as private residences, but the area that was the hub of activity, now known as Sycamore Mills, is listed as the "Ridley Creek State Park Historic District" on the National Register of Historic Places. On this hike you can visit the dam and view a few of the remaining structures.

In 1966, when the Commonwealth bought the 2,606 acres that was to become the park from the Jeffords family, the purchase included the Jeffords Estate Mansion. The English Tudor–style manor house was built between 1915 and 1918 in the middle of the property, and it remains there today in its current incarnation as the park office. And if you feel like exploring the grounds after your hike, there are self-guided tour directions available in the park office that direct you to the pump house, the old springhouse, the pond site, the old pump house, the greenhouse, and a cistern where water was stored to a capacity of 20

This dam provided water power for the eighteenth-century mill and for the small village now known as Sycamore Mills. The remaining early buildings are now private residences.

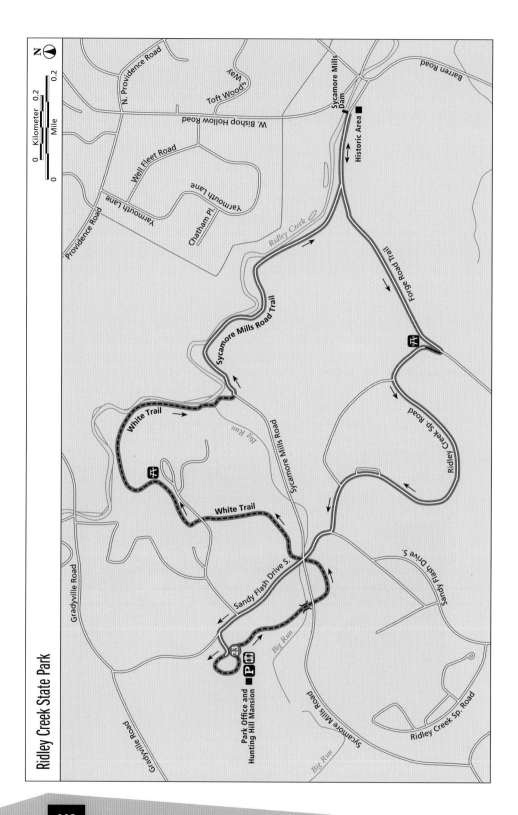

# Ridley Creek State Park

N. Providence Road

Toft Woods Way

W. Bishop Hollow Road

Well Fleet Road

Providence Road

Yarmouth Lane

Yarmouth Lane

Chatham Pl.

*Ridley Creek*

Sycamore Mills Road Trail

Sycamore Mills Dam

Historic Area

Forge Road Trail

White Trail

*Big Run*

Sycamore Mills Road

White Trail

Ridley Creek Sp. Road

Gradyville Road

Sandy Flash Drive S.

Sandy Flash Drive S.

23

Park Office and Hunting Hill Mansion

P

*Big Run*

Sycamore Mills Road

Ridley Creek Sp. Road

*Big Run*

Gradyville Road

0 Kilometer 0.2

0 Mile 0.2

N

feet deep. When a faucet was opened in the house, the pressure in the bottom of the cistern forced the water into the water pipes.

Your hike starts at the mansion. The trail leads you into the forest, where you will see both new-growth and old-growth oak, beech, walnut, maple, sycamore, hickory, and tulip poplar. Plus there are plenty of nonnative trees that were planted on the grounds by the Jeffords family to enhance the landscape.

At 1.4 miles you get your first glimpse of Ridley Creek and then you hike alongside the stream for 0.4 mile, passing benches set at picturesque spots along the creek, before you turn onto the multiuse trail that leads you to the historic area and the Sycamore Mills Dam. After that you have an uphill climb for 0.5 mile, followed by a right turn onto a paved road that leads you back to your starting point.

## MILES AND DIRECTIONS

**0.0** Start at the kiosk in the parking lot near the mansion. Walk down the steps and walk past the bathrooms on your left. Turn right and continue on the sidewalk.

**0.1** Arrive at the trail parking lot. Path becomes gravel.

**0.2** Enter the woods. Stay on the gravel trail.

**0.4** Cross the bridge. Cross over the Sycamore Mills Road. Continue straight. Go up a set of steps and turn left on the White Trail. At the Y take the right fork and follow the white blazes. Continue to follow the white blazes, ignoring the other trails.

**0.5** Cross Sycamore Mills Road a second time and arrive at a culvert. Walk through the culvert and turn left onto the White Trail.

**1.1** Arrive near Picnic Area 9 and turn left, staying on the White Trail.

**1.4** Arrive at Ridley Creek and continue to follow the white blazes.

**1.8** Turn left on Sycamore Mills Road Trail and walk alongside Ridley Creek.

**2.8** Arrive at the historic area and Sycamore Mills Dam. Then turn around and retrace your steps.

**3.0** Turn left onto the paved Forge Road Trail and begin an uphill climb.

**3.5** Arrive at Picnic Area 17. Get on the paved road and follow it to Sandy Flash Drive.

**4.6** Turn right onto Sandy Flash Drive and continue back to Hunting Hill Mansion and your vehicle.

**5.4** Arrive back at the parking lot and your vehicle.

There are two sections to hike on this outing. The actual arboretum is enclosed with a fence to keep out the whitetail deer, and other creatures who would like nothing better than to get inside to eat their breakfast, lunch, and dinner. To get to the hike outside the fence you walk through the arboretum to a gate in the fence, and once you're on the other side you're in a typical forest, with 17 miles of hiking trails that traverse a 550-acre natural area, complete with two pristine streams.

**Start:** The visitor center

**Distance:** 3.4-mile lollipop

**Hiking time:** 1.5 to 2 hours

**Difficulty:** Moderate

**Trail surface:** Paved walkway, forest footpath

**Best seasons:** Spring, summer, fall

**Other trail users:** Children's groups, outdoor enthusiasts

**Canine compatibility:** No pets or bicycles allowed

**Land status:** Nonprofit organization

**Fees and permits:** Adults: $11; seniors: $9; youth: $7; under 3: free

**Schedule:** Mar to Oct weekdays 9 a.m. to 5 p.m., weekends 9 a.m. to 6 p.m.; Nov to Feb weekdays 9 a.m. to 4 p.m., weekends 9 a.m. to 5 p.m.; closed Thanksgiving and December 24 and 25

**Map:** USGS Media

**Trail contacts:** Tyler Arboretum, 515 Painter Rd., Media, PA 19063; (610) 566-9134; www.Tyler Arboretum.org

**Finding the trailhead:** Take I-95 S and take exit 7 for I-476 N. Drive 0.6 mile and continue onto I-476 N. Drive 2.8 miles and take exit 3 toward Media/Swarthmore. Continue 0.3 mile and turn left onto East Baltimore Pike (signs for Media). Drive 0.9 mile and continue onto East Baltimore Avenue. Drive 1.3 miles and turn right on North Ridley Creek Road. Continue 0.8 mile and take the first left onto West Rose Tree Road. Drive 0.4 mile and take the second right onto Painter Road. Drive 1.7 miles and turn right to the destination on your right. Trailhead GPS: N39 56.080' / W75 26.491'

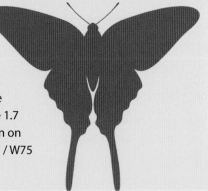

## THE HIKE

Quaker Thomas Minshall and a group of Friends left their homes in Chester County, England, to emigrate to the New World, where they could buy farmland and set up their own Quaker Community. The group first looked at the land along the riverbanks, but found it too low—and too crowded—for its needs. To get away from the areas the Quakers considered too unsuitable, they moved farther into the wooded areas. By March 1681 they had found three tracts of land that they combined for a total of 625 acres, which they purchased from William Penn.

Brothers Jacob and Minshall Painter had no idea that their efforts to start a tree and shrub farm—way back in 1831—would one day become one of the most popular ecological tourist attractions and childhood learning centers in the Philadelphia area. But that's what happened when the brothers inherited the land that their sixth-generation grandfather, Thomas Minshall, had passed down to them through his descendants.

Today, the Tyler Arboretum features 650 acres of plant collections, native wildflowers, a fragrant garden, a rhododendron garden, and, of course, champion trees. Visitors can spend the entire day exploring and enjoying the fenced-in arboretum on the network of paved walking trails that can accommodate families with strollers and the handicapped.

If you have young children be sure to bring them along so that they can learn about nature as they walk—or run—from one whimsical feature to the next. There is the Crooked Goblin Shack that looks like it might collapse at any minute; there

If you ever want to get away from it all, visit a butterfly enclosure: It's hard to imagine being surrounded by such fascinating creatures in such a beautiful space.

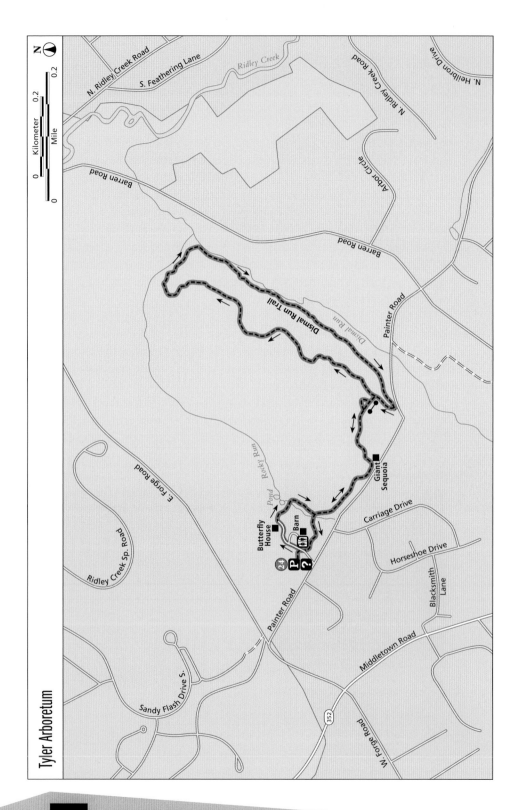

Tyler Arboretum

is Hobbit Hollow and the Lenape Teaching Station; there are oversize wooden chairs; and there are nine "Totally Terrific Tree Houses" with names like Imagination Station, Strummin' and Drummin', and the Cape May Bird House. For those who like to explore historic buildings, there is Latchford Hall, the Painter Library, the Stone Bank Barn, and other nineteenth century outbuildings. While you're at the barn, walk to its backside to view the oldest trees in the original arboretum.

Although your hike is outside the fenced area of the arboretum, there is only one entrance and exit so that everyone who comes here must pass through the visitor center. This hike begins at the visitor center, passes the Butterfly House, then the pond, where you cross over the feeder stream, Rocky Run. You next pass the giant sequoia at 0.5 mile, and from there you walk to Gate 6, which is 0.8 mile from the beginning.

You then pass through the gate and get on the orange-blazed Dismal Run Trail, which takes you into the 550 acres of natural areas with plenty of canopy trees to provide shade.

At 1.6 miles the trail takes a right turn and heads downhill; then it makes another right turn at 1.8, which heads you back toward the starting point. On this section you walk alongside the strangely named Dismal Run, which is in fact a pristine stream that should have been named Delightful Run. As soon as you cross a small feeder stream, the trail becomes an uphill climb to the top and Gate 6.

## MILES AND DIRECTIONS

**0.0**  Start at the visitor center. Turn left at the water fountain and walk past the Butterfly House.

**0.1**  Turn right and walk past the pond. Keep right and follow the signs for the Dismal Run Trail.

**0.5**  Pass by the giant sequoia.

**0.8**  Arrive at Gate 6 and the Dismal Run Trail. Pass through the gate, then turn left, following the orange blazes.

**1.6**  Trail turns right.

**1.8**  Trail turns right and you walk alongside Dismal Run.

**2.6**  Trail makes a sharp right turn. Walk 200 feet to Gate 6 and retrace your steps toward the visitor center.

**3.1**  Turn left and cross Rocky Run on a bridge. Walk through the meadow toward the left side of the barn. Get on the paved path and walk to the water fountain, then turn left and retrace your steps to your vehicle.

**3.4**  Arrive back at your vehicle.

## Stroud Preserve

*On this easy hike, which is mostly flat, you begin by crossing over the East Branch of Brandywine Creek. From there you hike past historic homes and barns as you make your way to a mowed path through a field of bright yellow coneflowers on a trail that leads to the pond. From there it's on through a woodland to the rolling hills of a hayfield where you hike the tree line alongside the field to complete your circle back to the main intersection and on to the trail that returns you to the parking lot.*

**Start:** The parking area

**Distance:** 3.0-mile lollipop

**Hiking time:** 1.5 hours

**Difficulty:** Easy

**Trail surface:** Dirt road, mowed path, forest footpath

**Best seasons:** Spring, summer, fall

**Other trail users:** Birders, horseback riders on designated trails

**Canine compatibility:** Leashed dogs permitted

**Land status:** Natural Lands Trust

**Fees and permits:** None

**Schedule:** Dawn to dusk daily

**Map:** USGS Unionville

**Trail contacts:** Stroud Preserve, 454 North Creek Rd., West Chester, PA 19382; (610) 353-5587; www .natlands.org

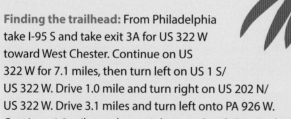

**Finding the trailhead:** From Philadelphia take I-95 S and take exit 3A for US 322 W toward West Chester. Continue on US 322 W for 7.1 miles, then turn left on US 1 S/ US 322 W. Drive 1.0 mile and turn right on US 202 N/ US 322 W. Drive 3.1 miles and turn left onto PA 926 W. Continue 1.3 miles and turn right onto South Birmingham Road. Drive 2.8 miles and turn left onto PA 842 W. Drive 0.1 mile and take a slight right onto North Creek Road; then drive 1.2 miles to the parking lot on your left. Trailhead GPS: N39 57.155' / W075 38.836'

### THE HIKE

The Stroud Preserve is one of forty-two nature preserves owned and managed by the Natural Lands Trust, a non-profit land conservation organization dedicated to protecting the forests, fields, streams, and wetlands in eastern Pennsylvania and southern New Jersey.

The Trust began in 1953 as the Philadelphia Conservationists, a group of avid birders who came together as volunteers to protect the marshes at Tinicum along the Delaware River. That effort became the John Heinz National Wildlife Refuge, and the group of volunteers soon found themselves leading a private conservation movement.

In the years that followed, the group preserved natural areas, wetlands, and forests along the East Coast. In those beginning years they transferred these saved lands to government agencies or other nonprofits, but by the early 1960s they established the Natural Lands Trust as an agency where the Trust could own and care for the woods, fields, streams, marshes, and seashores that they owned.

In the case of the Stroud Preserve, well-known geriatric physician Dr. Morris Stroud 3rd willed his West Chester farm, which he called Georgia Farm to the Trust in 1990 when he died at age 76. The farm was considered one of the most scenic spots in Chester County, where the Brandywine Creek ran through 330 acres of rolling pastureland.

Stroud also left his 1740s-era stone farmhouse to the Trust. The farmhouse was built by Thomas Worth in 1740 on property he inherited from his father, an English Quaker who had purchased 500 acres of "Penn's Woods" from William Penn himself.

The original farmhouse was a modest, two-story, two-bay structure built of locally quarried serpentine stone with a slate roof. The house has had a number

The trail leads you to a path through a meadow of coneflowers.

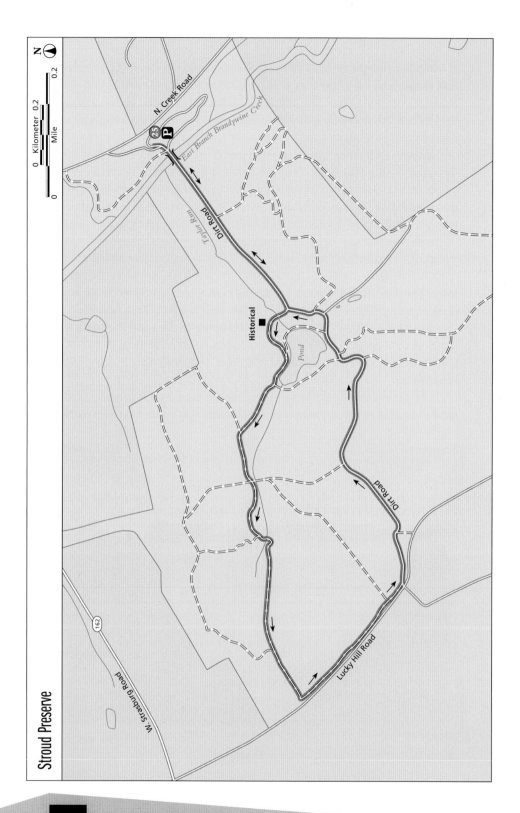

Stroud Preserve

N. Creek Road

East Branch Brandywine Creek

Taylor Run

Dirt Road

Historical

Pond

Dirt Road

Lucky Hill Road

W. Strasburg Road

162

N

0   Kilometer   0.2

0   Mile   0.2

0

of additions over the years, and today it is listed on the National Register of Historic Places.

You begin your hike in the parking lot, where you walk to the stone bridge that crosses the East Branch of Brandywine Creek, which is a fishing creek evidenced by the fact that you are likely to see fishermen casting their lines from the bridge.

From the bridge, you hike 0.5 mile to a Y intersection where you turn right and begin a small climb, where, once you reach the top, you can see the Georgia Farm farmhouse sitting higher up the knoll. There is a sign here indicating that, beginning with the driveway to the house, this area is a private residence that the Trust rents out.

Your hike cuts away from the knoll and leads you to a breathtaking view of the valley below, which is full of bright yellow coneflowers with the trail a mowed path through the plants. You then visit the pond and forest before you reach the hayfield and walk around it on the circle you create as you hike back toward the pond, then on to the T intersection and a right turn back to the beginning of the hike.

## MILES AND DIRECTIONS

**0.0**  Start at the parking area and cross the East Branch of Brandywine Creek.

**0.5**  Come to an intersection and turn right.

**0.6**  Turn left on a mowed path and walk through a field of wild yellow coneflowers. Arrive at a Y intersection by the pond. Stay to the right.

**0.7**  Turn left at the intersection and follow the yellow blazes.

**0.8**  Walk under the power line. Continue to follow the yellow blazes.

**1.0**  Arrive at a field. Turn right and walk along the tree line.

**1.4**  The trail turns left and follows beside Lucky Hill Road.

**1.7**  Turn left on a dirt access road.

**2.4**  Arrive at the intersection where you started. Turn right and retrace your steps to the parking area.

**3.0**  Arrive back at the parking area and your vehicle.

# 26

# Longwood Gardens

*On this short, easy hike you'll have the chance to experience the grandeur of one of the world's premier horticultural showplaces. Along the way you can visit twenty outdoor gardens—each fashioned in a unique landscape of similarly colored flowers— a 4½-acre glass encased conservatory, and the largest greenhouse in the world, and you can stop and smell the roses or any of the other 11,000 different types of plants. You will also pass by the Italian Water Gardens on your way to Hourglass Lake and the 86-acre Meadow Garden area before you climb the Eye of Water tower as you complete this one-of-a-kind hiking experience.*

**Start:** The Visitor Center parking lot
**Distance:** 1.9-mile loop
**Hiking time:** 2 to 3 hours
**Difficulty:** Easy
**Trail surface:** Paved trail, dirt trail; the paved pathways are handicapped accessible
**Best seasons:** Spring, summer, fall
**Other trail users:** Tourists
**Canine compatibility:** No dogs allowed

**Land status:** Longwood Gardens, Inc.
**Fees and permits:** Adults: $18; seniors: $15; students: $8; children under 4: free
**Schedule:** 9 a.m. to 6 p.m. daily
**Map:** USGS Kennett Square
**Trail contacts:** Longwood Gardens, 1001 Longwood Rd., Kennett Square, PA 19348; (610) 388-1000; longwoodgardens.org

**Finding the trailhead:** From Philadelphia take I-95 S to exit 3A for US 322 W toward Chester. Continue on US 322 W for 7.1 miles, then turn left onto US 1 S/ US 322 W. Drive 7.8 miles and take the exit toward Longwood Road. Continue 0.1 mile and take a slight right onto Longwood Road; continue 0.2 mile to your destination on the right. Trailhead GPS: N39 52.251' / W75 40.462'

## THE HIKE

The 1,077 acres that is now Longwood Gardens was originally part of the Lenni Lenape territory, where, according to historians, the Native Americans hunted, fished, and farmed the productive wilderness. William Penn acquired the land, and in 1700 he sold it to a fellow Quaker named George Pierce, who turned it into a working farm and homestead. In 1798 Pierce's descendants, brothers Joshua and Samuel Pierce, planted the first specimens of an arboretum there. By the 1850s they had amassed what many believed to be the finest collection of trees in the country.

The brothers had also begun to acquire native and exotic plants through exchanges with other collectors, and over time the collection, which they named Pierce's Park, had increased and was opened to the public. The park was eventually maintained by another Pierce descendant, George Pierce, but after his death the collection of trees was put under contract to be cut down in 1906.

It was at this point in 1906 that industrialist, designer, collector, farmer, and conservationist Pierre S. du Pont, grandson of the founder of Du Pont Chemical Company, Éleuthère Irénée du Pont, stepped forward and purchased the lumber contract. He also purchased the land and made the property his private estate.

From that point in 1906 to the 1930s, du Pont added extensively to the property. His first addition was the Flower Garden Walk, a 600-foot-long brick path through a variety of floral gardens that was added in 1907.

In 1921 du Pont finished construction on the Conservancy, a 4.5-acre greenhouse housing 20 indoor gardens and 5,500 types of plants. He then added the Italian Water Garden, fashioned after the Villa Gamberaia near Florence, which he had visited some years before. The 5-acre Main Fountain Garden, whose jets spray water 130 feet in the air, was added in 1929.

When du Pont died in 1954, he left most of his estate for the maintenance and improvement of the gardens and to ensure there would be no changes in his

The Chimes Tower has a 62-bell, 5-octave carillon that can be played by hand or with a new computerized system.

long-standing policy of having the gardens and greenhouses open to the public every day of the week.

The most difficult aspect of this hike is that once you have stopped at one of the many gardens, it's hard to get going again. Plus, there are so many to choose from: the Main Fountain Garden, the Italian Water Garden, the Meadow Garden, the Topiary Garden, the Rose Garden, the Hillside Garden, the Theatre Garden, the Peony Garden, and finally the Wisteria Garden. And those are just the outdoor gardens.

Your hike starts at the visitor center, where you turn right to visit the Peony Garden, then you walk through the arbor to the Wisteria Garden. Then you turn left onto the paved walkway, where you pass the Canopy Cathedral Treehouse. The next feature is the Italian Water Garden, where it is impossible not to stop.

From the Italian Water Garden, you get on the elevated walkway and hike to Hourglass Lake and the Meadow Garden trailhead, which is the starting point for a series of meandering trails that cover 83 acres. As soon as you see the meadow with its elevated boardwalks, you may want to take a detour here, but, there is no way you could hike this trail and see the rest of the attractions on your original hike. You must leave the Meadow Garden hike for another visit.

From this point, you hike 0.2 mile to another elevated walkway, reenter the main area, and head to the Peirce-du Pont House. From here you turn right and head to the Main Fountain Garden, then continue to a waterfall, a tower, and a bridge that spans across the waterfall. After that, you return to the visitor center.

## MILES AND DIRECTIONS

**0.0** Start at the visitor center. Turn right.

**0.1** Turn left and visit the Peony Garden, then turn right, pass through the arbor, then walk back to the main trail and turn left.

**0.3** Visit the Canopy Cathedral Tree House.

**0.5** Get on the elevated walkway to the Meadow Garden entrance and walk toward Hourglass Lake.

**0.6** Arrive at Hourglass Lake pavilion and trailhead then turn left and cross over Meadow Bridge.

**0.7** Arrive at a trail intersection and turn right on the main trail, which is wide and covered with sand.

**0.8** Get on the ramp to leave the Meadow Garden area. Walk toward the Peirce-du Pont House, then swing to the right and follow the main pathway.

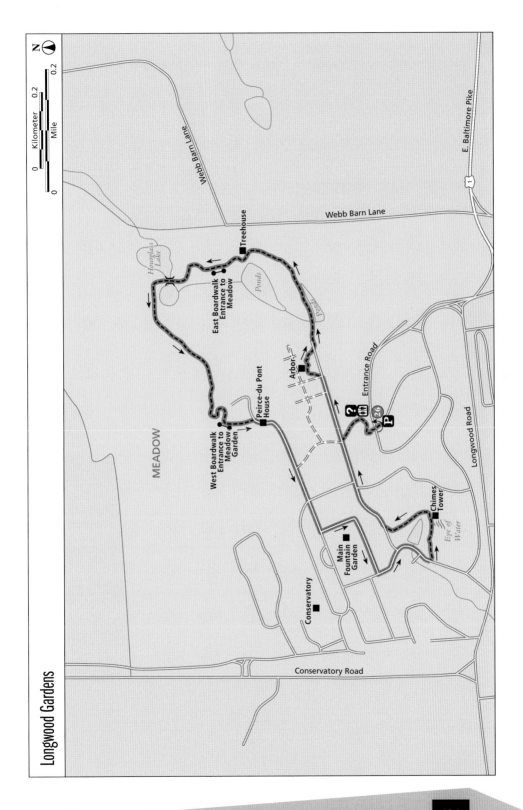

Longwood Gardens

N

Kilometer    0.2
0
0    0.2
Mile

Webb Barn Lane

Hourglass Lake

Treehouse

East Boardwalk Entrance to Meadow

Ponds

Ponds

MEADOW

Arbor

West Boardwalk Entrance to Meadow Garden

Peirce-du Pont House

Entrance Road

Longwood Road

Conservatory

Main Fountain Garden

Chimes Tower

Eye of Water

Conservatory Road

E. Baltimore Pike

1

**1.1** Turn left and walk the tree-lined walkway, then turn right at the end of Main Fountain Garden.

**1.2** Arrive at the end of the Main Fountain Garden. Turn left and walk toward the Chimes Tower. Stop beside the pond for a view of the waterfall. Continue on the trail and turn left at the "Eye of Water" sign, then take the steps to get behind the tower and onto Falls Bridge. From this point bear right.

**1.8** Arrive back at the visitor center.

**1.9** Arrive back at the parking lot and your vehicle.

# Southeast Hikes

After you have hiked the eight hikes in this section, you'll have a firsthand insight into what makes the City of Philadelphia a city like no other. For example, when you hike the Wissahickon Gorge, you'll see that the geology of this area forced the water to flow down the gorge and on into the Schuylkill River. Here, you'll understand how this rushing water provided the power to run mills along Wissahickon Creek before it emptied into the Schuylkill River, where a towpath was created and the town of Manayunk was born as more mills were set up.

The history of Pennypack Creek reads much the same as Wissahickon Creek: First there were water-power mills along its banks. Then along came other sources of energy—such as steam—and the waterwheels were abandoned. Then the City of Philadelphia stepped in to preserve the area along the stream.

That's the short version of how Lorimer and Pennypack Parks came into existence. When you hike here you'll see that the forest along the stream is a top-notch place to hike, bike, or ride your trusty steed. Another major stream, the Neshaminy, meets its end at the Delaware River in this section, just about 15 miles upriver from the city. If you're hiking in Neshaminy Park on a clear day, you can see the Philadelphia skyline.

When you hike the John Heinz National Wildlife Refuge, you'll learn that some early Europeans first settled here in what was then a swamp. Think of that disappointment: After the long, arduous, and sometimes life-threatening journey across the Atlantic Ocean, as you come ashore looking for the Promised Land, all you find are turtles, snakes, and all kinds of birds and waterfowl.

We included the Boxers' Trail because we wanted to hike the same path that heavyweight boxer "Smokin'" Joe Frazier jogged when he prepared for the heavyweight title fight with Muhammad Ali. That fight took place in Madison Square Garden on March 8, 1971. It was billed as the "Fight of the Century," and Frazier won, delivering to Ali his first loss.

There is a bonus on this hike: When you get to the turnaround point on the trail, look to your right and you'll see the mansion that infamous Revolutionary War traitor Benedict Arnold purchased, but because of his needing to leave the country in a hurry, he never lived in it.

# Andorra Natural Area

*If you're looking for a place in the city of Philadelphia where you can get away from it all, this hike just might be the place for you. This is an easy hike that takes you through a natural area, which once was a famous nursery, on a network of well-marked, color-coded trails. You'll get a chance to see a fenced enclosure that shows what the area would look like without the wildlife munching on the understory. The trail then leads you to the ruins of Black Farm, which you can explore before you reach the giant magnolia tree that has fallen and is today called the Fallen Magnolia.*

**Start:** The kiosk by the Environmental Center
**Distance:** 1.9-mile loop
**Hiking time:** 1 to 1.5 hours
**Difficulty:** Easy
**Trail surface:** Forest footpath, meadow path
**Best seasons:** Spring, summer, fall
**Other trail users:** Equestrians
**Canine compatibility:** Leashed dogs permitted
**Land status:** City of Philadelphia
**Fees and permits:** None
**Schedule:** Open daily, dawn to dusk; Environmental Center open Mon through Fri, 9 a.m. to 4 p.m.

**Maps:** USGS Germantown; Andorra Natural Area Trail Map
**Trail contacts:** Wissahickon Environmental Center (also known as the Tree House Visitor Center), 300 W. Northwestern Ave., Philadelphia, PA 19118; (215) 685-9285; www.fow.org/about-us/partners/wissahickon-environmental center. The Friends of the Wissahickon, 8708 Germantown Ave., Philadelphia, PA 19118; (215) 247-0417; www.fow.org.

**Finding the trailhead:** From Philadelphia take I-76 W ramp to Valley Forge. Keep left at the fork and follow the signs for I-76 W/Valley Forge and then merge onto I-76 W. Drive 4.5 miles and take exit 340A toward Lincoln Drive/Kelly Drive; then merge onto City Avenue. Keep right at the fork and follow the signs for Ridge Avenue, then turn left onto Ridge Avenue. Continue 0.9 mile and take a slight right onto Hermit Street. Continue 0.3 mile and turn left onto Henry Avenue. Continue 3.4 miles and take a slight right onto Henry–Ridge Avenue. Henry–Ridge Avenue turns slightly right and becomes Ridge Avenue. Drive 0.7 mile and turn right onto Northwestern Avenue, then drive 0.7 mile on a partially restricted road to the Tree House Visitor Center parking lot on your right. Trailhead GPS: N40 04.893' / W075 14.014'

## THE HIKE

In 1750 a farmhouse was built on the land that is now the Andorra Natural Area. In 1850 Richard Wistar bought the property, naming it the Andorra Farm. He planted many types of trees and built a long drive lined with beech trees meant to be the grand entrance to a large home. Wistar died in 1863; his mansion was never built.

In 1882 railroad tycoon Henry Houston purchased Andorra Farm. He saw its potential as a nursery. Houston hired manager William Harper, who later purchased the business and expanded the operation. At the time of Harper's death in 1934, Andorra Nursery was the largest tree farm in the East. The operation continued until 1961. When it dissolved, much of the 1,000 acres was sold for housing developments; the original Andorra property went to the Houston estate.

In the 1970s Houston's granddaughter, Eleanor Houston Smith, offered 100 acres to Fairmount Park to be used specifically as a natural area. With the help of the Smith's funding the Tree House, the former propagator's cottage was opened as the Wissahickon Environmental Center at the Andorra Natural Area in 1981.

The cottage got its unusual name because the Andorra Nursery propagator, Adolph Steinle, had built a small house on the nursery grounds. He built its enclosed porch around the trunk of a large sycamore tree that grew through a hole in the roof, so the Steinle family named their house the Tree House. In 1981 the sycamore had to be cut down, but a portion of the huge trunk remains inside for visitors to see.

This clearing in the forest was once a farm; the ruins are all that remains of the Black Farm homestead.

Today there are more than 230 species and 110 varieties of deciduous trees, evergreens, and shrubs left over from the nursery. Many of these trees, like the Japanese maple, are labeled. If you visit here in the spring, expect to see Solomon's seal, skunk cabbage, mayapples, wild ginger, spring beauties, and smooth yellow violets come to bloom. As for trees, you'll see giant scarlet oaks, black oaks and white oaks, the great beech, and the fallen cucumber magnolia, which has a diameter of over 4 feet.

If you're a birder, be sure and bring your binoculars and bird book. There are plenty of birds here, like the northern cardinal, the American redstart, the red-bellied woodpecker, and the scarlet tanager.

Your hike starts at the kiosk behind the Tree House as you get on the Red Trail, which at one point parallels Northwestern Avenue, and then cuts inward at a storm-water basin before it connects with the Purple Trail. You will then pass a fenced area, which some call an enclosed area, while others refer to it as a deer exclosure.

Regardless of what these fenced-in areas are called, their purpose is to keep animals away from an area so that those studying the forest can monitor just what wildlife do to a forest.

Next you visit the ruins of the Black Farm homestead, which was built in a beautiful meadow that was once farmland. From the ruins you get back on the Red Trail for a chance to see up close and personal the fallen magnolia. After the magnolia, you catch the Blue/Green Trail, which means the Blue Trail and the Green Trail are both heading in the same direction so that they overlap for a section of the trail before the Blue Trail makes a sharp right turn and the Green Trail continues as it was. Both trails eventually connect with the Red Trail, which is the trail that leads back to the kiosk where you began.

## MILES AND DIRECTIONS

**0.0**    Start at the kiosk near the Environmental Center. Walk to your left to a Y intersection and turn right on the Red Trail.

**0.1**    Arrive at a T intersection and turn left, then take an immediate right and follow the red blazes.

**0.2**    The Red Trail turns left. Disregard the Pink Trail off to your left. It will loop to meet the Red Trail a second time.

**0.5**    Turn right onto the Purple Trail. Disregard the Lavender Trail.

**1.0**    Pass by the deer exclosure on your right.

**1.2**    Come to the Black Farm ruins.

# Andorra Natural Area

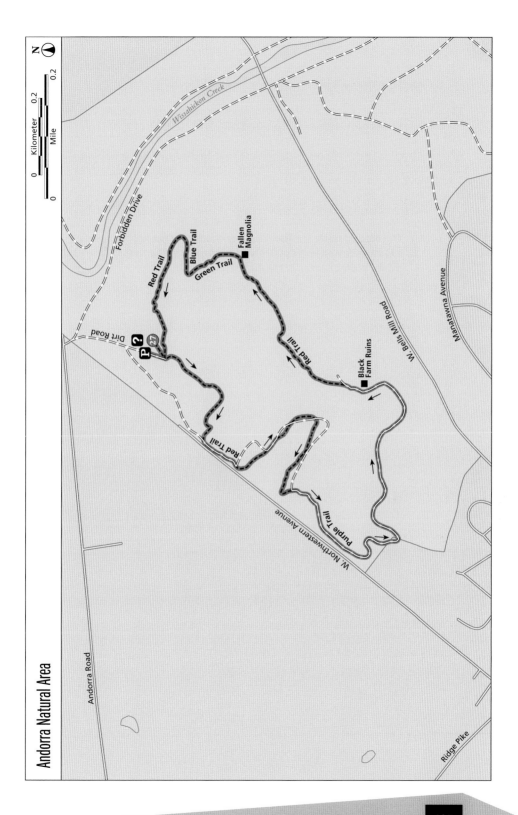

**1.3**     Come to an intersection with the Red Trail. Turn right on the Red Trail. Disregard the Yellow Trail.

**1.5**     Visit the fallen magnolia tree. Then take the Blue/Green Trail. At the next intersection turn right onto the Blue Trail.

**1.7**     Turn left on the Red Trail and follow it back to the Environmental Center.

**1.9**     Arrive back at the parking lot kiosk.

> *The highest point in Philadelphia is 440 feet at the Wissahickon Environmental Center, known also as the Tree House Visitor Center, in the Andorra Natural Area.*

# Wissahickon Gorge North Loop

*There are two major attractions on this hike that make this an absolute must for serious outdoor lovers. Hikers can investigate the history and historical significance of Northwest Philadelphia while they're overwhelmed by the natural history and majestic beauty of Wissahickon Gorge. Be sure to bring your camera. Centered around Wissahickon Gorge and the wide-flowing Wissahickon Creek, which runs 7 miles through Fairmount Park, this hike leads you to an historic stone arch and on to Indian Rock, where the Lenni Lenape Indians held council until they disappeared from the valley in the mid-eighteenth century. Here you can take a photo of Tedyuscung, a stone statue called the Kneeling Warrior; explore a 97-foot-long covered bridge built in 1737; or take a break near a small dam that sends water cascading 5 feet over its crest.*

**Start:** The kiosk in the upper parking lot on Valley Green Road
**Distance:** 3.7-mile loop
**Hiking time:** 3.5 to 4 hours
**Difficulty:** Moderate
**Trail surface:** Rocky footpath, gravel road
**Best season:** May to Oct
**Other trail users:** Mountain bikers, bike riders, joggers, equestrians, parents pushing baby strollers, horseback riders; since Forbidden Drive is considered handicapped accessible, you may encounter wheelchair hikers
**Canine compatibility:** Leashed dogs permitted
**Land status:** City of Philadelphia
**Fees and permits:** No fees or permits are required for hikers; free permits are required for bicyclists and equestrians in certain sections of the park; call for details
**Schedule:** Open daily, dawn to 1:00 a.m. curfew
**Maps:** USGS Germantown; *Map of the Wissahickon Valley*, Fairmount Park, Philadelphia, available from The Friends of the Wissahickon
**Trail contacts:** Wissahickon Environmental Center (also known as the Tree House Visitor Center), 300 W. Northwestern Ave., Philadelphia, PA 19118; (215) 685-9285; www.fow.org/about-us/partners/wissahickon-environmental center. The Friends of the Wissahickon, 8708 Germantown Ave., Philadelphia, PA 19118; (215) 247-0417; www.fow.org

**Finding the trailhead:** From Philadelphia take the I-76 W ramp to Valley Forge and keep left at the fork. Follow signs for I-76 W/Valley Forge and merge onto I-76 W. Drive 4.5 miles and take exit 340A toward Lincoln Drive/Kelly Drive, then merge onto City Avenue, keep left at the fork, and follow the signs for Lincoln Drive. Drive 3.0 miles and turn left onto McCallum Street. Continue 1.3 miles and turn left onto Wolcott Drive. Drive 0.3 mile and turn onto Valley Green Road; continue 0.1 mile to the upper parking lot on your right. Trailhead GPS: N40 04.893' / W075 12.821'

*By train*: From 30th Street Station, take Train 819 toward Chestnut Hill West at 9:47 a.m. Arrive at St. Martins Station at 10:14 a.m. Walk 0.8 mile from the station to the upper parking lot on Valley Green Road.

## THE HIKE

Fairmount Park stretches from the edge of downtown Philadelphia to the city's northwest corner, and at 4,500 acres it's the largest urban park in any city in the world. Before the land for the park was acquired by the City of Philadelphia in 1868, it was an industrial area comprised mostly of mills—paper mills, sawmills, textile mills—run by waterwheels. The mill owners lived on top of the gorge and built roadways and paths so they could walk or take their buggies down to their factories. Many of those trails remain today. In fact, Forbidden Drive, the main thoroughfare that runs on the west side of Wissahickon Creek, was once a popular carriage road.

Bedrock here is comprised of schist, mica, quartzite, and granite, which is conveniently called the Wissahickon Formation.

The world-famous Philadelphia Museum of Art lies at the southern end of Fairmount Park atop the Faire Mount plateau. The mammoth structure, modeled after the ancient Greek temples, covers 10 acres and is home to 200 galleries, housing an amazing 300,000 works of art, including Van Gogh, Renoir, Picasso, and Rubens, to name but a few. If you visit Philadelphia, this museum is a must-see.

There's a pretty good chance, however, that you've already seen the museum. The 1976 film *Rocky*, written by and starring Sylvester Stallone, contains a now-famous scene where heavyweight contender Rocky Balboa runs up Benjamin Franklin Parkway to the front of the museum, continuing up the museum's ninety-nine steps to the terrace. That's where he raises both fists and exalts himself to "Gonna Fly Now," the highly recognizable *Rocky* theme song. Meanwhile, back in the real world, you probably won't hear the *Rocky* theme song as you continue your hike, but you may be enraptured by the tumbling waters of Wissahickon Creek as you make your way upstream, past outcrops, and along the forested trails that rise up the gorge away from the creek.

You begin this hike at the kiosk at the upper parking lot on Valley Green Road. You then walk 0.2 mile downhill on the paved path, turn right at the trail sign, and cross a small bridge over a feeder stream. As soon as you cross the stream you notice bedrock of schist, mica, quartzite, and granite along the trail; these are conveniently called the "Wissahickon formation." They are a result of the eroding action of the gorge that over time wore away the softer layers, creating the gorge and exposing the harder rocks.

At 0.9 mile you come to an intersection where one trail continues and the other trail, the one you want, veers left toward Wissahickon Creek. Continue on this streamside trail until you reach Rex Avenue and the stone arch above the stone steps that lead to the trail that takes you to the Kneeling Warrior. These steps have been closed for a while; for this reason the hike directs you to make a right turn on Rex Avenue, then a left turn followed by a series of switchbacks that take you to the same trail as the steps would have.

After your time at the Kneeling Warrior, you continue on the trail until you reach a hairpin left turn that leads you down the gorge to Wissahickon Creek. Here you turn left and walk alongside the creek until you reach 2.0 miles, where you turn right to cross the creek on the covered bridge that was originally built in 1737 and restored by the Friends of the Wissahickon in 1939. At this point you turn left and hike on Forbidden Drive until you reach 3.4 miles and the Valley Green area.

The big white building you see is the Valley Green Inn, which was built in 1850 and continues the tradition that began in the mid-nineteenth century, when there were dozens of roadhouses along Fairmount Drive and farther south along the Schuylkill River where Wissahickon Creek ends its 7-mile journey.

# Wissahickon Gorge North Loop

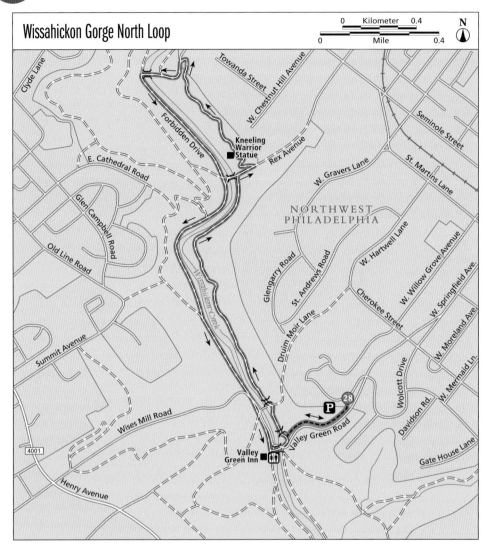

There are outdoor bathrooms and picnic tables here, and of course you can always take your post-hike meal at the Valley Green Inn. From the inn you cross over Wissahickon Creek on the vehicle bridge and continue uphill till you meet the paved pathway, where you began, and follow it to the upper parking lot and your vehicle.

## MILES AND DIRECTIONS

**0.0**    Begin at the kiosk at the lower end of the upper parking lot and walk downhill.

**0.2**    Turn right at the trail sign and cross a small bridge. Follow the green blazes.

**0.5**    Arrive at a trail intersection. Go left across a small bridge.

**0.9**    Come to a trail intersection. Veer left and head toward Wissahickon Creek.

**1.2**    Arrive at the bridge at Rex Avenue. Do not take the stone steps. Instead, turn right on Rex Avenue, walk uphill, and make a sharp left turn onto the trail and begin a series of switchbacks.

**1.4**    Arrive at the Kneeling Warrior statue. After the statue, continue straight on the trail, following the green and white blazes.

**1.8**    Make a hairpin turn to the left and descend to Wissahickon Creek.

**2.0**    Arrive at the covered bridge. Cross over the creek and turn left onto Forbidden Drive.

**3.4**    Arrive at the Valley Green Inn. Cross the vehicle bridge over the creek and retrace your steps to the parking lot.

**3.7**    Arrive back at the parking lot.

> ### Mussels to the Rescue
> *The Delaware River Estuary is home to freshwater mussels, which are similar to oysters and clams. Unlike their marine cousins, mussels are also found in local streams. Mussels have two important environmental jobs: fortifying the streambed by holding the soil in place and purifying the water. They do this by sucking water in, thus removing various impurities from it, and then releasing clean water back into the stream. There was once over a dozen species of mussels in Pennsylvania, but today only one species survives in Pennsylvania, Delaware, and New Jersey. Many factors have been blamed for this, not the least of which is water pollution. Today, organizations such as the Pennsylvania Delaware Estuary are working to restore freshwater mussels by transplanting mussels from healthy beds to polluted waterways.*

# Manayunk Towpath

On this flat hike you'll walk on the first canal and towpath begun in the United States. Your hike starts from the gentrified downtown area of Manayunk, a former working-class neighborhood that is now a popular spot for upscale restaurants, night clubs, and shopping. As you make your way farther out of town, you can immerse yourself in the history of the industrial era as you pass rail lines, old canal locks, the ruins of the lock tender's house and the sluice house, and old textile mills. There are also land-scaped areas along the trail, with trees and benches that provide a shaded resting spot with a wide-open view of the Schuylkill River.

**Start:** The parking lot on the Manayunk Canal in Downtown Manayunk

**Distance:** 4.0 miles out-and-back

**Hiking time:** 1.5 to 2 hours

**Difficulty:** Easy

**Trail surface:** Gravel, boardwalks, hard ground

**Best seasons:** Spring, summer, fall

**Other trail users:** Bike riders, joggers, walkers

**Canine compatibility:** Leashed dogs permitted

**Land status:** City of Philadelphia

**Fees and permits:** No fees or permits, but you must pay to park your vehicle in the parking lot.

**Schedule:** Open daily year-round

**Map:** USGS Germantown

**Trail contacts:** Manayunk Development Corporation, 4312 Main St., Philadelphia, PA 19127; (215) 487-9137; manayunk.com

**Finding the trailhead:** From Philadelphia take the I-76 W ramp to Valley Forge. Keep left at the fork and follow the signs for I-76 W/ Valley Forge. Drive 6.3 miles and take exit 338 for Belmont Avenue toward Green Lane. Drive 0.1 mile and turn right onto Green Lane. Continue on Green Lane and take the first right onto Main Street. Continue on Main Street until you get to 4436 Main Street. Turn right on Carson Street and drive across the towpath, then drive on the vehicle bridge to get across the canal to get to the parking lot. Trailhead GPS: N40 01.559' / W75 13.563'

## THE HIKE

Manayunk Main Street Historic District is listed in the National Register of Historic Districts. Manayunk is relatively isolated from Center City Philadelphia and is less densely populated. The earliest European settlers arrived here in the 1690s. In 1841 Manayunk separated from Roxborough Township to become its own borough. Prior to this the town was known as Flat Rock because of the flat rock shelf in the Schuylkill River, which makes up the western border. In 1824 residents voted to change the name of the borough to Manayunk, which is derived from the Lenni Lenape word *manaiung*, which means "the place where we drink water."

During the Industrial Revolution, Manayunk grew from a town of eleven houses along the Schuylkill River to a manufacturing center of about fifty companies producing goods, mostly yarn and other textiles. The town benefited also from the development of the Manayunk Canal, which was used to move goods along the river. Another boon for Manayunk came when the Philadelphia and Reading Railroad was built between Manayunk and Reading. When the Great Depression came along, industry began to wane and disappeared completely after World War II. Despite this setback the neighborhood continued to grow, mainly because land along the Schuylkill River was available.

On this hike, you will see remnants of the canal along the river, as well as the railroad depot in Shawmont, the turn-around point for this beautiful in-and-out hike.

This paved and landscaped hike/bike trail reflects the town's goal to be an upscale destination.

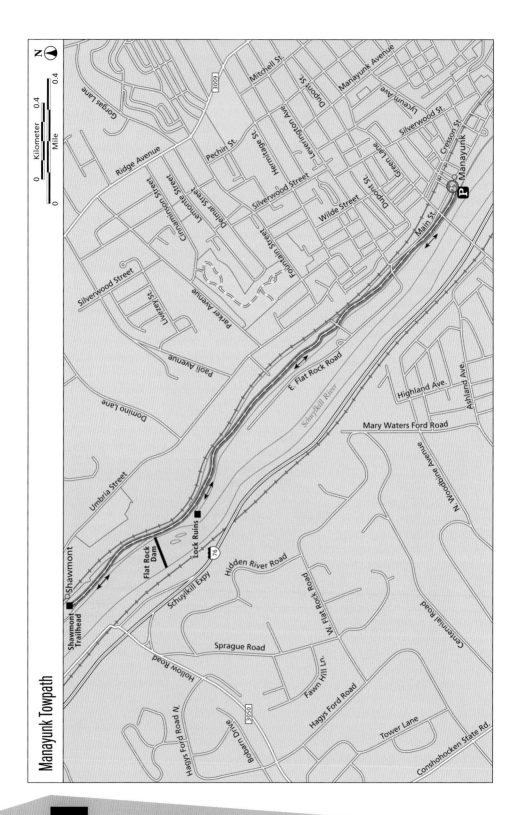

Manayunk Towpath

You begin your hike by walking across the bridge over the canal. You then turn right and walk on the towpath until you get to Ring Street, where you turn around and hike in the other direction. It is along this stretch that you can explore the canal side of these stone buildings that were the textile mills and factories that operated here in the nineteenth century.

As you continue hiking, you soon leave the historic downtown area and enter into a woodland area that supports a number of different ecological areas. As you come to the Riparian Slope forest, you'll find trees such as red maple, sycamore, and box elder and exotics like tree of heaven. These trees act as stabilizers for the steep slope.

A little farther along you see that vines cover the slope. The dominant ones here are Japanese honeysuckle, Asiatic bittersweet, cucumber vine, and briars. When you pass through the meadow, you'll see wildflowers and roadside weeds such as evening primrose and crown vetch. You will also see Japanese knotweed, purple loosestrife, and creeping water primrose growing along the banks of the canal.

Just before you get to the view of Flat Rock Dam, you hike through a lowland forest of box elder, silver maple, and sycamore trees, as well as an herbaceous layer of stinging nettle, touch-me-not, and poison ivy. When you get to the Shawmont Trailhead, you turn around and retrace your steps back to the beginning. If you're tired of looking down, on your return you can look upward or toward the canal to see if you can spot any of these birds that have been reported here: the belted kingfisher, the great blue heron, the green heron, and the cedar waxwing.

Of course, if you look closely between the trees you will see the sluice house channel, then the ruins of the sluice house behind a fence.

## MILES AND DIRECTIONS

**0.0** Start at the downtown parking lot that is accessed by a bridge over the canal. After you park your vehicle, walk across the bridge and turn right on the towpath. (At the time of this writing, there was a construction barricade at Ring Street.)

**0.1** Arrive at Ring Street and turn around.

**1.5** Note the lock ruins on your left.

**1.7** Arrive at the Flat Rock Dam on your left.

**2.0** Arrive at the Shawmont Trailhead. Turn around and retrace your steps.

**4.0** Arrive back at the parking lot and your vehicle.

# Boxers' Trail

*This moderate hike begins in the Strawberry Mansion neighborhood in East Fairmount Park in the city of Philadelphia. Here, you walk on sidewalks that lead past baseball fields and picnic areas as you begin a slight uphill climb to the woodsy section, where you get off the sidewalk and pick up the dirt trail that leads you uphill into the forest. Along this section you see colorful signs that announce you will soon get a chance to explore a number of eighteenth-century mansions in what was once an affluent section of the city known as the Schuylkill Highlands. But before the mansions, you get to an overlook where you can see the colorful boats plying the waters of the Schuylkill River.*

**Start:** The Boxers' Memorial Headstone in East Fairmount Park

**Distance:** 3.2-mile lollipop

**Hiking time:** 2.5 to 3 hours

**Difficulty:** Moderate

**Trail surface:** Sidewalk, dirt path, forest footpath, mowed meadow path

**Best season:** May to Oct

**Other trail users:** Mountain bikers, tourists

**Canine compatibility:** Leashed dog permitted

**Land status:** City of Philadelphia

**Fees and permits:** No fees or permits required

**Schedule:** Open daily from dawn until 1:00 a.m. curfew

**Map:** USGS Philadelphia

**Trail contacts:** East Fairmount Park, Philadelphia, PA, 19121; (215) 686-1776; phila.gov

**Finding the trailhead:** From Center City Philadelphia drive east on South Penn Square toward South Broad Street/Avenue of the Arts for 0.2 mile, to where South Penn Square turns slightly left and becomes John F. Kennedy Boulevard. Continue straight to stay on John F. Kennedy Boulevard, then turn north onto North 16th Street, then turn left onto Benjamin Franklin Parkway. Drive 0.3 mile to the traffic circle, take the second exit, and stay on Benjamin Franklin Parkway and drive 0.6 mile to the next traffic circle. Take the first exit onto John B. Kelly Drive/Kelly Drive. Continue 1.8 miles and turn right onto Fountain Green Drive. Drive 0.4 mile and take a slight left onto Reservoir Drive, then continue 0.7 mile and take the second right onto West Dauphin Drive. Drive 0.1 mile to the Boxers' Memorial headstone in East Fairmount Park on your left. Trailhead GPS: N39 59.529' / W75 11.227'

## THE HIKE

Strawberry Mansion was built in 1750 and is the largest mansion in East Fairmount Park. It was originally called Somerton by its original owner, Charles Thomson, who was secretary of the Continental Congress and known as the "Sam Adams of Pennsylvania." In 1798 William Lewis, president-judge of the United States District Court of Pennsylvania, bought the home from Thomson and named it Summerville.

The present name, Strawberry Mansion, stems from the time—after 1842—when a Mrs. Grimes bought the property and turned it into a dairy farm of sorts and sold strawberries covered with cream from the farm. In 1868 the mansion and the land surrounding it was sold to the City of Philadelphia and became part of Fairmount Park.

Today when you say "Strawberry Mansion," most people familiar with this part of Philadelphia assume you are talking about the neighborhood that surrounds the mansion, which is known as Strawberry Mansion.

The first mansion you visit on this hike was built in 1798 by Major Edward Burd on 45 acres of land that he owned. He named the house Ormiston, after his grandfather Colonel James Burd's Scottish estate near Edinburgh. Major Burd was born in Philadelphia in 1750, and in 1778 he was appointed prothonotary.

Prominent Philadelphia merchant George Thomson built his Philadelphia Federal style home in 1810. Since 2002, "Rockland" has been home to the Psychoanalytic Center of Philadelphia.

Burd died in 1833, and the City of Philadelphia bought the mansion from his heirs in 1869.

The Georgian-style house has a spacious drawing room that spans the width of the house; it also has a smaller drawing room with a large door that opens on to a veranda that has a view of the Schuylkill River.

After Ormiston, you return to the trail and then begin a 0.5-mile uphill climb through the forest to the Schuylkill River overlook. If you're lucky enough to get here at the right time, you may see boats passing by on their way upstream or down.

After the overlook you hike 0.2 mile through a meadow on a trail that leads to Mount Pleasant Drive. From this vantage point, if you look to your right, you can see the great Georgian home known as Mount Pleasant. This mansion was built in the eighteenth century by Captain John MacPherson, a privateer who was a friend of John Adams, second president of the United States.

In 1779 Benedict Arnold purchased the house and gave it to his bride as a wedding gift, but due to the charges of treason leveled against him, Arnold and his bride fled to England without ever living in the house. A later owner was John Williams, a great-nephew of Benjamin Franklin and first superintendent of West Point Military Academy.

Next you turn left onto the sidewalk that runs alongside Mount Pleasant Drive and continue to the next mansion, Rockland. Built in 1810 by prominent Philadelphia merchant George Thomson, Rockland is an excellent example of what was then called Philadelphia Federal-style domestic architecture.

In 2002 the Psychoanalytic Center of Philadelphia established Rockland as its new home and completed its restoration in 2005. Today the center maintains its administration offices and carries on its educational and community-related activities at Rockland.

After Rockland, the trail goes behind Rockland and onto a trail in the forest that leads you back to the original trail, where you turn right to retrace your steps back to your vehicle.

Boxers' Trail follows a network of trails dating back to the 1870s, when users strolled through wooded glens between the historic mansions and enjoyed picturesque views of the Schuylkill River. One hundred years later, in the winter of 1970, heavyweight boxer "Smokin'" Joe Frazier took this trail for his early morning jogs to prepare for his historic fight with Muhammad Ali on March 8, 1971.

Since then other boxers and would-be world champions have jogged on the trail, and each year the Fairmount Park Conservancy helps organize a Boxers' Trail 5K to honor Philadelphia's most-famous prizefighter.

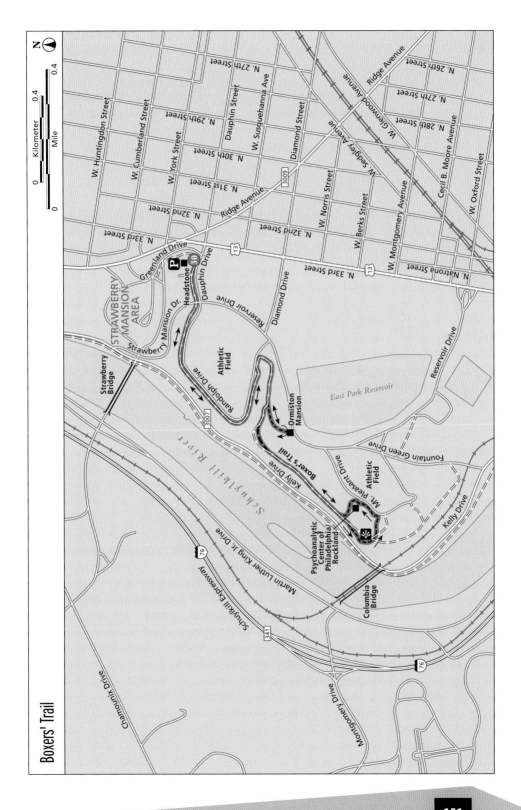

Boxers' Trail

**0.0**  Start at the Boxers' Memorial headstone in East Fairmount Park at the corner of Greenland Drive and Dauphin Drive. Walk on the sidewalk toward the Indian equestrian statue, then cross Strawberry Mansion Drive. There will be baseball fields on your left.

**0.7**  Still on the sidewalk, turn right at the path where the woods end, just before Reservoir Drive.

**0.9**  Arrive at a Y. Take the left trail up the hill and visit Ormiston mansion, then retrace your steps back down the hill to the trail.

**1.1**  Arrive back at the trail and turn left.

**1.2**  Arrive at a second Y and take the left fork uphill.

**1.6**  Come to the overlook above the Schuylkill River. Then turn left at the Mount Pleasant sign and enter an open meadow. Walk along the tree line to the sidewalk, then turn left again on Mount Pleasant Drive.

**1.8**  Reach the Psychoanalytic Center of Philadelphia/Rockland. Walk on the grass behind Rockland to find the opening in the woods that is the path back to Boxers' Trail. Retrace your steps back to the beginning.

**3.2**  Arrive back at the Boxers' memorial headstone where you started.

# John Heinz National Wildlife Refuge: Impoundment Loop

31

Want a hike where you can take your children and your parents? This is it. Along this easy, flat hike, you're surrounded by nature's beauty and the excitement of spotting some of the 280 species of birds that have been seen here. In season you can check out the migratory birds as they make their spring and fall journeys. On this 1,200-acre refuge, you can bike, fish, or take a canoe and do your bird watching and amphibian and reptile sighting from the water. Once written off as a useless swamp, the refuge will surprise you with more than fifty species of wildflowers, an abundance of deciduous trees, and wildlife from white-tailed deer to turtles.

**Start:** The gate that separates the trail from the parking lot
**Distance:** 3.5-mile loop
**Hiking time:** 1.5 to 2 hours
**Difficulty:** Easy
**Trail surface:** Wide, level dirt and gravel roads
**Best seasons:** Spring, summer, fall
**Other trail users:** Cyclists, joggers, birders, dog-walkers, fishermen
**Canine compatibility:** Leashed dogs permitted
**Land status:** National wildlife refuge

**Fees and permits:** No fees or permits required
**Schedule:** Sunrise to sunset daily
**Maps:** USGS Landsdowne, PA and USGS Philadelphia, PA; John Heinz National Wildlife Reserve map available at the contact station
**Trail contacts:** John Heinz National Wildlife Reserve at Tinicum, 8601 Lindbergh Blvd., Philadelphia, PA 19153; (215) 365-3118; www.fws.gov/northeast/heinz

**Finding the trailhead:** From Philadelphia get on I-76 E and take exit 347A on the left toward I-95 S/PA 291/Penrose Avenue/International Airport. Drive 0.4 mile and continue onto South 26th Street. Drive 0.9 mile and turn right onto Penrose Avenue. Continue 2.4 miles to where Penrose Avenue turns right and becomes Island Avenue. Drive 0.4 mile and turn left onto Bartram Avenue. Continue 0.3 mile and turn right onto South 84th Street. Drive 0.7 mile and turn left onto Lindbergh Boulevard. Drive 0.3 mile, turn right, take a slight left, then turn left again, and arrive at the parking lot on your right. Trailhead GPS: N39 53.573' / W075 15.448'

## THE HIKE

The Tinicum National Environmental Center was established by an act of Congress in 1972 to protect the last 200 acres of freshwater tidal marsh in Pennsylvania. In 1991 the name was changed to the John Heinz National Wildlife Refuge to honor the late senator who helped preserve Tinicum Marsh. The history of the marsh can be traced back to the mid-1600s, when early settlers built a dike and drained part of the marsh for grazing. At that time the marsh was more than 5,700 acres, but with the rapid urbanization of the area that followed World War I, the marsh was reduced to a mere 200 acres.

In 1955 Gulf Oil donated 145 acres adjacent to the eastern end of the marsh, and the area soon became a haven for wildlife. But in 1969 plans were on the table to route I-95 right through the marsh. This started a series of injunctions and public hearings that ended in 1972 when Congress gave the secretary of the interior authorization to acquire the 1,200 acres that comprise the marsh today.

One of the popular ways to explore the refuge is by canoe, on the 4.5-mile section of Darby Creek that winds through the marsh. If you've got a canoe, bring it; there's a canoe launch, but there are no canoe rentals. Also, keep in mind that the refuge waters are tidal and navigable only within two hours of high tide. If you plan to canoe, it's best to contact the visitor contact station. They can provide you with a canoe map and ten points of interest, or you can download the canoe map from the refuge's website listed below. Fishing is permitted, and you can use the same map for fishing.

Once written off as a worthless swamp, the refuge propagates over 50 species of wildflowers.

From your canoe you'll see a diversity of waterfowl, wildlife, and amphibians. You may come upon the eastern painted turtle or the state-endangered red-bellied turtle sunning himself on a log. Chances are you'll see one of these ducks: the hooded merganser, pintail, shoveler, or mallard. There are three nonvenomous snakes that call the marsh home: the northern water snake, the eastern garter snake, and the northern brown snake. Eight species of toads, frogs, and turtles have been identified here as well.

In addition to the indigenous population, the refuge is along the Atlantic Flyway and serves as a stopover for migratory birds in the spring and fall. Sightings have included the great blue heron, Canada geese, egrets, killdeer, and sandpipers. More than 280 species of birds have been sighted, with 80 of those species recorded as nesting in or near the marsh. Bring your binoculars and bird-watching book: You might just see a bird here you've never seen before, like a great crested flycatcher, a Philadelphia vireo, or a yellow-throated warbler.

There are a number of environmental education opportunities here for young and old. Educators and group leaders use the refuge as an outdoor classroom to enhance student learning. Field trips are free, but you need to reserve a place for your group in advance. Also, it's recommended that anyone planning on leading an educational field trip meet with the refuge staff for an introduction to the refuge.

There are ongoing free programs with titles like Nature Photo Walk, Birding Basics, Waterfowl Wonderment, and Minnow Evolution. There are even free professional-development workshops for educators offered throughout the year. Add to all this a resource library, located in the visitor center, with more than 200 activity guides, videos, and other resources, and you have the perfect place to spend a day.

## MILES AND DIRECTIONS

**0.0** Start at the parking lot and walk to the gate. Pass around the gate and walk on the crushed stone trail.

**0.3** Pass the boardwalk on your left.

**0.4** Pass the fishing pier on Darby Creek on your right.

**0.8** Pass the observation tower on your left.

**1.4** Turn left and cross the dike.

**1.7** Pass an observation platform on your left.

**1.8** Turn left onto the Trolley Bed Trail.

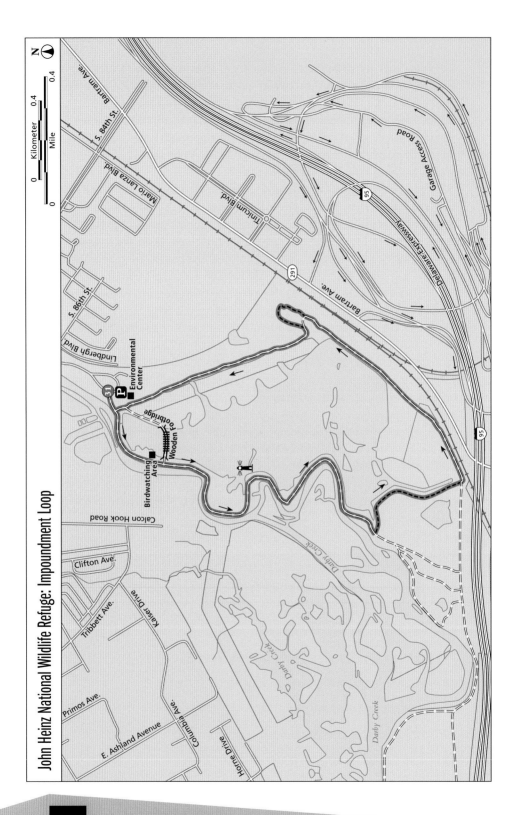

# John Heinz National Wildlife Refuge: Impoundment Loop

**2.5**   Turn left onto Haul Road.

**3.1**   Pass a trail on your left.

**3.3**   Pass the visitor center on your right.

**3.5**   Arrive back at the parking lot.

*Estuaries: Where the River Meets the Ocean*
*Estuaries are created when the tide mixes the salt water*
*from the ocean with freshwater from rivers. Because this*
*mix of the two waters creates such an ideal habitat for*
*so many species, 75 percent of commercial fishing in the*
*United States is done in estuaries. The biggest threat to*
*estuaries today is the building of homes and recreational*
*areas along the coastline, but organizations such as the*
*Partnership for the Delaware enlist volunteers to conduct*
*surveys, collect data, and most important, reconstruct*
*shorelines.*

*There are a number of highlights on this moderate hike that just about anybody could do. After you hike through the activity and picnic area of the park, you cross Pennypack Creek on an interesting footbridge to the wooded area where you can get up close to Council Rock, a 100-foot-high gneiss outcrop where chiefs of the local Lenni Lenape Indians met on the topside to celebrate or to seek or give counsel. You then hike uphill to get on top of the boulder to check out the view. From here, the hike leads you back across the footbridge and alongside Pennypack Creek to connect for a short time with the Pennypack Trail before you cut away and reenter the forest before you return to the paved park roads and the parking lot where you started.*

**Start:** The parking lot on Moredon Road

**Distance:** 2.5-mile figure-eight

**Hiking time:** 1 to 1.5 hours

**Difficulty:** Moderate

**Trail surface:** Paved park roads, forest footpath, crushed limestone trail

**Best seasons:** Spring, summer, fall, winter

**Other trail users:** Dog-walkers, joggers, fishermen, equestrians, cross-country skiers, sled riders

**Canine compatibility:** Leashed dogs permitted in all areas of the park except the main activity field and picnic area

**Land status:** Montgomery County Park

**Fees and permits:** No fees or permits

**Schedule:** 8 a.m. to sunset daily

**Maps:** USGS Frankford; park map at ranger station

**Trail contacts:** Lorimer Park, 183 Moredon Rd., Huntingdon Valley, PA 19006; (215) 947-3477; www.montcopa.org

**Finding the trailhead:** From Philadelphia get on I-95 N and take exit 32 toward Academy Road/Linden Avenue. Keep left at the fork and follow the signs for Academy Road. Drive 0.4 mile. Continue straight onto Academy Road. Drive 1.6 miles and turn left onto Grant Avenue. Drive 2.5 miles and continue onto Welsh Road for 0.2 mile. Take a slight left onto Alburger Avenue and continue 0.3 mile. Take the first left onto Verree Road. Continue 0.5 mile and turn right onto Bloomfield Avenue. Drive 0.6 mile and continue onto Moredon Road. Continue on Moredon Road for 0.3 mile and turn left into the parking lot. Trailhead GPS: N40 05.788' / W75 04.464'

## THE HIKE

In 1936 George Horace Lorimer, a former graduate of Yale and editor in chief of the *Saturday Evening Post*, left his 132-acre weekend retreat to Montgomery County to be used as a public park. He actually owned 2,000 acres of farmland in the area but began to sell off portions, as the farm was losing money. Because of its beauty, the area known as King's Oak became a retreat for his family. It was this section of his estate that he left to the county to be preserved for the public's enjoyment. He wanted the park to be a peaceful place where visitors could observe birds and other wildlife as well as the trees and flowers. Today the park encompasses 230 acres of woods, streams, and meadows.

The central feature of the park is Council Rock, overlooking Pennypack Creek. It is said that back in the sixteenth century, this rock was a meeting place for the Lenni Lenape chiefs. Today this majestic, 100-foot rock formation is a popular backdrop for wedding photos. The park boasts huge trees, hiking and biking trails, fishing in the stocked Pennypack Creek, and even a hiking trail for visitors with handicaps.

There are over 8 miles of trails within the park, including a section of the Pennypack Trail that runs alongside the western edge of the park. The trails lead hikers through deep, shaded woods alongside bubbling streams and to scenic overlooks. Scattered among all of this are more than seventy picnic tables where you can stop and enjoy a meal and take a well-deserved break.

Council Rock is a 100-foot high gneiss outcrop where chiefs of the local Lenni Lenape met on the topside to celebrate or to seek or give counsel.

If you're a birder, look for the northern bobwhite, the gray catbird, the eastern kingbird, and the great crested flycatcher. These particular species delight in eating the shiny red berries (also called drupes) of the spicebush, which is part of the understory of the forest, which also includes mountain laurel and witch hazel.

Arching over these shrubs are over seventy species of trees, including typical northern hardwoods such as red oak, white oak, and black oak, as well as maple, black gum, pine, and tulip poplar.

Your first stop on this hike is Council Rock, which provides a photo op for wedding photos of the bride and bridegroom, as well as less-formal shots of families with their children or hikers before or after they achieve the topside of the rock and hike the topside forest.

After the giant rock, you walk alongside Pennypack Stream for 0.2 mile on a trail that leads you under Moredon Road before you take the footpath that leads you uphill to the gravel road that is the Pennypack Trail. From this point you continue 0.4 mile to a sign on the trail that directs hikers to turn left and reenter the forest.

Once you cross Pennypack Creek, turn left and note the "Handicapped" sign in a streamside clearing that provides deep shade, benches, and handrails. From this setting you hike 0.4 mile and cross the stream on a bridge, then turn left once again as you head uphill to the parking lot where you started out.

## MILES AND DIRECTIONS

**0.0** Start by crossing Moredon Road via the crosswalk. Stay on the paved park trail going downhill. *Note:* Do not get on the Pennypack Trail, which runs alongside the park. Continue on to the paved vehicle road leading to the park picnic area. Turn left and walk past the restrooms on your left.

**0.2** After you pass the restrooms, turn right and circle around the picnic area. Then walk alongside Pennypack Creek. It is here where you get your first look at Council Rock.

**0.3** Turn left and cross over Pennypack Creek on Michael's Bridge for a different view of Council Rock. Then turn right and visit a small replica of a covered bridge over a small feeder stream. Then turn left and walk uphill.

**0.5** Bear to the right. Do not take the hairpin right turn. You will soon see private homes on your left.

**0.8** Turn right and drop down into the forest.

**0.9** Arrive back at the road where you started before you made the loop. Make a sharp left and return downhill; cross the creek on Michael's Bridge, then turn left and walk alongside the creek.

# Lorimer Park

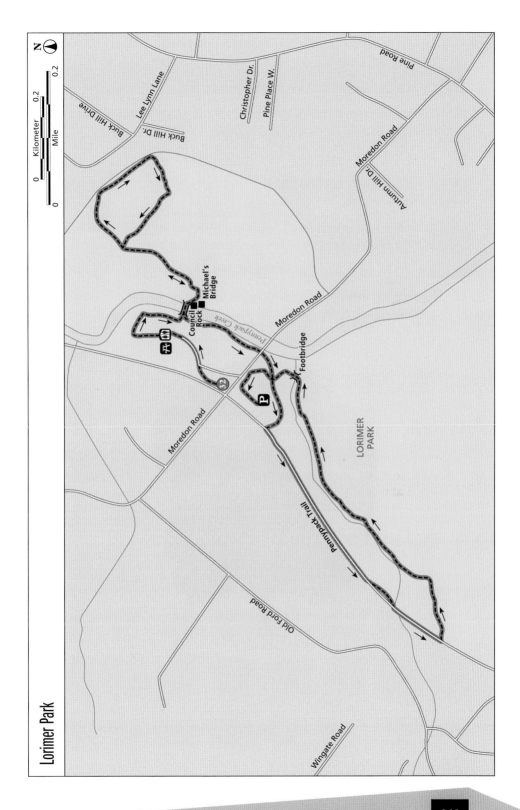

**1.2** Connect with a trail that goes under Moredon Road, then bear right.

**1.3** Come to an intersection and continue straight.

**1.4** Take the footpath on the right that leads uphill. *Note:* This is near the bird blind, before the maintenance storage area.

**1.5** Arrive at the top and turn left onto the Pennypack Trail.

**1.9** Come to a hiker's sign and turn left, then turn left again on the trail back the way you came.

**2.0** Arrive at a setting with benches alongside the stream. Continue straight with the stream on your left. Note the "Handicapped" sign.

**2.4** Turn left on the bridge and cross the stream.

**2.5** Turn left and walk uphill to arrive back at the parking lot and your vehicle.

# Pennypack Park

*This easy, mostly flat hike begins at an open park-like setting where there are picnic tables placed in the shade of huge trees that rise alongside Pennypack Creek. You start out on the paved hiking/biking trail where, at this point, there are just as many walkers, bike riders, dog walkers, and parents pushing strollers as there are serious hikers, sporting colorful backpacks and opaque water bottles. As is often the case at popular trails, the farther you hike the less company you'll have, especially on this hike when just under a mile you leave the trail for a forest footpath and a short uphill climb through the forest. This section is also an equestrian trail, where proper trail etiquette dictates that hikers should step off the trail and give the horse and its rider the right-of-way.*

**Start:** The hiking/biking trailhead
**Distance:** 3.8-mile lollipop
**Hiking time:** 2 to 2.5 hours
**Difficulty:** Easy
**Trail surface:** Paved hiking/biking trail, dirt forest path
**Best seasons:** Spring, summer, fall
**Other trail users:** Mountain bikers, bike riders, equestrians, strollers, joggers
**Canine compatibility:** Leashed dogs permitted

**Land status:** City of Philadelphia
**Fees and permits:** No fees or permits
**Schedule:** Open daily from 8:00 a.m. to sunset
**Map:** USGS Frankford
**Trail contacts:** Fairmount Park Information; (215) 683-0200; www.visitphilly.comoutdoors-activities/philadelphia/fairmountpark

**Finding the trailhead:** From Philadelphia get on I-95 N and take exit 30 for Cottman Avenue toward PA 73/Rhawn Street and drive 0.3 mile. Continue on Cottman Avenue for 0.9 mile and make a slight right onto Ryan Avenue. Drive 1.3 miles and continue straight onto Borbeck Avenue. Drive 0.3 mile and turn right onto Bustleton Avenue/SR 1009/SR 1009. Continue 0.2 mile and take the third left onto Rhawn Street. Drive 1.6 miles and turn right onto Verree Road. Continue 0.6 mile and turn left onto Susquehanna Road. Drive 0.4 mile and turn right onto Pine Road. Continue 0.5 mile and take the third right into the parking lot. Trailhead GPS: N40 05.378' / W075 04.149'

## THE HIKE

Pennypack Creek is a 22.6-mile-long creek that rises from headwater springs and wetlands in Horsham, Warminster, and Upper Southampton, then flows southeast through eastern Montgomery County, lower Bucks County, and the northeast section of Philadelphia before discharging into a broad mudflat on the Delaware River.

The creek got its name from the Lenape word *penepekw*, meaning "downward-flowing water" or "deep, dead water; water without much current." Early cartographers gave various spellings for the name, including *Pennishpaska*, *La Riviere de Pennicpacka*, and *Pennishpaca Kyl*.

When William Penn founded the province of Pennsylvania in 1682, the Pennypack Valley was already occupied by Swedish colonists who continued to live in the valley as the English settlement began. Despite the lack of navigability beyond the fall line near the Franklin Avenue Bridge, early settlers built mills along the Pennypack, including William Penn who built his Pemmapecka Mill in 1701.

As a result of this early development, the Pennypack Valley was a center of industry throughout the nineteenth and early twentieth centuries. But with the development of steam power during the Industrial Revolution, water power's influence on industry declined. As a result, many of the mills on the Pennypack closed, and by 1905 the land around the creek was acquired by the City of Philadelphia to ensure the protection of Pennypack Creek and the preservation of the

Deep shade over a paved trail: What more could you ask for?

surrounding 1,600 acres of woodlands, meadows, wetlands, and fields that were preserved to create Pennypack Park.

Those preservation efforts have paid off. Today Pennypack Park is alive and well with over 150 species of nesting and migratory bird sightings reported, including the ruby-throated hummingbird, the great blue heron, warblers, the pileated woodpecker, ducks, geese, hawks, great horned owls, and the screech owl.

The park is famous for its large, scattered deer herd, but it's also home to a large variety of mammals, including several kinds of bats, red foxes and gray foxes, rabbits, muskrats, woodchucks, raccoons, skunks, opossums, and long-tailed weasels.

The park includes an impressive mixed-oak forest of black oak, red oak, white oak, chestnut oak, the tulip tree, and American beech, with an understory of shrubs including blueberry shrubs, maple-leaf viburnum, and southern arrowwood.

Pennypack Creek is not only a beautiful stream, it is also a fisherman's delight. One reason for that is that the Pennsylvania Fish Commission stocks Pennypack Creek each year, in the spring and fall, with rainbow trout, brown trout, and golden rainbow trout. Other fish that have been caught are red-breasted sunfish, green sunfish, rock bass, largemouth bass, carp, and white sucker.

This hike begins at the hiking/biking trailhead with the creek on your left. At 0.2 mile you cross the creek as it winds its way snake-like from one end of the park to the other. At 0.9 mile you turn left and stay on the paved trail that takes you under Verree Road. (Before you turn left, you can see that before this underpass was put in, bikers and hikers had to cross the busy road.)

Immediately after the underpass you turn right onto the combination hiking and equestrian trail, which is a narrow dirt path that cuts through the thick underbrush. It's uphill for 0.2 mile before the trail leaves the underbrush and you enter the forest. At 1.8 miles you arrive at a major trail intersection where you turn left onto the paved hiking/biking trail, then turn left again and cross a modern bridge on your way back to the Verree Road underpass. While this stretch has a few uphill sections, the trail is in deep shade and runs very close to the stream, making this short section the most beautiful stretch of the hike. After you come up from the Verree Road underpass, retrace your steps back to the parking area and your vehicle.

🌿 **Green Tip:**
*Observe wildlife from a distance. Don't interfere in their lives—both of you will be better off for it.*

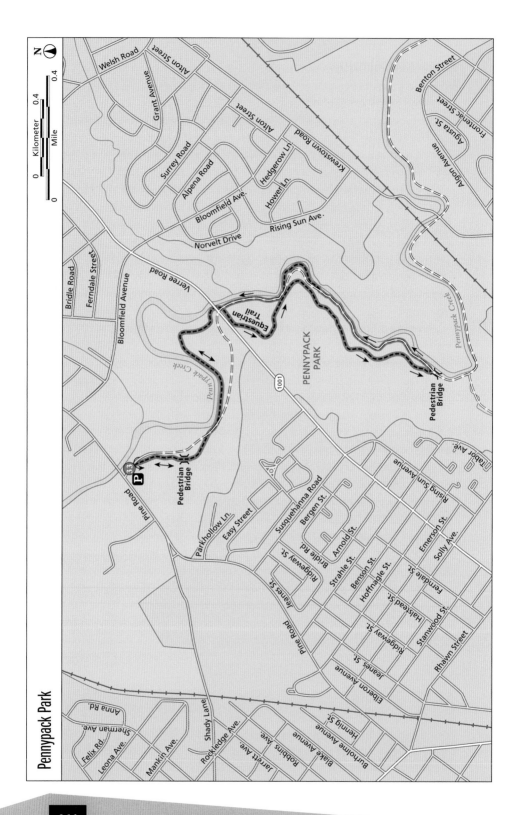

# Pennypack Park

## MILES AND DIRECTIONS

**0.0**  Start at the trailhead for the paved hiking/biking trail.

**0.2**  Cross a washout gully on a pedestrian bridge.

**0.9**  Come to a trail intersection. Go left at the Y. The trail goes under Verree Road. As soon as you arrive on the other side of the road, take the dirt hiking/equestrian trail off to your right, into the forest.

**1.2**  You enter a mixed-oak forest of mature trees.

**1.8**  Come to a major trail intersection. Cross over a small bridge/culvert on the trail. Then turn left and left again onto the paved hiking/biking trail and cross a newer bridge. You then head back to the park with the creek on your right.

**2.7**  Go under Verree Road and retrace your steps back to where you started.

**3.8**  Arrive back at the parking lot and your vehicle.

*This easy, flat hike first takes you to a short spur that leads you to a site on the banks of the Delaware River where you can see the skyscrapers of downtown Philadelphia, 15 miles downriver. If you pause here long enough, you may notice the effect the Atlantic Ocean's tides have on the river as it raises or lowers the water level of the Delaware River at the rate of an inch a minute. The hike continues to the point where Neshaminy Creek meets the river, then it's on through a natural area and pine plantation as you make the loop back to where you started. Along the way you will discover the unique plants and animals that are found only in a freshwater estuary.*

**Start:** The kiosk by the parking lot
**Distance:** 2.3-mile loop
**Hiking time:** 1.5 hours
**Difficulty:** Easy
**Trail surface:** Paved park roads, sidewalks, dirt pathways, forest footpath
**Best seasons:** Spring, summer, fall
**Other trail users:** Fishermen, tourists
**Canine compatibility:** Leashed dogs permitted; pets prohibited in the swimming area

**Land status:** Pennsylvania State Park
**Fees and permits:** No fees or permits
**Schedule:** 8 a.m. to sunset daily
**Map:** USGS Beverly
**Trail contacts:** Neshaminy State Park, 3401 State Rd., Bensalem, PA 19020; (215) 639-4538; www.visit PAparks.com

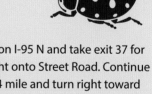

**Finding the trailhead:** From Philadelphia get on I-95 N and take exit 37 for PA 132/Street Road. Drive 0.2 mile and turn right onto Street Road. Continue 0.6 mile and turn left onto State Road. Drive 0.4 mile and turn right toward Park Drive. Go 0.1 mile and turn left toward Park Drive. Turn left onto Park Drive and continue 440 feet, then take the first right onto Park Drive to the parking lot on the left. Trailhead GPS: N40 04.670' / W74 55.222'

**Special considerations:** During winter months there is a limited archery season in the park in designated 100-acre sectors that will be marked off and may be shifted from one area to another. During hunting season five archers, who are registered with the Pennsylvania Game Commission, will hunt for a week, then five different archers will be chosen for the next week, and so on. The hunting sectors will be posted. Be sure to wear safety orange during this time. Contact the park office for more details.

## THE HIKE

For repayment of a debt to his father, William Penn received a land grant in the American Colonies from the king of England, King Charles II, but instead of assuming that the king's grant gave him property rights, Penn had what many people considered a crazy idea: He would buy the land from its current owners, the American Indians.

In 1682 William Penn made his first purchase from the Lenape chiefs for the land that was bounded on the south by Neshaminy Creek. A year later Penn's second purchase of land was bounded on the north by Neshaminy Creek, making what is now Neshaminy Creek State Park the core of the future Commonwealth of Pennsylvania.

Robert R. Logan, who was a descendant of William Penn's secretary, gave a large portion of land to the Commonwealth of Pennsylvania in 1936. His home is no longer on the land that became Neshaminy State Park, but the original drive to his home, which is paved, serves as a hiking trail and park service road.

Along the eastern edge of the park is Dunksferry Road. More than 300 years ago, a man named Dunken Williams operated a ferry across the Delaware River. Dunksferry Road is named after him and is one of the oldest roads in Pennsylvania.

This hike allows you to get an up-close look at a unique habitat: an estuary in the Delaware Valley. Even though you are 116 miles from the Atlantic Ocean, you are at sea level here. When the tide rises and falls at the ocean in New Jersey, it

Hikers take a break and sit on a log on the banks of the Delaware River as they check out the Philadelphia skyline 15 miles downriver.

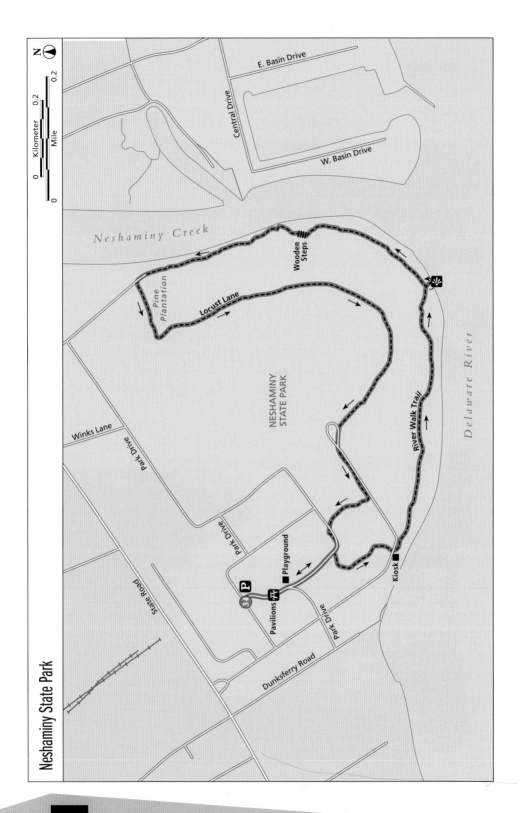

Neshaminy State Park

also rises and falls an inch a minute along the river shoreline here. The shoreline is an estuary; the water is fresh, not salty like the water of the lower estuary, which is closer to the ocean.

American Indians used the rise and fall of tides to trap fish. The Indians built low fences in the river. At high tide, the fish swam over the top of the fence, then as the tide went out, the fish were trapped behind the fence and easily speared.

You begin this hike in the parking lot near the kiosk. From there you walk past Pavilion No. 3. At 0.2 mile you turn right toward the river and get on the River Walk Trail. At 0.7 you get off the River Walk Trail on a short spur that takes you to the beach on the banks of the river. There are large driftwood logs here where you can sit and soak in the sound the waves make as they come to shore. If you have your camera, you can get a shot of the skyscrapers in downtown Philadelphia.

Back on the trail you hike toward Neshaminy Creek, where you may spot sandpipers, herons, egrets, and colorful wood ducks. On the other side of the creek, you see the marina with its 370 slips that boaters can rent each season. At this point along the creek, you are hiking through a forest of willows, alders, ashes, and silver maples that thrive in the moist creek-side soil. The trail continues into the Pine Plantation, and then you turn left onto Locust Lane, then left again to get on the paved road. From this point you turn right, then right again as you retrace your steps back to the parking lot and your vehicle.

## MILES AND DIRECTIONS

**0.0**  Start at the kiosk by the parking lot. Take the paved park road past the playground and the pavilions.

**0.2**  Turn right at the Y.

**0.3**  Come to a kiosk and a paved road. Continue straight and get on the dirt River Walk Trail.

**0.7**  Come to a trail spur that takes you to a site on the banks of the Delaware River for a photo opportunity.

**1.0**  Turn right by a set of wooden steps.

**1.2**  Turn left and walk through the Pine Plantation.

**1.3**  Turn left on Locust Lane.

**1.9**  Turn left at the macadam loop.

**2.0**  Turn right.

**2.1**  Turn right again and retrace your steps back to your vehicle.

**2.3**  Arrive back at the parking lot and your vehicle.

# William Penn's Grand Plan

In 1681, when King Charles II of England granted William Penn the charter for the New World colony that would become Pennsylvania, Penn already had a plan for how this new world should be set up and governed. Based on his Quaker beliefs, his plan was to create a society that was godly in its beliefs and virtuous in its deeds. Penn knew it wouldn't be difficult to attract fellow Quakers to the New World. As religious dissenters of the Church of England, they were targets of the church much like the Separatists and Puritans.

One of the first problems Penn faced, a full year before he arrived in the New World, was that even though King Charles II of England had granted him 45,000 acres, the Lenni Lenape Indians who were established there proclaimed that they owned the land. Knowing that it was critical that he establish a peaceful relationship with the Lenape, Penn began a correspondence wherein he laid out his ideas as well as his beliefs for establishing a peaceful coexistence between the settlers and the Indians. One such letter read, "I desire to gain your Love and Friendship by a kind, Just and Peaceable Life."

As a zealous advocate of Quakerism, Penn believed in a liberal government where men like himself could be both idealistic and practical—working diligently on their lofty ideas for the betterment of mankind, while at the same time maintaining a practical and pragmatic lifestyle that would ensure religious freedom.

Despite his beliefs in democracy and religious tolerance, Penn was also a member of the landed gentry and had control over how the land was bought and sold, how the city was plotted and populated, how its government worked, and how its laws and public institutions were set up.

In many ways Penn had control of his grand enterprise, but he did not have as much control as he wanted, and he had to continually change his plans and engage in endless squabbles with landowners, including Lord Baltimore, who tried to take territorial rights from Pennsylvania and annex the land into his holdings.

When Penn began to devise his grand utopian city, Philadelphia, he had to outmaneuver agents from Maryland who wanted nothing more than to acquire the land that was situated at the convergence of the Delaware and Schuylkill Rivers. When Penn wrote about his choice of land for the grand new city, he wrote "in the most Convenient place upon the river for health & Navigation."

To secure new routes to interior Pennsylvania, Penn tried to buy land for the Lenape on the Susquehanna River, where they could build a trading post closer to the Iroquois Nation in New York that was closer than Albany. However, New York state agents beat him out by claiming that the land in question was a gift from the Iroquois.

In 1701 Penn brokered his last treaty, which conveyed land and controlled trade at the expense of the New York agents he had dealt with, and lost out to, in the original negotiations. Penn's deal rewarded "his" Indians, and his policies made Pennsylvania, in the words of renown missionary John Heckewelder, "the last delightful asylum" for Native Americans.

By 1701 Penn made his final voyage back to England. In 1712 he suffered a stroke and died in 1718.

# New Jersey Hikes

There are four great hikes in this section, and while each hike could be classified as an historic hike, each is uniquely different from the others. Two hikes, Washington Crossing Historic Park and The Princeton Woods, are from the Revolutionary War; the first hike leads you across the Delaware River at the exact spot where Washington and his troops crossed on their way to their surprise victory in Trenton. The second hike takes you to Washington's second major victory eight days later in Princeton. On this hike, as you make your way to the battlefield, you pass through The Princeton Woods where well-known intellectuals connected to the Institute for Advanced Study, including Albert Einstein, sometimes walked.

On the Delaware River Valley hike, you walk the canal towpaths on both sides of the Delaware River. At the northern terminus of the hike, you cross the Delaware River on the famous Centre Bridge; at the southern terminus of this hike you cross the Delaware River on the historic New Hope–Lambertville Bridge, built originally in 1904.

Along the way, on both sides of the river you pass by relics and historic sites left over from the Great Canal Period.

In the early 1800s three forts were built on each shore of the Delaware River and on Pea Island in the river. These forts were built to protect the Delaware Bay and shipping interests. The forts sat dormant until the Civil War came along and Fort Delaware was used as a Union prison and eventually held 32,000 Confederate soldiers. Conditions were harsh at the prison and many prisoners died of cholera and were buried at Finn's Point National Cemetery at Fort Mott.

Fort Mott has remained as it was back in the 1800s, so as part of the hike visitors can explore the gun emplacements, the moat, and the other buildings and tunnels that were erected during the Protectionist Period to safeguard this entry to the United States.

# Delaware River Valley: Lambertville to Stockton

*This is an easy, flat hike. It is rated moderate due to its length. If you have two vehicles and want to shorten this hike, park one of your vehicles in the parking lot near Errico's Market in Stockton, then drive south on Route 29 to the original parking lot starting point. This will give you a 4.8-mile hike. On the other hand, if you want to do the entire length, you need to know there is very little shade on this trail, so the earlier in the day you start the better, and once you get away from the towns, there is no place to get water. The bottom line is this is a great hike where you can explore the historic canal system, then hike across an historic bridge over the Delaware River, then pass through a number of quaint villages, where it will take all of your willpower not to linger.*

**Start:** At the parking area at the towpath under Route 202, near the Jimison Farm
**Distance:** 7.1-mile loop
**Hiking time:** 3.5 to 4 hours
**Difficulty:** Moderate, due to the length
**Trail surface:** Dirt towpath, railroad bed, sidewalks, bridges
**Best seasons:** Spring, summer, fall, winter
**Other trail users:** Joggers, bike riders, strollers, cross-country skiers
**Canine compatibility:** Leashed dogs permitted
**Land status:** New Jersey State Park
**Fees and permits:** No fees or permits

**Schedule:** Dawn to dusk daily
**Map:** USGS Stockton and Lambertville, NJ
**Trail contacts:** D & R Canal State Park Office, 625 Canal Rd., Somerset, NJ 08873; (732) 873-3050; www.state.nj.us/dep/parksand forests/parks/drcanal.html. Delaware and Raritan Canal Commission, PO Box 539, Rte. 29, Prallsville Mills, Stockton, NJ 08559; (609) 397-2000; www.dandrcanal.com/index.html. Delaware Canal State Park, 11 Lodi Hill Rd., Upper Black Eddy, PA 18972; (610) 982-5560; www.dcnr.state.pa.us/ stateparks/parks/delawarecanal .aspx

**Finding the trailhead:** From Philadelphia take I-95 N to exit 1 for New Jersey 29 N toward Lambertville. Drive 0.3 mile, keep left at the fork, and then merge onto River Road. Drive 8.9 miles and continue onto NJ 29 N. Continue 0.8 mile and turn left onto Bridge Street. Take the second right onto North Main Street. Drive 1.0 mile and continue onto NJ 29 N/River Road, then turn left onto River Road and continue 0.2 mile to the parking area on the left. Trailhead GPS: N40 22.792' / W074 57.075'
**Special considerations:** Spring flooding will close this hike.

## THE HIKE

In the Colonial era of the 1700s, rivers like the Delaware played an important role in providing power for sawmills, paper mills, iron works, and just about any early industry that needed power to function. To get across those rivers, early entrepreneurs built ferries and transported farmers, factory workers, and assorted other travelers along with their horses and buggies and other belongings, from one side to the other. Soon villages sprang up at the ferry landings, many of them carrying the name of the ferry operator.

But the days of the ferries were numbered, and by the early 1800s bridges replaced the ferries. In 1814 the Centre Bridge Company built a 950-foot long covered wooden bridge across the Delaware River on the former site of Reading's Ferry. They called the bridge the Centre Bridge because it was exactly halfway between the Trenton and the Phillipsburg bridges.

With the opening of the Erie Canal in 1825, "Canal Fever" hit the United States. In 1830 the State of New Jersey decided it would build a canal from the Delaware River to the Raritan River; the work would be done by local farmers and newly arrived immigrants, mostly Irish, who would use picks and shovels. The canal was finished in 1834 and became the final link in the intercoastal waterway that extended from Massachusetts to Georgia.

For nearly a century after it opened, the Delaware & Raritan Canal was one of the country's busiest canals, carrying coal from Pennsylvania's anthracite coal region across New Jersey and to the eastern seaboard to be shipped north to

Hikers stop for an up-close look at the Alexauken Creek Aqueduct.

feed New York's industrial boom. From 1860 to 1870, 80 percent of the Raritan's total cargo was coal from Pennsylvania.

Meanwhile, in Pennsylvania, the Delaware Canal was completed in 1832. It connected with the Lehigh Navigation System at Easton and helped develop the anthracite coal industry in the Upper Lehigh Valley by providing a convenient and economical way to transport coal to Philadelphia, New York, and the eastern seaboard.

But by the mid-1800s, when railroads appeared in both Pennsylvania and New Jersey, it soon became clear that railroads were a more efficient way to transport goods, and it became increasingly difficult to profitably operate canals. The last paying canal boat completed its journey through the Delaware Canal on October 17, 1931. The state of Pennsylvania bought 40 miles of the canal in 1931 and bought the remaining 20 miles in 1940. In 1989 the state named the canal, and its surrounding 830 acres, the Delaware Canal State Park.

On this hike the first thing you come to at 0.2 mile is the aqueduct that carries water from the Delaware River into the Delaware Raritan Feeder Canal. It looks like a concrete dam with a very powerful waterfall cascading over the top. At 0.3 mile you pass by Bum Junction, as you enter the outskirts of the City of Lambertville, population just under 4,000. At the 1.0-mile mark, you are in the downtown section with its antiques shops, boutiques, and restaurants.

The New Hope–Lambertville Bridge was built in 1904 as a steel replacement for the first two wooden bridges here that were swept away by floods. It is 1,053 in length, has a weight limit of 4 tons, and cost 63,818 dollars to build. Each day 13,990 vehicles cross the bridge.

When New Hope started its existence as a river town, it was called Coryell's Ferry, after the family who ran the ferry. But after a fire in the 1790s destroyed three mills, the owner rebuilt the mills and, just for luck, named the town New Hope. His plan worked, because today New Hope is a booming river town with plenty of upscale restaurants, art galleries, canal-related tourist attractions, and the Bucks County Playhouse.

From New Hope you walk north and arrive at the Centre Bridge at 4.5 miles. Like its southern counterpart this bridge started its existence as a wooden bridge in 1814; it was rebuilt in 1830, rebuilt again in 1841 after a flood, then rebuilt again in 1923 after a lightning fire, then finally rebuilt into its current state in 1927. It is 950 feet long.

From the bridge you walk to the town of Stockton, and at 4.7 miles you reach the old railroad station, which these days is a market and sandwich shop. From the old station you get on the abandoned rail bed and hike south. At 5.3 miles you cross over a deck girder bridge, and at this point the rail bed connects with the towpath that leads you back to where you started.

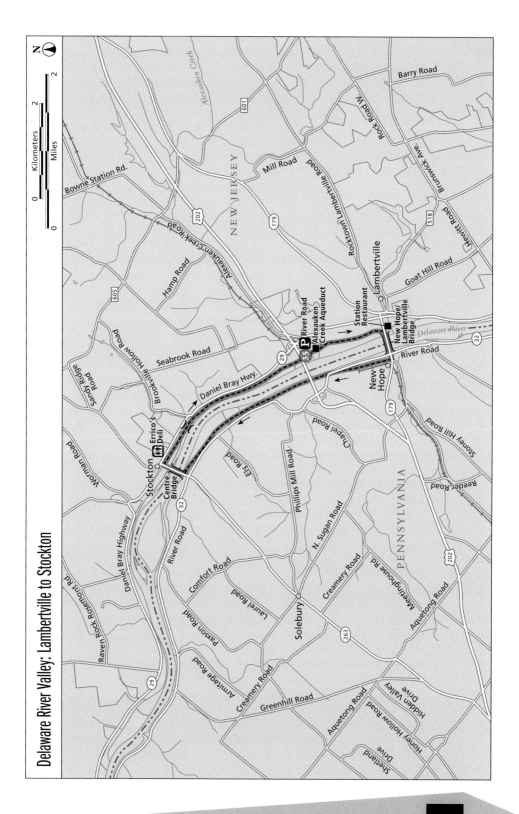

Delaware River Valley: Lambertville to Stockton

## MILES AND DIRECTIONS

**0.0** Start at the parking area at the towpath under US 202 near the Jimison Farm.

**0.2** Arrive at the Alexauken Creek aqueduct.

**0.3** Pass under a railroad girder bridge.

**1.0** Cross Bridge Street to the sidewalk on the other side and then turn right. Cross over the canal then pass the Station Restaurant, the former railroad station, on your left.

**1.2** Cross over the Delaware River on the New Hope–Lambertville Bridge.

**1.3** In New Hope continue west on East Bridge Street. Continue straight, crossing over Main Street. You are now on West Bridge Street, which is also SR 179. Continue straight up the hill on the sidewalk.

**1.4** Before the bridge over the Delaware Canal, turn right and cross West Bridge Street, then descend onto a driveway that leads to the towpath.

**2.4** Pass under US 202.

**3.0** Pass under a bridge to the private residence of William L. Lathrop, a prominent member of New Hope's artist colony in the early 1900s.

**3.6** Pass under a bridge that is a driveway to a private residence.

**4.0** Pass under a second bridge that is a driveway to a private residence.

**4.5** Go up the steps to the Centre Bridge and cross the Delaware River on the pedestrian walkway.

**4.6** Arrive in Stockton. Continue walking straight ahead on Bridge Street. Pass the Delaware Raritan Feeder Canal and the post office on your right.

**4.7** Arrive at the old Stockton railroad station, which is now Errico's Deli. There are bathrooms and picnic tables here.

**5.3** Pass over a deck girder bridge. Here the rail bed joins the towpath.

**7.1** Pass under US 202 and arrive back to the parking lot where you started.

> **🌱 Green Tip:**
> *Pack out what you pack in—even food scraps, because they can attract wild animals.*

# Washington Crossing Historic Park

*On this moderate hike you walk the same trail that General George Washington and his Continental Army walked to get to the Pennsylvania side of the Delaware River, where they boarded sturdy cargo boats and made their way to the New Jersey side. Of course, you will cross the river on a bridge, then get on a causeway that takes you to higher ground and back on Washington's trail, which is called the Continental Lane Trail. The trail then enters the forest, where you walk alongside a stream until the trail ends in the park and you turn around and follow the stream through the forest before you make a short uphill climb to return to where you got on the Continental Trail. From this point you retrace your steps back to the visitor center.*

**Start:** The parking lot, then walk to the George Washington statue in front of the visitor center
**Distance:** 4.2-mile lollipop
**Hiking time:** 2 to 2.5 hours
**Difficulty:** Moderate
**Trail surface:** Sidewalks, paved roads, wood chips, forest footpath
**Best seasons:** Spring, summer, fall
**Other trail users:** Tourists, birders, cross-country skiers
**Canine compatibility:** Leashed dogs permitted
**Land status:** Pennsylvania Historical and Museum Commission; New Jersey State Park

**Fees and permits:** No fees or permits to hike
**Schedule:** Dawn to dusk daily
**Maps:** USGS Lambertville, PA; Pennington, NJ
**Trail contacts:** Washington Crossing Historic Park, 112 River Rd., PO Box 103, Washington Crossing, PA 18977; (215) 493-4076. Washington Crossing State Park, Washington Crossing-Pennington Road, Titusville, NJ 08560; (609) 737-0616; www.state.nj.us/dep/parksandforests/parks/washcros.html

**Finding the trailhead:** From Philadelphia get on I-95 N and take exit 51 toward New Hope. Drive 0.3 mile and turn left onto Taylorsville Road; watch for New Hope signs. Drive 1.1 miles and turn right onto Mount Eyre Road. Continue 0.2 mile and turn left onto PA 32 N. Continue 2.0 miles to your destination. Trailhead GPS: N40 17.716' / W074 52.342'

## THE HIKE

The American Revolution began on April 19, 1775, when British troops marched from Boston, Massachusetts to Lexington and Concord to seize war supplies stored by local militias. Shots were fired and the revolution began with the Continental Congress proclaiming that the Colonies were fighting in self-defense. To coordinate their war effort, Congress took control of the army and named Virginia's George Washington commander-in-chief.

In July 1775, when Washington arrived in Boston to take command of the Continental Army, he found many difficulties. There were three types of fighting units: Continental troops, state militia groups, and soldiers who had enlisted for short periods of time. There was a shortage of food, supplies, weapons, and money, and because of the poor condition of his ill-fed, ill-clothed army, his soldiers were quick to succumb to disease, such as smallpox, malaria, and dysentery. All of these factors combined led to a high desertion rate.

Just eight months later, in March 1776, the occupying British Army boarded a fleet of ships and left Boston. Washington figured that while their departure was good news in Boston, it was going to be bad news for some other city, and he predicted their next attack would be in New York. His prediction was right.

In June, 25,000 British troops landed on Staten Island. Throughout the summer and fall of 1776 the Continental Army stumbled through a series of disastrous battles, including defeats in Brooklyn, Manhattan, Harlem Heights, Fort Washington, and Fort Lee. The only good thing that came from all these defeats

The Hibbs House, built in Taylorsville in 1828 to house local artisans, their family, and an apprentice.

was that Washington had been rescued from battle at the East River by a seago-ing unit from Massachusetts known as the Marblehead Mariners, and it was this rescue that gave him the idea that in order to beat the British, he needed a river nearby from which to attack.

Washington and his troops arrived in Trenton, New Jersey, on December 7, 1776. Using the Marblehead Mariners, he ordered all his ships to tie up on the Pennsylvania side, and any ship they could not use was to be set ablaze.

On December 25, 1776, Washington was in Pennsylvania preparing his attack on the British and their Hessian mercenaries in Trenton, New Jersey, 9 miles downriver from his headquarters near McConkey Ferry Inn. He had set in motion a three-pronged attack, whereby his troops would cross the Delaware in Durham boats under the cover of night and arrive at the enemy outposts early in the morning to catch them by surprise.

Washington's plan was that two other generals, along with their troops and artillery, would set up at Trenton Ferry and Bristol and would also cross the Delaware and rendezvous with his company at the Trenton encampment of the Hessian forces. But because of the freezing rain and ice flows in the raging river, General Ewing believed the attack would certainly be called off. General Cadwalader's infantry men did make it across the river, but they returned to the Pennsylvania side and abandoned the attack because they were unable to get their cannons across the river.

At sundown Washington—along with 2,400 men, 18 artillery pieces, and 50 horses—made it to the New Jersey side and began the 9-mile march to Trenton. The Battle of Trenton began at 8 a.m. and at the end of two hours of fighting, the Hessians surrendered. Washington and his exultant troops returned to their encampment near McConkey's Ferry Inn, their boats laden with 980 Hessian pris-oners, more than a thousand muskets, six brass cannon, food and clothing, and other needed supplies.

Once you're on the New Jersey side of this hike, the terrain changes to a park-like setting surrounded by a forest with a deep ravine where Steel Run Creek runs through the bottom of it as it makes its way to the Delaware River. It is this stream and its proximity to the Delaware that makes this site a natural stopover for migrating birds.

The surrounding forest is made up of mixed hardwoods, as well as red cedar, eastern white pine, Japanese larch, Norway spruce, and red pine, and at the start of the Continental Lane Trail, the trail is flanked on both sides by giant pines.

From the start of the Continental Lane Trail at 0.8 mile, you hike into the forest and arrive at the stone bridge at 2.0 miles, which is the turnaround point. From there you follow the stream to 3.0 miles, where you hike uphill, and at 3.3 miles you arrive back at the start of the Continental Lane Trail. From here you retrace your steps to the visitor center and then the parking lot.

**0.0**  From the parking lot walk to the front of the visitor center and come to the statue of George Washington. Walk on the sidewalk toward the Delaware River, then turn right on the sidewalk to pass through Washington Crossing Historic Park, a section of historical houses, outbuildings, and artifacts.

**0.3**  Arrive at Route 532 and turn left onto Washington Crossing Bridge to cross the Delaware River.

**0.5**  The bridge continues over the Delaware & Raritan Canal. Turn left on the other side to cross the street and continue to a raised walkway that takes you safely over Route 29 and into Washington Crossing State Park on the New Jersey side. The walkway ends, and you get on the paved trail, which turns left as you arrive at two informational kiosks that list Washington's artillery, staff officers, and companies in his campaign.

**0.8**  Cross the paved road and note the old stone barn on your left. A short section of the Green Trail leads you to the Continental Lane Trail, which is made of wood chips, with a row of trees and shrubs along each side.

**0.9**  Start on the Continental Lane Trail.

**1.0**  Note the New Jersey visitor center on your right. Continue straight on the Continental Lane Trail.

**1.5**  Turn right on the Yellow Trail.

**2.0**  Arrive at the stone bridge, then turn around and retrace your steps on the Yellow Trail.

**2.4**  Pass the Continental Lane Trail on your left. Stay on the Yellow Trail, then cross the paved road.

**2.5**  Pass the outdoor theater on your right. You can now see the Steel Run Creek on your right. Cross the stream on exposed stones and continue to follow the signs for the Yellow Trail.

> **Green Tip:**
> *If at all possible, camp in established sites. If there are none, then camp in an unobtrusive area at least 200 feet (70 paces) from the nearest water source.*

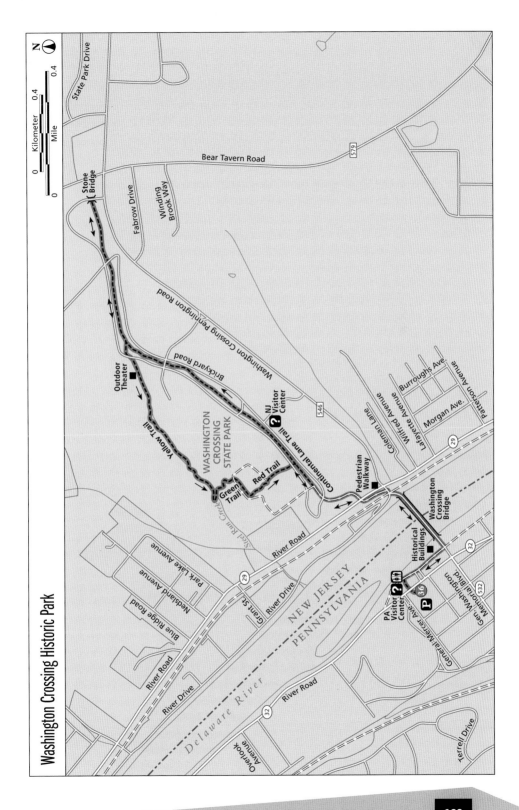

Washington Crossing Historic Park

**36**

**3.0** Recross the stream and get to the Green Trail, which makes a small loop, after which you turn right and climb up the hill.

**3.2** Arrive at the top of the hill and come to a trail junction. Turn right to stay on the Green Trail. In a few feet, you will arrive at the Red Trail and turn left. Look for a section of tall pine trees, then cross an open meadow toward the pines.

**3.3** Arrive at the Continental Lane Trail and turn right, then retrace your steps back to the visitor center where you started.

**4.2** Arrive back at the parking lot.

# The Princeton Woods

*On this easy hike you will walk through two distinctly different time periods in American history. You start out at the Clarke House, the scene of the January 3, 1777, clash between American and British forces that came to be known as the Battle of Princeton. You then hike on the former rail bed of the "Fast Line" or trolley system that ran between Trenton and Princeton, as you make your way to the Institute for Advanced Study, which was established in 1930 to accommodate the likes of J. Robert Oppenheimer, the "father of the atomic bomb" and Albert Einstein, who lived in Princeton from 1933 until his death in 1955.*

**Start:** The parking lot and walk toward the Clarke House Museum
**Distance:** 3.6-mile loop
**Hiking time:** 3 hours
**Difficulty:** Easy
**Trail surface:** Wide paths, sidewalks, pavement, former trolley tracks
**Best seasons:** Spring, summer, fall, winter
**Other trail users:** Tourists, bike riders, cross-country skiers
**Canine compatibility:** Leashed dogs permitted
**Land status:** New Jersey State Park and Institute for Advanced Study property

**Fees and permits:** No fees or permits
**Schedule:** Dawn to dusk daily
**Map:** USGS Princeton, NJ
**Trail contacts:** Princeton Battlefield State Park, 500 Mercer Rd., Princeton, New Jersey, 08540; (609) 921-0074; www.state.ny.us/dep/parksandforests/parks/princeton.html. Institute for Advanced Study, Einstein Dr., Princeton, NJ 08540; (609) 734-8000; www.ias.edu.

**Finding the trailhead:** Get on I-95 N and take exit 8B for CR 583/Princeton Pike. Drive 0.3 mile and merge onto CR 583/Princeton Pike. Continue 3.7 miles and turn right. Go 325 feet and turn right, then go 436 feet to your destination on the left. USGS Trailhead GPS: N40 19.766' / W74 40.582'

## THE HIKE

Hot on the heels of his perilous crossing of the Delaware River and surprise victory at Trenton on December 26, 1776, General George Washington was ready for another encounter with the British and their Hessian forces. Anticipating a second attack from Washington, Lord Cornwallis reestablished his troops in Trenton and the stage was set for a second battle. But Washington outsmarted Cornwallis once again and, using the same secrecy as he had before, he slipped past Trenton and attacked a much smaller British force at Princeton on January 3, 1777. In the end, Washington's army killed, captured, or wounded over 500 British troops and won the Battle at Princeton.

Princeton University, which was originally named the College of New Jersey, came about in 1746 and was one of the nine "Colonial Colleges" that were established before the American Revolution. After a number of relocations, the college was established in Princeton in 1756 and subsequently its name was changed to Princeton University. Today Princeton is referred to as a private research university, and it is rated alternately as the top or top two or three universities in the country.

Although it is not affiliated with Princeton University, the Institute for Advanced Study was established here in 1930 as a center for worldwide theoretical research. And as such it attracted the top thinkers of the day, such as J. Robert

The Mercer Memorial site is dedicated to General Hugh Mercer, who died of battlefield wounds. The oak tree under which Mercer lay while wounded was a landmark here for centuries, but the Mercer Oak fell from old age in the year 2000.

Oppenheimer, considered the "father of the atomic bomb"; John Von Neumann, who helped develop the modern digital computer; and perhaps the best-known scientist of all time, Albert Einstein, who developed his mass-energy equivalent theorem that $E=MC^2$ in 1905 while still living in Germany.

Einstein lived in Princeton from 1933 until his death in 1955. It is said that the 589-acre parcel of land known as Institute Woods is where Einstein and the other geniuses came to loosen their ties and spend long afternoons contemplating the mysteries of science while strolling the same paths hikers do today. Institute Woods abuts Princeton Battlefield State Park and is part of this hike, so if you are in the woods, you're in Institute Woods.

The original Princeton settlement on the Stony Brook was just west of the woods. Most of the land was farmed or planted as orchard at one time. The soil here is a mixture of eroded shale, clay, and sand; the mixture is rich with phosphates and has good drainage to sustain a luxuriant growth of canopy trees, understory, wildflowers, and vegetation.

There are more than forty-five species of trees here, including aspen and gray birch in areas that were farmed as recently as 1940; there is also a beech stand with some of its trees dating back to the 1720s. Throughout the forest you may notice there are lines of large trees. These are the trees that once defined the fencerows when the fields around them were open. You will also see oaks and hickories and an understory of dogwoods, plus sweet gum, red maple, and beech. But the most imposing of all the trees is a stand of tulip trees, which are among the tallest trees in Eastern forests. Also, if you do this hike in the spring, you will see an abundance of wildflowers such as yellow trout lilies, light pink spring beauties, mayapples, and wild yellow irises.

If you're a birder, you're in for a treat on this hike, as more than 42 species of birds make their homes here, but of course during migratory season that number jumps to over 200, with the warbler population equal to any place of comparable size in the United States. Two of the most sought-after sightings here are the Kentucky warbler and the golden swamp warbler.

Among the transitory birds, quite a few species—such as blue jays, rufous-sided towhees, and wood thrushes—stay over the summer to breed in the woods. The brightest spring visitors you may see are the northern orioles, rose-breasted grosbeaks, and scarlet tanagers, which have a voracious appetite for gypsy moths.

At 2.4 miles you leave the woods and hike to the cul-de-sac where Einstein and the other research scientists lived, then you turn left onto the Trolley Track Trail and pass the grounds of the Institute for Advanced Study on your right. At 3.0 miles you turn right on the bike path and immediately see the field that was the site of the Battle at Princeton. Today it's an empty field that looks just like any other field in the area, but for those who revere history, it's a place where if you close your eyes you can see what really happened here on that bitter-cold day in January 1777.

The trail continues toward Mercer Road, named for General Mercer, who was killed in action that day. At 3.3 miles you cross the road and visit the Ionic Colonnade and gravesite that is the Princeton Battlefield Monument. After your visit you recross Mercer Road and walk the entry lane back to the parking lot and your vehicle.

## MILES AND DIRECTIONS

**0.0**   Start at the parking lot and walk between the pines heading toward the Clarke House Museum. The trail goes between the Clarke House Museum and the outbuilding.

**0.2**   Enter the woods and turn right on the Trolley Track Trail.

**0.3**   Turn left onto the Cornfield Trail, which bears to the left and becomes the Pipeline Trail.

**0.6**   Turn right on an unnamed trail, which bears left.

**0.7**   Turn right onto the Far Trail.

**1.0**   Turn left onto the Stony Brook Trail.

**1.4**   Arrive at Haning (Swinging) Bridge. Turn left and take the Swinging Bridge Trail.

**1.6**   Cross a wooden bridge and turn right onto the Pipeline Trail.

**1.8**   Turn right onto the Firebreak Trail.

**2.0**   The trail turns left and skirts alongside the Charles H. Rogers Wildlife Refuge on your right.

**2.2**   Turn left onto a path that is the Elizabethtown Water Company Pipeline.

> 🐸 **Green Tip:**
> *When hiking in a group, walk single file on established trails to avoid widening them. If you come upon a sensitive area, spread out so you don't cut one path through the landscape. Don't create new trails where there were none before.*

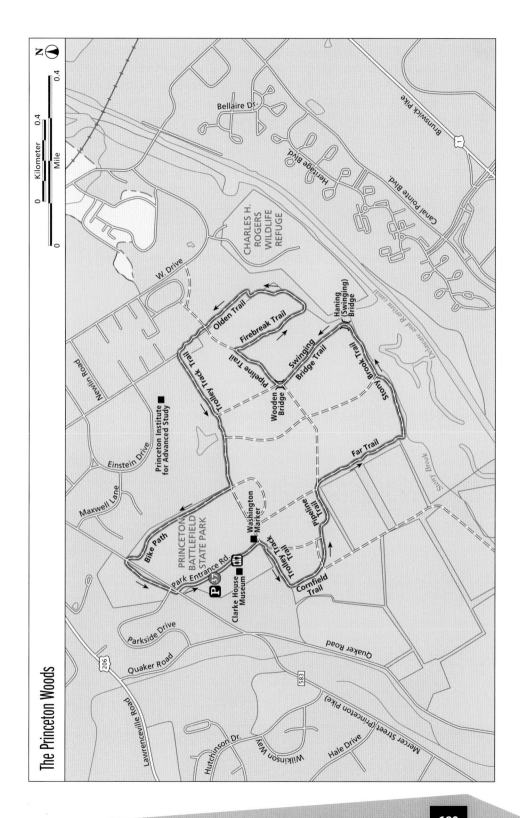

# The Princeton Woods

**2.4** Cross the Pipeline Trail (you are now on the Olden Trail) and continue through the tree line on a small boardwalk, then walk directly forward into the cul-de-sac where Albert Einstein lived.

**2.5** Come to the black mailbox numbered 330 and turn left onto the Trolley Track Trail.

**3.0** Turn right onto the bike path. Princeton Battlefield State Park is on your left.

**3.3** Cross Mercer Street Road at the crosswalk, then visit the Princeton Battlefield Monument.

**3.5** Recross Mercer Street Road and walk the lane to your vehicle.

**3.6** Arrive at parking lot and your vehicle.

# Finn's Point

*You hike along the tree-lined perimeter of Fort Mott State Park to the Delaware River, where you walk on a sea wall and take in the views. From there you take the Interpretive Trail through a small forest and on to the serenity of Finn's Point National Cemetery. Then it's back to the fort for a tour of the massive gun emplacements, Officer's Row, the moat, and other mysterious buildings, tunnels, and towers.*

*While this hike includes a forest trail and dirt road, the actual tour of Fort Mott is on paved pathways and could be considered handicapped accessible.*

**Start:** Fort Mott State Park parking lot
**Distance:** 2.5-mile loop
**Hiking time:** 2 hours
**Difficulty:** Easy
**Trail surface:** Gravel road, macadam road, forest path, grass paths, sandy beach
**Best seasons:** Spring, summer, fall
**Other trail users:** Tourists, bike riders, dog walkers
**Canine compatibility:** Leashed dogs permitted; no dogs permitted in the national cemetery
**Land status:** New Jersey State Park and federal cemetery

**Fees and permits:** None
**Schedule:** 8 a.m. to 7:30 p.m., daily; park office is open 8:30 a.m. to 4 p.m., daily
**Map:** USGS Delaware City, Del-NJ
**Trail contacts:** Fort Mott State Park, 454 Fort Mott Rd., Pennsville, NJ 08070; (856) 935-3218; www .state.nj.us/dep/parksandforests/ parks/fortmott.html. Finn's Point National Cemetery, Fort Mott Road, Salem, NJ 08079; (609) 877-5460; www.cem.va.gov/nchp/ finnspoint.htm.

**Finding the trailhead:** From Philadelphia head east on South Penn Square toward Avenue of the Arts/South Broad Street. Take a slight left onto John F. Kennedy Boulevard. Take the first right onto North Broad Street. Turn right onto the I-676 E/US 30 E ramp to I-95. Merge onto I-676/US 30 E. Entering New Jersey, take the ramp onto I-676. Merge onto I-76 E. Take exit 1A on the left to merge onto I-295 S toward Del Memorial Bridge. Take exit 1 to merge onto NJ 49 E/North Broadway toward Pennsville/Salem. Turn right onto Fort Mott Road. Turn right to stay on Fort Mott Road. Arrive at Fort Mott. Turn right then turn left into the parking lot. Trailhead GPS: N 39 36.166' / W 75 32.968'

## THE HIKE

The history of Fort Mott and Finn's Point National Cemetery began in the early 1800s when the Federal Government decided that it needed to protect the Delaware Bay and the Delaware River ports, so it commissioned three forts to be built in and along the Delaware River. The first to be completed, Fort Delaware, was built on Pea Patch Island in the Delaware River in 1848.

When the Civil War started in 1861, Fort Delaware became a Union prison for captured Confederate soldiers. The fort-turned-prison, which held at its peak over 32,000 Confederate prisoners, was damp and overcrowded, and in short order it became a breeding ground for disease—mainly cholera. At this point a decision was made to bury the dead in the soldiers' cemetery on Finn's Point, and eventually all the confederate dead from Fort Delaware were buried there, along with 135 Union guard soldiers and later 7 German prisoners of war.

The third fort, now known as Fort DuPont, was initially named Ten Gun Battery during the Civil War, when its task was to fortify Fort Delaware. The fort, which is on the Delaware side of the river, later served as a deployment center and prisoner-of-war camp during World War II. After the war the three forts were declared surplus property and were eventually bought by the state and turned into state parks.

As you walk on the seawall along with the Delaware River, you pass a mysterious 750-foot-long, 35-foot-wide concrete and earth embankment. At this point the trail takes you past this structure, but you will explore it inside and out when you return from the cemetery to the fort.

The serenity of a hike in Finn's Point National Cemetery can refresh your soul.

You leave Fort Mott on the Interpretive Trail, which passes through a small forested area with a pond, and make your way to Finn's Point National Cemetery. As you approach the cemetery, you are at once overwhelmed by the 85-foot granite obelisk, which was erected in 1910 and honors the Confederate soldiers buried here. It is offset by 135 stark-white tombstones that are set on the opposite side of the cemetery along a stone fence; and in the northwest corner, there are thirteen more tombstones where thirteen German prisoners of war who died at Fort Dix during World War II are buried.

The Union monument is just as impressive. It is a circular white marble gazebo with columns around the perimeter and a granite monolith set in the center.

After the cemetery you return to Fort Mott and begin the tour that takes you past Officer's Row and on to the mysterious embankment, which you soon learn was constructed to house and protect three 10-inch and three 12-inch guns that were installed on disappearing carriages.

These guns had an effective range of 7 to 8 miles and shot projectiles that weighed 600 to 1,000 pounds. Two steel observation towers were built so that observers could be stationed on the top platform to direct the aiming of the guns. There were also two batteries of 3-inch and 5-inch rapid-fire guns set up to counter faster-moving smaller warships that might evade the larger guns.

In its day Fort Mott was a self-contained military community. The post had over thirty buildings, including barracks, noncommissioned and officers' housing, a hospital, a post exchange, a library, a guard house, a stable, a YMCA, and a school for soldiers' children.

## New Jersey Coastal Heritage Trail & Welcome Center

Visitors to the Fort Mott Welcome Center may enjoy exhibits highlighting South Jersey history, especially maritime themes, the construction of Fort Mott, a biography of Gershom Mott, and a video program. Fort Mott is the southern anchor for the New Jersey Coastal Heritage Trail & Welcome Center. The New Jersey Coastal Trail is a partnership between New Jersey's Department of Environmental Protection and the National Park Service.

Each year in September Fort Mott State Park hosts the Historic Soldiers Weekend. The event features historic encampments of all eras, period vehicles, weapons demonstrations, a World War II skirmish, military vendors, veteran guest speakers, book signings, and live music. For more information go to www.SoldiersWeekend.com, or call Fort Mott at (856) 935-3218.

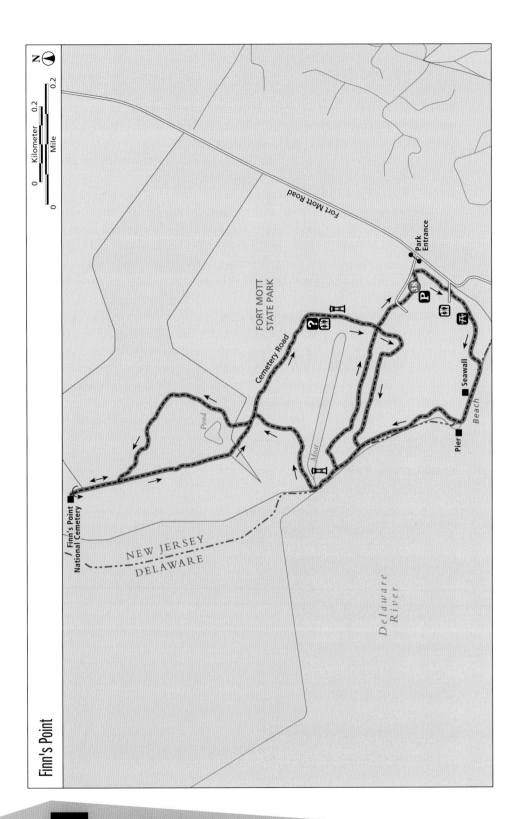

Finn's Point

## MILES AND DIRECTIONS

**0.0**  Walk from the parking area to the gravel road that runs alongside the tree line. Walk past the restrooms on your right.

**0.2**  Come to the end of the tree line. Turn left and head toward the sandy beach. Turn right at the beach.

**0.3**  Turn right onto the path just before the pier. Then turn left onto the paved road. Then walk along the seawall.

**0.7**  Turn right onto the gravel trail and enter the forest.

**0.8**  Reenter the forest. The trail turns left. Pass trail marker No. 3, then No. 4.

**0.9**  Cross the road. Pass trail marker No. 7.

**1.0**  Cross a little wooden bridge. Pass a bench that sits beside a small pond. Come to a trail intersection. Stay to the left. Pass trail marker No. 10.

**1.1**  Pass trail marker No. 11.

**1.2**  Turn right on the macadam road and pass trail marker No. 13 on your way to Finn's Point National Cemetery. After you visit the cemetery, walk on the road back the way you came.

**1.7**  Pass the maintenance shack on your right.

**1.8**  Turn right at the visitors center and walk on the path.

**2.1**  Arrive at the tour area. Walk toward the river, then turn right at the gun emplacement and take a set of wooden steps to the topside of the emplacement. Walk to the end of the emplacement and take another set of the steps down to the walking path and turn right.

**2.2**  Turn right again onto the trail between the mounds. Pass the brick building, then walk through the tunnel.

**2.5**  Arrive back at your vehicle.

> 🍃 **Green Tip:**
> *Be courteous of others. Many people visit natural areas for quiet, peace, and solitude, so avoid making loud noises and intruding on others' privacy.*

# Delaware Hikes

There are only two hikes in this section, but these two have just about everything serious hikers look for when setting out for a day in the woods. There are 14 miles of trails within Brandywine Creek State Park; these interconnected trails lead hikers to two nature preserves and a freshwater marsh, where you can check out wildflowers, songbirds, and, if you're there in the right season, migrating hawks and other raptors.

Brandywine Creek is a great park for children, even if you come here in winter. There is sled riding and cross-country skiing for children and adults; in summer there are kayak expeditions, campouts, educational hikes, fishing, and disc golf, as well as indoor activities.

Like Brandywine Creek State Park, White Clay Creek has an outdoor activity for any outdoor aficionado, including hiking, long-distance bike riding, trout fishing, experiencing a magnificent pine plantation, and exploring the history of the area at the Arc Monument. And, if that isn't enough to keep you going, visit the Carpenter Recreation Area on Wednesday evening at 6:30 p.m. for an outdoor concert sponsored by the Friends of White Clay Creek State Park. If you're still looking for something extra to do, you can visit the Chambers House Nature Center on Creek Road north of Hopkins Road on the weekend from 11 a.m. to 4 p.m., spring through fall. Here you can learn the history of the Chambers family, starting with the first Quaker immigrant to settle in the valley, John Chambers, and progressing to his great-grandson, Joseph Chambers, who built the house in 1813.

Over the next two centuries, descendants of John Chambers operated their farms, which were known as Hopyard, Hillvale, Pennview, Hillside, and Hilltop, located along the White Clay Creek and what is now Chambers Rock Road.

# Brandywine Creek State Park

*There are a number of interesting and fascinating features on this easy hike, but the most striking feature is the gray-stone walls that run alongside and throughout the park. The walls were constructed by Italian masons for the du Pont family back in the 1800s, when the land that is now the park was their dairy farm. Add to this, rolling hills, beautifully maintained trails through woodlands, the Tulip Tree Woods Nature Preserve, and of course, the centerpiece of the park, Brandywine Creek, and you are all set for a very pleasant hike. Be sure to bring your camera, your children, and a picnic lunch.*

**Start:** The kiosk by the nature center and park office

**Distance:** 2.2-mile loop

**Hiking time:** 1.5 hours

**Difficulty:** Easy

**Trail surface:** Forest footpath, sidewalk

**Best seasons:** Spring, summer, fall, winter

**Other trail users:** Birders, cross-country skiers, horseback riders

**Canine compatibility:** Leashed dogs permitted

**Land status:** Delaware State Park

**Fees and permits:** Park entrance fees are charged from March 1 through November 30

**Schedule:** 8 a.m. to sunset daily

**Map:** USGS Wilmington North, DE

**Trail contacts:** Brandywine Creek State Park, 41 Adams Dam Rd., Wilmington, DE 19803; (302) 577-3534; www.destateparks.com/park/brandywine-creek

**Finding the trailhead:** Get on I-95 S and take exit 8B for US 202 N/Concord Pike toward Wilmington. Continue 0.8 mile, then keep right and follow the signs for Delaware 141 S/Foulk Road. Drive 0.7 mile and turn left onto Children's Drive, then turn right onto Rockland Road. Continue 1.6 miles and take a slight right onto Adams Dam Road. Drive 0.5 mile and turn right. Continue 0.1 mile, turn left, and drive 0.5 mile to your destination on the right. Trailhead GPS: N39 48.454' / W75 34.767'

In March 1638 the first Europeans settled in the area where Brandywine Creek meets the Delaware River. They named their settlement New Sweden to reflect the fact that, while there were some Finns and Dutch in the group, the majority of the 600 colonists were Swedish. It is this early colony that is credited with introducing the log cabin to their new country, and by 1687 they had built their first mill on Brandywine Creek.

In 1735 English Quakers, along with dissident Protestants, settled here and established Brandywine Village along with a number of flour mills. This group concentrated on milling grain into flour that was hauled to them from Conestoga Valley in wagons soon to be called Conestoga Wagons. The group soon established a reputation of milling only the finest flour, which they named Brandywine Superfine, and marketed it all along the East Coast and to the West Indies.

In 1802 Éleuthère Irénée du Pont purchased a mill that had been destroyed by fire; he paid the former owner, Jacob Broom, $6,740 for the mill site and 95 acres and set up the Eleutherian Mills to turn gunpowder into explosives. Sales grew during the Mexican-American War and the Crimea War, and during the Civil War the firm sold over 4,000,000 barrels of explosives to the Federal Government.

The gray-stone walls were built by Italian masons for the du Pont family in the 1800s, when the land was their dairy farm.

Over the years as many as 100 mills were established on the Brandywine, producing paper, flour, and textiles, but with the onset of the Industrial Revolution and the use of steam for power, the water-powered mills became a thing of the past.

On September 11, 1777, General George Washington and his Continental Army fought the British forces under Sir William Howe in the Battle of Brandywine. Howe's objective was to capture Philadelphia, which was at that time the capital of the new country. Washington's plan was to stop him at Chadds Ford on Brandywine Creek. The Americans lost, and Howe captured the city on September 26, beginning an occupation that lasted until June 1778.

Today the mills are all gone or reverted to ruins and there are no invading armies. The Brandywine River Valley remains a major tourist area, attracting tourists from all over the country with the stunning natural beauty of the rolling hillsides, charming fieldstone houses, backcountry roads, rural open lands, and the invitation to kayak the Brandywine, bicycle the dirt roads, and hike the shaded trails of Brandywine Creek State Park.

The land that is now the 933-acre state park was once a large dairy farm owned by the du Pont family until the State of Delaware bought the property in 1965.

Your hike begins behind the nature center and park office as you follow the paved sidewalk into the forest and get a close look at a section of the gray-stone wall that parallels the trail for 0.3 mile.

That lasts until 1.3 miles, where you can take a spur trail off the Hidden Pond Trail and walk a short distance to the Hidden Pond, where if the sun is just right, you can get a great photo. After the pond the trail leads you to the Tulip Tree Nature Preserve, where you will see tulip trees that are over 190 years old (not to mention tulip trees are the tallest trees in the eastern United States). After the preserve you meet up with yet another gray-stone wall at 2.1 miles, where you turn left and follow the path that leads you back to the nature center and park office.

> 🌿 **Green Tip:**
> *When hiking with your dog, stay in the center of the path and keep Fido close by. Dogs that run loose can harm fragile soils and spread pesky plants by carrying their seeds.*

# Brandywine Creek State Park

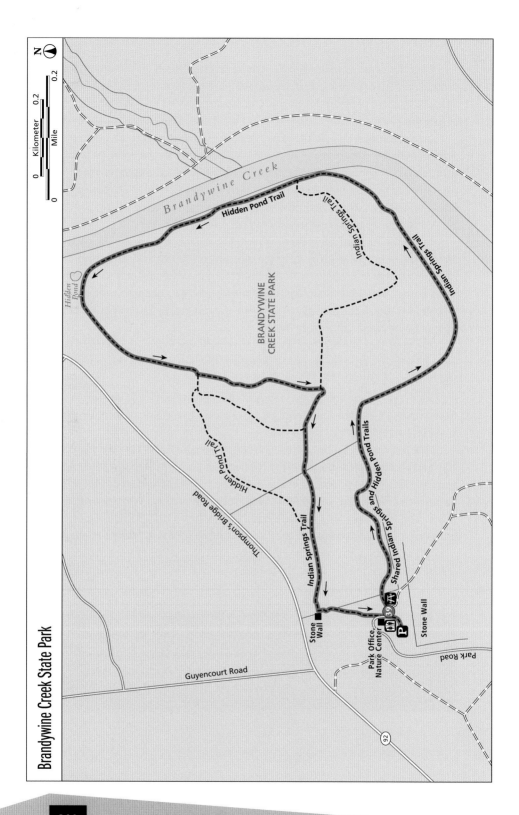

**0.0**   Start at the kiosk by the nature center and park office. Take the shared yellow-blazed Indian Springs Trail and pink-blazed Hidden Pond Trail. Follow the sidewalk into the trees. Note the stone wall and picnic area on your right.

**0.1**   A trail goes off to your left. Continue straight.

**0.3**   The trail comes to the site where the stone wall ends. The trail turns left, and you arrive at a trail intersection where you continue straight.

**0.4**   Come to an intersection. The pink-blazed Hidden Pond Trail goes off to the left. You go right and stay on the Indian Springs Trail.

**1.0**   The Hidden Pond Trail comes in from your left. Get on the Hidden Pond Trail and continue straight.

**1.3**   Pass the unnamed trail and the bridge on your right that takes you to the Hidden Pond.

**1.6**   Turn left onto a connector trail that leads you to the Indian Springs Trail.

**1.8**   Turn right on the Indian Springs Trail.

**2.1**   Arrive at the stone wall and turn left.

**2.2**   Arrive back at the nature center and park office.

*Delaware is the lowest state in the United States, with an average altitude of about 60 feet above sea level. Even its highest point, Ebright Azimuth, is the second lowest in the country at 442 feet.*

# White Clay Creek State Park

On this moderate hike you start out on Creek Road, an abandoned railroad grade that parallels White Clay Creek and leads you to a trail that takes you to the Arc Monument, an engraved monolith that marks the boundary between Pennsylvania and Delaware. On your way to the monument, you pass an old springhouse where you can hear and see the cold, clear water bubbling from the earth. After the monument the trail passes through a magnificent pine plantation, where the forest floor is covered with a thick layer of pine needles that makes you feel as if you're walking on a plush carpet. Then it's downhill to the banks of White Clay Creek, where you can stop and watch fishermen try their luck with the rainbow and brown trout that are stocked in the creek each spring.

**Start:** The kiosk in the parking lot

**Distance:** 2.5-mile lollipop

**Hiking time:** 1.5 hours

**Difficulty:** Moderate

**Trail surface:** Gravel road, forest footpath

**Best seasons:** Spring, summer, fall, winter

**Other trail users:** Tourists, bike riders, cross-country skiers

**Canine compatibility:** Leashed dogs permitted

**Land status:** Delaware State Park

**Fees and permits:** $3 for Delaware residents, $6 for nonresidents

**Schedule:** 8 a.m. to sunset daily

**Map:** USGS Newark West

**Trail contacts:** White Clay Creek State Park, 880 New London Rd., Newark, DE 19711; (302) 368-6900; www.destateparks.com/park/white-clay-creek

**Finding the trailhead:** From Philadelphia get on I-95 S and take exit 3 to merge onto DE 273 W toward Newark. Drive 3.9 miles and turn right onto Capitol Trail. Continue 0.2 mile and take the first left onto East Cleveland Avenue. Drive 1.2 miles and turn right onto SR 896/New London Road. Drive 2.0 miles, turn right onto Wedgewood Road, and continue 1.0 mile to your destination on the left. Trailhead GPS: N39 42.919' / W75 45.624'

**Special considerations:** There is a shotgun hunting season, comprised of specific weeks between November and January of the next year. Certain trails are closed on these dates. Trailheads will be posted "Trails Closed Active Hunting Area." However, all trails will be open on Sunday.

There is an archery hunting season, comprised of certain weeks between October and January of the next year. Trailheads will be posted "Trails Closed Active Hunting Area."

## THE HIKE

The original Mason-Dixon Line was set as a border between Pennsylvania and Maryland in an effort to settle an eighty-year land dispute between the two colonies. It also included the western border of present-day Delaware, as it was then a part of the Pennsylvania colony. The ongoing dispute between the Penn family of Pennsylvania and the Calvert family of Maryland over the border of the two colonies finally erupted into war in 1730, known as the Cresap's War. After years of conflict England's King George II negotiated a cease-fire in 1738.

Shortly thereafter the Penns and Calverts commissioned two Englishmen, Charles Mason and Jeremiah Dixon, to mark the official border. Mason, an astronomer, and Dixon, a surveyor, used celestial measurements to establish an accurate 233-mile-long border between Pennsylvania and Maryland and an 83-mile-long border between Maryland and Delaware. The new border was marked by large blocks of limestone set at every mile and more elaborate crown stones set at every 5 miles.

In 1892 the US Coast and Geodetic Survey set the Arc Cornerstone in White Clay Creek State Park to mark the Delaware-Pennsylvania state boundary line at the intersection of the east-west southern boundary of Pennsylvania, with the 12-mile Circle boundary line centered on New Castle, Delaware. The stone is a dressed Brandywine granite that is 54 inches tall, with a 14-inch square base that reduces to a 12-inch square at its top; "Pennsylvania" is etched on the north side and "Delaware" is etched on the south side.

This must be a good spot to fish on White Clay Creek; you can see where fishermen have worn the grass away.

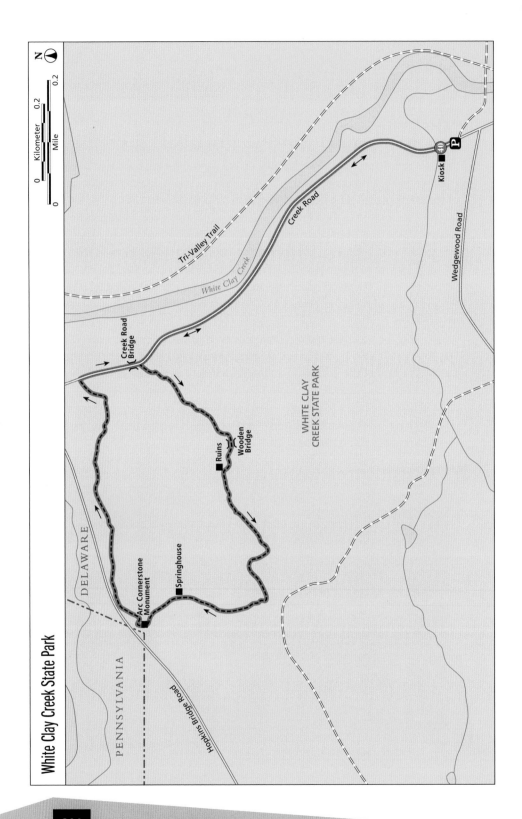

White Clay Creek State Park

You start your journey to the monument by walking around a gate across Creek Road, which is the abandoned rail bed of the Pennsylvania and Delaware section of the former Pomeroy and Newark Railroad, which went out of business in 1939. The gravel road parallels White Clay Creek and gets real close at 0.3 mile, where there is a fishermen's trail and an open area on the bank where you can sit on a bench and enjoy the nearby waterfall.

From this point you continue north on Creek Road until 0.6 mile, just before a wooden bridge, where you turn left and follow the round trail markers as you begin a short uphill climb to a small wooden bridge and stone ruins at 0.8 mile. At 1.3 miles you pass the springhouse on your right, and at 1.4 miles you arrive at the Arc Cornerstone Monument; after the monument you hike with Hopkins Bridge Road on your left, pass through the pine plantation, and continue downhill until you reach Creek Road, where you turn right to follow your footsteps back to the parking lot and your vehicle.

## MILES AND DIRECTIONS

**0.0** Start at the kiosk in the parking lot. Facing the kiosk, turn right and walk to the gate across the wide gravel trail. Walk around the gate and follow the blue blazes on Creek Road.

**0.3** A fisherman's trail on your right leads to a bench and a site to view White Clay Creek.

**0.6** Just before the wooden bridge, turn left onto the trail.

**0.8** Arrive at a major trail intersection. Turn right and cross the wooden bridge and come to stone ruins.

**1.1** Turn left at the trail intersection toward the Arc Cornerstone Monument.

**1.3** Pass the springhouse on your right.

**1.4** Arrive at the Arc Cornerstone Monument. Then turn right and walk with Hopkins Bridge Road on your left.

**1.7** Come to a trail intersection. Continue straight.

**1.8** Turn right onto Creek Road.

**1.9** Cross a wooden bridge and retrace your steps back to the parking lot.

**2.5** Arrive back at the parking lot and your vehicle.

> *Delaware became the first state in the Union when it was first to ratify the Constitution on December 7, 1787.*

# The Art of Hiking

When standing nose to nose with a mountain lion, you're probably not too concerned with the issue of ethical behavior in the wild. No doubt you're just terrified. But let's be honest. How often are you nose to nose with a mountain lion? For most of us, a hike into the "wild" means loading up the SUV with expensive gear and driving to a toileted trailhead. Sure, you can mourn how civilized we've become—how GPS units have replaced natural instinct and Gore-Tex stands in for true grit—but the silly gadgets of civilization aside, we have plenty of reason to take pride in how we've matured. With survival now on the back burner, we've begun to understand that we have a responsibility to protect, no longer just conquer, our wild places—that they, not we, are at risk. So please, do what you can. The following section will help you understand better what it means to "do what you can" while still making the most of your hiking experience. Anyone can take a hike, but hiking safely and well is an art requiring preparation and proper equipment.

## TRAIL ETIQUETTE

**Leave no trace.** Always leave an area just like you found it—if not better than you found it. Avoid camping in fragile, alpine meadows and along the banks of streams and lakes. Use a camp stove versus building a wood fire. Pack up all of your trash and extra food. Bury human waste at least 100 feet from water sources under 6 to 8 inches of topsoil. Don't bathe with soap in a lake or stream—use prepackaged moistened towels to wipe off sweat and dirt, or bathe in the water without soap.

**Stay on the trail.** It's true, a path anywhere leads nowhere new, but purists will just have to get over it. Paths serve an important purpose; they limit impact on natural areas. Straying from a designated trail may seem innocent, but it can cause damage to sensitive areas—damage that may take years to recover, if it can recover at all. Even simple shortcuts can be destructive. So, please, stay on the trail.

**Leave no weeds.** Noxious weeds tend to overtake other plants, which in turn affects animals and birds that depend on them for food. To minimize the spread of noxious weeds, hikers should regularly clean their boots, tents, packs, and hiking poles of mud and seeds. Also brush your dog to remove any weed seeds before heading off into a new area.

**Keep your dog under control.** You can buy a flexi-lead that allows your dog to go exploring along the trail, while allowing you the ability to reel him in should another hiker approach or should he decide to chase a rabbit. Always obey leash laws and be sure to bury your dog's waste or pack it in resealable plastic bags.

**Respect other trail users.** Often you're not the only one on the trail. With the rise in popularity of multiuse trails, you'll have to learn a new kind of respect, beyond the nod and "hello" approach you may be used to. First investigate whether you're on a multiuse trail, and assume the appropriate precautions. When you encounter motorized vehicles (ATVs, motorcycles, and 4WDs), be alert. Though they should always yield to the hiker, often they're going too fast or are too lost in the buzz of their engine to react to your presence. If you hear activity ahead, step off the trail just to be safe. Note that you're not likely to hear a mountain biker coming, so be prepared and know ahead of time whether you share the trail with them. Cyclists should always yield to hikers, but that's little comfort to the hiker. Be aware. When you approach horses or pack animals on the trail, always step quietly off the trail, preferably on the downhill side, and let them pass. If you're wearing a large backpack, it's often a good idea to sit down. To some animals, a hiker wearing a large backpack might appear threatening. Many national forests allow domesticated grazing, usually for sheep and cattle. Make sure your dog doesn't harass these animals, and respect ranchers' rights while you're enjoying yours.

## GETTING INTO SHAPE

Unless you want to be sore—and possibly have to shorten your trip or vacation—be sure to get in shape before a big hike. If you're terribly out of shape, start a walking program early, preferably eight weeks in advance. Start with a fifteen-minute walk during your lunch hour or after work and gradually increase your walking time to an hour. You should also increase your elevation gain. Walking briskly up hills really strengthens your leg muscles and gets your heart rate up. If you work in a storied office building, take the stairs instead of the elevator. If you prefer going to a gym, walk the treadmill or use a stair machine. You can further increase your strength and endurance by walking with a loaded backpack. Stationary exercises you might consider are squats, leg lifts, sit-ups, and push-ups. Other good ways to get in shape include biking, running, aerobics, and, of course, short hikes. Stretching before and after a hike keeps muscles flexible and helps avoid injuries.

## PREPAREDNESS

It's been said that failing to plan means planning to fail. So do take the necessary time to plan your trip. Whether going on a short day hike or an extended backpack trip, always prepare for the worst. Simply remembering to pack a copy of the *US Army Survival Manual* is not preparedness. Although it's not a bad idea if you plan on entering truly wild places, it's merely the tourniquet answer to a problem. You need to do your best to prevent the problem from arising in the first place. In order to survive—and to stay reasonably comfortable—you need to concern yourself with the basics: water, food, and shelter. Don't go on a hike without having these bases covered. And don't go on a hike expecting to find these items in the woods.

**Water.** Even in frigid conditions, you need at least two quarts of water a day to function efficiently. Add heat and taxing terrain and you can bump that figure up to one gallon. That's simply a base to work from—your metabolism and your level of conditioning can raise or lower that amount. Unless you know your level, assume that you need one gallon of water a day. Now, where do you plan on getting the water?

Preferably not from natural water sources. These sources can be loaded with intestinal disturbers, such as bacteria, viruses, and fertilizers. *Giardia lamblia,* the most common of these disturbers, is a protozoan parasite that lives part of its life cycle as a cyst in water sources. The parasite spreads when mammals defecate in water sources. Once ingested, giardia can induce cramping, diarrhea, vomiting, and fatigue within two days to two weeks after ingestion. Giardiasis is treatable with prescription drugs. If you believe you've contracted giardiasis, see a doctor immediately.

**Treating water.** The best and easiest solution to avoid polluted water is to carry your water with you. Yet, depending on the nature of your hike and the duration, this may not be an option—one gallon of water weighs 8½ pounds. In that case, you'll need to look into treating water. Regardless of which method you choose, you should always carry some water with you in case of an emergency. Save this reserve until you absolutely need it.

There are three methods of treating water: boiling, chemical treatment, and filtering. If you boil water, it's recommended that you do so for ten to fifteen minutes. This is often impractical because you're forced to exhaust a great deal of your fuel supply. You can opt for chemical treatment, which will kill giardia but will not take care of other chemical pollutants. Another drawback to chemical treatments is the unpleasant taste of the water after it's treated. You can remedy this by adding powdered drink mix to the water. Filters are the preferred method for treating water. Many filters remove giardia, organic and inorganic contaminants, and don't leave an aftertaste. Water filters are far from perfect, as they can easily become clogged or leak if a gasket wears out. It's always a good idea to carry a backup supply of chemical treatment tablets in case your filter decides to quit on you.

**Food.** If we're talking about survival, you can go days without food, as long as you have water. But we're also talking about comfort. Try to avoid foods that are high in sugar and fat like candy bars and potato chips. These food types are harder to digest and are low in nutritional value. Instead, bring along foods that are easy to pack, nutritious, and high in energy (e.g., bagels, nutrition bars, dehydrated fruit, gorp, and jerky). If you are on an overnight trip, easy-to-fix dinners include rice mixes with dehydrated potatoes, corn, pasta with cheese sauce, and soup mixes. For a tasty breakfast, you can fix hot oatmeal with brown sugar and reconstituted milk powder topped off with banana chips. If you like a hot drink in the morning, bring along herbal tea bags or hot chocolate. If you are a coffee junkie, you can purchase coffee that is packaged like tea bags. You can prepackage all of your meals in heavy-duty resealable plastic bags to keep food from spilling in your pack. These bags can be reused to pack out trash.

**Shelter.** The type of shelter you choose depends less on the conditions than on your tolerance for discomfort. Shelter comes in many forms—tent, tarp, lean-to, bivy sack, cabin, cave, etc. If you're camping in the desert, a bivy sack may suffice, but if you're above the tree line and a storm is approaching, a better choice is a three- or four-season tent. Tents are the logical and most popular choice for most backpackers, as they're lightweight and packable—and you can rest assured that you always have shelter from the elements. Before you leave on your trip, anticipate what the weather and terrain will be like and plan for the type of shelter that will work best for your comfort level (see Equipment later in this section).

**Finding a campsite.** If there are established campsites, stick to those. If not, start looking for a campsite early—around 3:30 or 4:00 p.m. Stop at the first decent site you see. Depending on the area, it could be a long time before you find another suitable location. Pitch your camp in an area that's level. Make sure the area is at least 200 feet from fragile areas like lakeshores, meadows, and stream banks. And try to avoid areas thick in underbrush, as they can harbor insects and provide cover for approaching animals.

If you are camping in stormy, rainy weather, look for a rock outcrop or a shelter in the trees to keep the wind from blowing your tent all night. Be sure that you don't camp under trees with dead limbs that might break off on top of you. Also, try to find an area that has an absorbent surface, such as sandy soil or forest duff. This, in addition to camping on a surface with a slight angle, will provide better drainage. By all means, don't dig trenches to provide drainage around your tent—remember you're practicing zero-impact camping.

If you're in bear country, steer clear of creek beds or animal paths. If you see any signs of a bear's presence (i.e., scat, footprints), relocate. You'll need to find a campsite near a tall tree where you can hang your food and other items that may attract bears, such as deodorant, toothpaste, or soap. Carry a lightweight nylon rope with which to hang your food. As a rule, you should hang your food at least 20 feet from the ground and 5 feet away from the tree trunk. You can put food and other items in a waterproof stuff sack and tie one end of the rope to the stuff sack. To get the other end of the rope over the tree branch, tie a good size rock to it, and gently toss the rock over the tree branch. Pull the stuff sack up until it reaches the top of the branch and tie it off securely. Don't hang your food near your tent! If possible, hang your food at least 100 feet away from your campsite. Alternatives to hanging your food are bear-proof plastic tubes and metal bear boxes.

Lastly, think of comfort. Lie down on the ground where you intend to sleep and see if it's a good fit. For morning warmth (and a nice view to wake up to), have your tent face east.

## FIRST AID

I know you're tough, but get 10 miles into the woods and develop a blister and you'll wish you had carried that first-aid kit. Face it, it's just plain good sense. Many companies produce lightweight, compact first-aid kits. Just make sure yours contains at least the following:

- adhesive bandages
- moleskin or duct tape
- various sterile gauze and dressings
- white surgical tape
- an Ace bandage
- an antihistamine
- aspirin
- Betadine solution
- a first-aid book
- antacid tablets
- tweezers
- scissors
- antibacterial wipes
- triple-antibiotic ointment
- plastic gloves
- sterile cotton tip applicators
- syrup of ipecac (to induce vomiting)
- thermometer
- wire splint

Here are a few tips for dealing with and hopefully preventing certain ailments:

**Sunburn.** Take along sunscreen or sunblock, protective clothing, and a wide-brimmed hat. If you do get a sunburn, treat the area with aloe vera gel, and protect the area from further sun exposure. At higher elevations, the sun's radiation can be particularly damaging to skin. Remember that your eyes are vulnerable to this radiation as well. Sunglasses can be a good way to prevent headaches and permanent eye damage from the sun, especially in places where light-colored rock or patches of snow reflect light up in your face.

**Blisters.** Be prepared to take care of these hike-spoilers by carrying moleskin (a lightly padded adhesive), gauze and tape, or adhesive bandages. An effective way to apply moleskin is to cut out a circle of moleskin and remove the center—like a doughnut—and place it over the blistered area. Cutting the center out will reduce the pressure applied to the sensitive skin. Other products can help you combat blisters. Some are applied to suspicious hot spots before a blister forms to help decrease friction to that area, while others are applied to the blister after it has popped to help prevent further irritation.

**Insect bites and stings.** You can treat most insect bites and stings by applying hydrocortisone 1 percent cream topically and taking a pain medication such as ibuprofen to reduce swelling. If you forgot to pack these items, a cold compress or a paste of mud and ashes can sometimes assuage the itching and discomfort. Remove any stingers by using tweezers or scraping the area with your fingernail or a knife blade. Don't pinch the area, as you'll only spread the venom.

Some hikers are highly sensitive to bites and stings and may have a serious allergic reaction that can be life threatening. Symptoms of a serious allergic reaction can include wheezing, an asthmatic attack, and shock. The treatment for this severe type of reaction is epinephrine. If you know that you are sensitive to bites and stings, carry a prepackaged kit of epinephrine, which can be obtained only by prescription from your doctor.

**Ticks.** Ticks can carry diseases such as Rocky Mountain spotted fever and Lyme disease. The best defense is, of course, prevention. If you know you're going to be hiking through an area littered with ticks, wear long pants and a long-sleeved shirt. You can apply a permethrin repellent to your clothing and a Deet repellent to exposed skin. At the end of your hike, do a spot check for ticks (and insects in general). If you do find a tick, grab the head of the tick firmly—with a pair of tweezers if you have them—and gently pull it away from the skin with a twisting motion. Sometimes the mouthparts linger, embedded in your skin. If this happens, try to remove them with a disinfected needle. Clean the affected area with an antibacterial cleanser and then apply triple-antibiotic ointment. Monitor the area for a few days. If irritation persists or a white spot develops, see a doctor for possible infection.

**Poison ivy, oak, and sumac.** These skin irritants can be found most anywhere in North America and come in the form of a bush or a vine, having leaflets in groups of three, five, seven, or nine. Learn how to spot the plants. The oil they secrete can cause an allergic reaction in the form of blisters, usually about twelve hours after exposure. The itchy rash can last from ten days to several weeks. The best defense against these irritants is to wear clothing that covers the arms, legs, and torso. For summer, zip-off cargo pants come in handy. There are also nonprescription lotions you can apply to exposed skin that guard against the effects of poison ivy/oak/sumac and can be washed off with soap and water. If you think you were in contact with the plants, after hiking (or even on the trail during longer hikes) wash with soap and water. Taking a hot shower with soap after you return home from your hike will also help to remove any lingering oil from your skin. Should you contract a rash from any of these plants, use an antihistamine to reduce the itching. If the rash is localized, create a light bleach/water wash to dry up the area. If the rash has spread, either tough it out or see your doctor about getting a dose of cortisone (available both orally and by injection).

**Snakebites.** Snakebites are rare in North America. Unless startled or provoked, the majority of snakes will not bite. If you are wise to their habitats and keep a careful eye on the trail, you should be just fine. When stepping over logs, first step on the log, making sure you can see what's on the other side before stepping down. Though your chances of being struck are slim, it's wise to know what to do in the event you are.

If a nonvenomous snake bites you, allow the wound to bleed a small amount and then cleanse the wounded area with a Betadine solution (10 percent povidone iodine). Rinse the wound with clean water (preferably) or fresh urine (it might sound ugly, but it's sterile). Once the area is clean, cover it with triple-antibiotic ointment and a clean bandage. Remember: Most residual damage from snakebites, venomous or otherwise, comes from infection, not the snake's venom. Keep the area as clean as possible and get medical attention immediately.

If somebody in your party is bitten by a venomous snake, follow these steps:

1. Calm the patient.

2. Remove jewelry, watches, and restrictive clothing, and immobilize the affected limb. Do not elevate the injury. Medical opinions vary on whether the area should be lower or level with the heart, but the consensus is that it should not be above it.

3. Make a note of the circumference of the limb at the bite site and at various points above the site as well. This will help you monitor swelling.

4. Evacuate the person. Ideally he or she should be carried out to minimize movement. If the person appears to be doing okay, he or she can walk. Stop and rest frequently, and if the swelling appears to be spreading or symptoms increase, change your plan and find a way to get him or her transported.

5. If you are waiting for rescue, make sure to keep the person comfortable and hydrated (unless he or she begins vomiting).

Snakebite treatment is rife with old-fashioned remedies: You used to be told to cut and suck the venom out of the bite site or to use a suction cup extractor for the same purpose; applying an electric shock to the area was even in vogue for a while. Do not do any of these things. Do not apply ice, do not give the person painkillers, and do not apply a tourniquet. All you really want to do is keep the person calm and get help. If you're alone and have to hike out, don't run—you'll only increase the flow of blood throughout your system. Instead, walk calmly.

**Dehydration.** Have you ever hiked in hot weather and had a roaring headache and felt fatigued after only a few miles? More than likely you were dehydrated. Symptoms of dehydration include fatigue, headache, and decreased coordination and judgment. When you are hiking, your body's rate of fluid loss depends on the outside temperature, humidity, altitude, and your activity level. On average a hiker walking in warm weather will lose four liters of fluid a day. That fluid loss is easily replaced by normal consumption of liquids and food. However, if you are walking briskly in hot, dry weather and hauling a heavy pack, you can lose one to three liters of water an hour. It's important to always carry plenty of water and to stop often and drink fluids regularly, even if you aren't thirsty.

**Heat exhaustion** is the result of a loss of large amounts of electrolytes and often occurs if a person is dehydrated and has been under heavy exertion. Common symptoms of heat exhaustion include cramping, exhaustion, fatigue, lightheadedness, and nausea. You can treat heat exhaustion by getting out of the sun and drinking an electrolyte solution made up of one teaspoon of salt and one tablespoon of sugar dissolved in a liter of water. Drink this solution slowly over a period of one hour. Drinking plenty of fluids (preferably an electrolyte solution/sports drink) can prevent heat exhaustion. Avoid hiking during the hottest parts of the day, and wear breathable clothing, a wide-brimmed hat, and sunglasses.

**Hypothermia** is one of the biggest dangers in the backcountry, especially for day hikers in the summertime. That may sound strange, but imagine starting out on a hike in midsummer when it's sunny and 80°F out. You're clad in nylon shorts and a cotton T-shirt. About halfway through your hike, the sky begins to cloud up, and in the next hour a light drizzle begins to fall and the wind starts to pick up. Before you know it, you are soaking wet and shivering—the perfect recipe for hypothermia. More advanced signs include decreased coordination, slurred speech, and blurred vision. When a victim's temperature falls below 92°F, the blood pressure and pulse plummet, possibly leading to coma and death.

To avoid hypothermia, always bring a windproof/rainproof shell; a fleece jacket; long underwear made of a breathable, synthetic fiber; gloves; and hat when you are hiking in the mountains. Learn to adjust your clothing layers based on the temperature. If you are climbing uphill at a moderate pace you will stay warm, but when you stop for a break you'll become cold quickly, unless you add more layers of clothing.

If a hiker is showing advanced signs of hypothermia, dress him or her in dry clothes and make sure he or she is wearing a hat and gloves. Place the person in a sleeping bag in a tent or shelter that will protect him or her from the wind and other elements. Give the person warm fluids to drink and keep him or her awake.

**Frostbite.** When the mercury dips below 32°F, your extremities begin to chill. If a persistent chill attacks a localized area, say, your hands or your toes, the circulatory system reacts by cutting off blood flow to the affected area—the idea being to protect and preserve the body's overall temperature. And so it's death by attrition for the affected area. Ice crystals start to form from the water in the cells of the neglected tissue. Deprived of heat, nourishment, and now water, the tissue literally starves. This is frostbite.

Prevention is your best defense against this situation. Most prone to frostbite are your face, hands, and feet, so protect these areas well. Wool is the traditional material of choice because it provides ample air space for insulation and draws moisture away from the skin. Synthetic fabrics, however, have made great strides in the cold-weather clothing market. Do your research. Wearing a pair of light silk liners under your regular gloves is a good trick for keeping warm. The liners afford some additional warmth, but more important, they allow you to remove your mitts for tedious work without exposing the skin.

If your feet or hands start to feel cold or numb due to the elements, warm them as quickly as possible. Place cold hands under your armpits or bury them in your crotch. If your feet are cold, change your socks. If there's plenty of room in your boots, add another pair of socks. Do remember, though, that constricting your feet in tight boots can restrict blood flow and actually make your feet colder more quickly. Your socks need to have breathing room if they're going to be effective. Dead air provides insulation. If your face is cold, place your warm hands over your face, or simply wear a head stocking.

Should your skin go numb and start to appear white and waxy, chances are you've got or are developing frostbite. Don't try to thaw the area unless you can maintain the warmth. In other words, don't stop to warm up your frostbitten feet only to head back on the trail. You'll do more damage than good. Tests have shown that hikers who walked on thawed feet did more harm, and endured more pain, than hikers who left the affected areas alone. Do your best to get out of the cold entirely and seek medical attention—which usually consists of performing a rapid rewarming in water for twenty to thirty minutes.

The overall objective in preventing both hypothermia and frostbite is to keep the body's core warm. Protect key areas where heat escapes, like the top of the head, and maintain the proper nutrition level. Foods that are high in calories aid the body in producing heat. Never smoke or drink alcohol when you're in situations where the cold is threatening. By affecting blood flow, these activities ultimately cool the body's core temperature.

**Altitude sickness (AMS).** High lofty peaks, clear alpine lakes, and vast mountain views beckon hikers to the high country. But those who like to venture high may become victims of altitude sickness (also known as acute mountain sickness—AMS). Altitude sickness is your body's reaction to insufficient oxygen in the blood due to decreased barometric pressure. While some hikers may feel lightheaded, nauseous, and experience shortness of breath at 7,000 feet, others may not experience these symptoms until they reach 10,000 feet or higher.

Slowing your ascent to high places and giving your body a chance to acclimatize to the higher elevations can prevent altitude sickness. For example, if you live at sea level and are planning a weeklong backpacking trip to elevations between 7,000 and 12,000 feet, start by staying below 7,000 feet for one night, then move to between 7,000 and 10,000 feet for another night or two. Avoid strenuous exertion and alcohol to give your body a chance to adjust to the new altitude. It's also important to eat light food and drink plenty of nonalcoholic fluids, preferably water. Loss of appetite at altitude is common, but you must eat!

Most hikers who experience mild to moderate AMS develop a headache and/or nausea, grow lethargic, and have problems sleeping. The treatment for AMS is simple: Stop heading uphill. Keep eating and drinking water, and take medication for the headache. You actually need to take more breaths at altitude than at sea level, so breathe a little faster without hyperventilating. If symptoms don't improve over twenty-four to forty-eight hours, descend. Once the person descends about 2,000 to 3,000 feet, his or her signs will usually begin to diminish.

Severe AMS comes in two forms: high altitude pulmonary edema (HAPE) and high altitude cerebral edema (HACE). HAPE, an accumulation of fluid in the lungs, can occur above 8,000 feet. Symptoms include rapid heart rate, shortness of breath at rest, AMS symptoms, dry cough developing into a wet cough, gurgling sounds, flu-like or bronchitis symptoms, and lack of muscle coordination. HAPE is life threatening, so descend immediately, at least 2,000 to 4,000 feet. HACE usually occurs above 12,000 feet but sometimes occurs above 10,000 feet. Symptoms are similar to HAPE but also include seizures, hallucinations, paralysis, and vision disturbances. Descend immediately—HACE is also life threatening.

**Hantavirus pulmonary syndrome (HPS).** Deer mice spread the virus that causes HPS, and humans contract it from breathing it in, usually when they've disturbed an area with dust and mice feces from nests or surfaces with mice droppings or urine. Exposure to large numbers of rodents and their feces or urine presents the greatest risk. As hikers, we sometimes enter old buildings, and often deer mice live in these places. We may not be around long enough to be exposed, but do be aware of this disease. About half the people who develop HPS die. Symptoms are flu-like and appear about two to three weeks after exposure. After initial symptoms, a dry cough and shortness of breath follow. Breathing is difficult. If you even think you might have HPS, see a doctor immediately!

## NATURAL HAZARDS

Besides tripping over a rock or tree root on the trail, there are some real hazards to be aware of while hiking. Even if where you're hiking doesn't have the plethora of venomous snakes, poisonous plants, insects, and grizzly bears found in other parts of the United States, there are a few weather conditions and predators you may need to take into account.

**Lightning.** Thunderstorms build over the mountains almost every day during the summer. Lightning is generated by thunderheads and can strike without warning, even several miles away from the nearest overhead cloud. The best rule of thumb is to start leaving exposed peaks, ridges, and canyon rims by about noon. This time can vary a little depending on storm buildup. Keep an eye on cloud formation, and don't underestimate how fast a storm can build. The bigger they get, the more likely a thunderstorm will happen. Lightning takes the path of least resistance, so if you're the high point, it might choose you. Ducking under a rock overhang is dangerous, as you form the shortest path between the rock and ground. If you dash below tree line, avoid standing under the only or tallest tree. If you are caught above tree line, stay away from anything metal you might be carrying; move down off the ridge slightly to a low, treeless point; and squat until the storm passes. If you have an insulating pad, squat on it. Avoid having both your hands and feet touching the ground at once and never lay flat. If you hear a buzzing sound or feel your hair standing on end, move quickly, as an electrical charge is building up.

**Flash floods.** On July 31, 1976, a torrential downpour unleashed by a thunderstorm dumped tons of water into the Big Thompson watershed near Estes Park, Colorado. Within hours a wall of water moved down the narrow canyon, killing 139 people and causing more than 30 million dollars in property damage. The spooky thing about flash floods, especially in Western canyons, is that they can appear out of nowhere from a storm many miles away. While hiking or driving in canyons, keep an eye on the weather. Always climb to safety if danger threatens. Flash floods usually subside quickly, so be patient and don't cross a swollen stream.

**Bears.** Most of the United States (outside of the Pacific Northwest and parts of the Northern Rockies) does not have a grizzly bear population, although some rumors exist about sightings where there should be none. Black bears are plentiful, however. Here are some tips in case you and a bear scare each other. Most of all, avoid surprising a bear. Talk or sing where visibility or hearing is limited, such as along a rushing creek or in thick brush. In grizzly country especially, carry bear spray in a holster on your pack belt where you can quickly grab it. While hiking, watch for bear tracks (five toes), droppings (sizable with leaves, partly digested berries, seeds, and/or animal fur), or rocks and roots along the trail that show signs of being dug up (this could be a bear looking for bugs to eat). Keep a clean camp, hang food or use bear-proof storage containers, and don't sleep in the clothes you wore while cooking. Be especially careful to avoid getting between a mother and her cubs. In late summer and fall, bears are busy eating to fatten up for winter, so be extra careful around berry bushes and oakbrush. If you do encounter a bear, move away slowly while facing the bear, talk softly, and avoid direct eye contact. Give the bear room to escape. Since bears are very curious, it might stand upright to get a better whiff of you, and it may even charge you to try to intimidate you. Try to stay calm. If a black bear attacks you, fight back with anything you have handy. Do *not* play dead. Unleashed dogs have been known to come running back to their owners with a bear close behind. Keep your dog on a leash or leave it at home.

**Mountain lions.** Mountain lions appear to be getting more comfortable around humans, as long as deer (their favorite prey) are in an area with adequate cover. Usually elusive and quiet, lions rarely attack people. If you meet a lion, give it a chance to escape. Stay calm and talk firmly to it. Back away slowly while facing the lion. If you run, you'll only encourage the cat to chase you. Make yourself look large by opening a jacket, if you have one, or waving your hiking poles. If the lion behaves aggressively, throw stones, sticks, or whatever you can while remaining tall. If a lion does attack, fight for your life with anything you can grab.

**Moose.** Because moose have very few natural predators, they don't fear humans like other animals. You might find moose in sagebrush and wetter areas of willow, aspen, and pine, or in beaver habitats. Mothers with calves, as well as bulls during mating season, can be particularly aggressive. If a moose threatens you, back away slowly and talk calmly to it. Keep your pets away from moose.

**Other considerations.** Hunting is a popular sport in the United States, especially during rifle season in October and November. Hiking is still enjoyable in those months in many areas, so just take a few precautions. First, learn when the different hunting seasons start and end in the area in which you'll be hiking. During this time frame, be sure to wear at least a blaze-orange hat, and possibly put an orange vest over your pack. Don't be surprised to see hunters in camo outfits carrying bows or rifles around during their season. If you would feel more comfortable without hunters around, hike in national parks and monuments or state and local parks where hunting is not allowed.

## NAVIGATION

Whether you are going on a short hike in a familiar area or planning a week-long backpack trip, you should always be equipped with the proper navigational equipment—at the very least a detailed map and a sturdy compass.

**Maps.** There are many different types of maps available to help you find your way on the trail. Easiest to find are USDA Forest Service maps and BLM (Bureau of Land Management) maps. These maps tend to cover large areas, so be sure they are detailed enough for your particular trip. You can also obtain National Park Service maps as well as high-quality maps from private companies and trail groups. These maps can be obtained either from outdoor stores or ranger stations.

US Geological Survey topographic maps are particularly popular with hikers—especially serious backcountry hikers. These maps contain the standard map symbols such as roads, lakes, and rivers, as well as contour lines that show the details of the trail terrain like ridges, valleys, passes, and mountain peaks. The 7.5-minute series (1 inch on the map equals approximately ⅖ mile on the ground) provides the closest inspection available. USGS maps are available by mail (US Geological Survey, Map Distribution Branch, PO Box 25286, Denver, CO 80225), or at mapping.usgs.gov/esic/to_order.html.

If you want to check out the high-tech world of maps, you can download software-mapping programs that let you select a route on your computer, print it out, then take it with you on the trail. Some software mapping programs let you insert symbols and labels, download waypoints from a GPS unit, and export the maps to other software programs.

The art of map reading is a skill that you can develop by first practicing in an area you are familiar with. To begin, orient the map so it's lined up in the correct direction (i.e., north on the map is lined up with true north). Next, familiarize yourself with the map symbols and try and match them up with terrain features around you such as a high ridge, mountain peak, river, or lake. If you are practicing with a USGS map, notice the contour lines. On gentler terrain these contour lines are spaced farther apart, and on steeper terrain they are closer together. Pick a short loop trail, and stop frequently to check your position on the map. As you practice map reading, you'll learn how to anticipate a steep section on the trail or a good place to take a rest break, and so on.

**Compasses.** First off, the sun is not a substitute for a compass. So, what kind of compass should you have? Here are some characteristics you should look for: a rectangular base with detailed scales, a liquid-filled housing, protective housing, a sighting line on the mirror, luminous alignment and back-bearing arrows, a luminous north-seeking arrow, and a well-defined bezel ring.

You can learn compass basics by reading the detailed instructions included with your compass. If you want to fine-tune your compass skills, sign up for an orienteering class or purchase a book on compass reading. Once you've learned the basic skills of using a compass, remember to practice these skills before you head into the backcountry.

Handheld GPS units are now very common as well and can provide nearly pinpoint accuracy (within 30 to 60 feet).

There are many different types of GPS units available, and they range in price from 100 to 400 dollars. In addition to acting as a compass, the unit allows you to plot your route, easily retrace your path, track your traveling speed, find the mileage between waypoints, and calculate the total mileage of your route.

Before you purchase a GPS unit, keep in mind that these devices don't pick up signals indoors, in heavily wooded areas, on mountain peaks, or in deep valleys. Also, batteries can wear out or other technical problems can develop. A GPS unit should be used in conjunction with a map and compass, not in place of those items.

**Pedometers.** A pedometer is a small, clip-on unit with a digital display that calculates your hiking distance in miles or kilometers based on your walking stride. Some units also calculate the calories you burn and your total hiking time. Pedometers are available at most large outdoor stores and range in price from 20 to 40 dollars. Most smartphones come with a pedometer already installed; if your phone doesn't have this feature, you can download the app from your app store.

## TRIP PLANNING

Planning your hiking adventure begins with letting a friend or relative know your trip itinerary so he or she can call for help if you don't return at your scheduled time. Your next task is to make sure you are outfitted to experience the risks and rewards of the trail. This section highlights gear and clothing you may want to take with you to get the most out of your hike.

### Day Hikes
- bear repellent spray (if hiking in grizzly country)
- camera
- compass/GPS unit
- day pack
- first-aid kit
- fleece jacket
- food
- guidebook
- hat
- headlamp/flashlight with extra batteries and bulbs
- insect repellent
- knife/multipurpose tool
- map
- matches in waterproof container and fire starter
- pedometer
- rain gear
- space blanket
- sunglasses
- sunscreen
- swimsuit and/or fishing gear (if hiking to a lake)
- watch
- water
- water bottles/water hydration system

### Overnight Trip

- backpack and waterproof rain cover
- backpacker's trowel
- bandanna
- bear bell
- bear repellent spray (if hiking in grizzly country)
- biodegradable soap
- clothing—extra wool socks, shirt, and shorts
- collapsible water container (2–3 gallon capacity)
- cook set/utensils
- ditty bags to store gear
- extra plastic resealable bags
- gaiters
- garbage bag
- ground cloth
- journal/pen
- long underwear
- nylon rope to hang food
- permit (if required)
- pot scrubber
- rain jacket and pants
- sandals to wear around camp and to ford streams
- sleeping bag
- sleeping pad
- small bath towel
- stove and fuel
- tent
- toiletry items
- water filter
- waterproof stuff sack
- whistle

## EQUIPMENT

With the outdoor market currently flooded with products, many of which are pure gimmickry, it seems impossible to both differentiate and choose. Do I really need a tropical-fish-lined collapsible shower? (No, you don't.) The only defense against the maddening quantity of items thrust in your face is to think practically—and to do so before you go shopping. The worst buys are impulsive buys. Since most name brands will differ only slightly in quality, it's best to know what you're looking for in terms of function. Buy only what you need. You will, don't forget, be carrying what you've bought on your back. Here are some things to keep in mind before you go shopping.

**Clothes.** Clothing is your armor against Mother Nature's little surprises. Hikers should be prepared for any possibility, especially when hiking in mountainous areas. Adequate rain protection and extra layers of clothing are a good idea. In summer a wide-brimmed hat can help keep the sun at bay. In the winter months the first layer you'll want to wear is a "wicking" layer of long underwear that keeps perspiration away from your skin. Wear long underwear made from synthetic fibers that wick moisture away from the skin and draw it toward the next layer of clothing, where it then evaporates. Avoid wearing long underwear made of cotton, as it is slow to dry and keeps moisture next to your skin.

The second layer you'll wear is the "insulating" layer. Aside from keeping you warm, this layer needs to "breathe" so you stay dry while hiking. A fabric that provides insulation and dries quickly is fleece. It's interesting to note that this one-of-a-kind fabric is made out of recycled plastic. Purchasing a zip-up jacket made of this material is highly recommended.

The last line of layering defense is the "shell" layer. You'll need some type of waterproof, windproof, breathable jacket that will fit over all of your other layers. It should have a large hood that fits over a hat. You'll also need a good pair of rain pants made from a similar waterproof, breathable fabric. Some Gore-Tex jackets cost as much as 500 dollars, but you should know that there are more affordable fabrics out there that work just as well.

Now that you've learned the basics of layering, you can't forget to protect your hands and face. In cold, windy, or rainy weather, you'll need a hat made of wool or fleece, and insulated, waterproof gloves that will keep your hands warm and toasty. As mentioned earlier, buying an additional pair of light silk liners to wear under your regular gloves is a good idea.

**Footwear.** If you have any extra money to spend on your trip, put that money into boots or trail shoes. Poor shoes will bring a hike to a halt faster than anything else. To avoid this annoyance, buy shoes that provide support and are lightweight and flexible. A lightweight hiking boot is better than a heavy, leather mountaineering boot for most day hikes and backpacking. Trail running shoes provide a little extra cushion and are made in a high-top style that many people wear for hiking. These running shoes are lighter, more flexible, and more breathable than hiking boots. If you know you'll be hiking in wet weather often, purchase boots or shoes with a Gore-Tex liner, which will help keep your feet dry.

When shopping for boots, be sure to wear the same type of socks you'll be wearing on the trail. If the boots you're buying are for cold weather hiking, try the boots on while wearing two pairs of socks. Speaking of socks, a good cold weather sock combination is to wear a thinner sock made of wool or polypropylene covered by a heavier outer sock made of wool or a synthetic/wool mix. The inner sock protects the foot from the rubbing effects of the outer sock and prevents blisters. Many outdoor stores have some type of ramp to simulate hiking uphill and downhill. Be sure to take advantage of this test, as toe-jamming boot fronts can be very painful and debilitating on the downhill trek.

Once you've purchased your footwear, be sure to break it in before you hit the trail. New footwear is often stiff and needs to be stretched and molded to your foot.

**Hiking poles.** Hiking poles help with balance and, more important, take pressure off your knees. The ones with shock absorbers are easier on your elbows and knees. Some poles even come with a camera attachment to be used as a monopod. And heaven forbid you meet a mountain lion, bear, or unfriendly dog, the poles can make you look a lot bigger.

**Backpacks.** No matter what type of hiking you do, you'll need a pack of some sort to carry the basic trail essentials. There are a variety of backpacks on the market, but let's first discuss what you intend to use it for. Day hikes or overnight trips?

If you plan on doing a day hike, a day pack should have some of the following characteristics: a padded hip belt that's at least 2 inches in diameter (avoid packs with only a small nylon piece of webbing for a hip belt); a chest strap (the chest strap helps stabilize the pack against your body); external pockets to carry water and other items that you want easy access to; an internal pocket to hold keys, a knife, a wallet, and other miscellaneous items; an external lashing system to hold a jacket; and, if you so desire, a hydration pocket for carrying a hydration system (which consists of a water bladder with an attachable drinking hose).

For short hikes some hikers like to use a fanny pack to store just a camera, food, a compass, a map, and other trail essentials. Most fanny packs have pockets for two water bottles and a padded hip belt.

If you intend to do an extended, overnight trip, there are multiple considerations. First off, you need to decide what kind of framed pack you want. There are two backpack types for backpacking: the internal frame and the external frame. An internal frame pack rests closer to your body, making it more stable and easier to balance when hiking over rough terrain. An external frame pack is just that, an aluminum frame attached to the exterior of the pack. Some hikers consider an external frame pack to be better for long backpacking trips because it distributes the pack weight better and allows you to carry heavier loads. It's often easier to pack, and your gear is more accessible. It also offers better back ventilation in hot weather.

The most critical measurement for fitting a pack is torso length. The pack needs to rest evenly on your hips without sagging. A good pack will come in two or three sizes and have straps and hip belts that are adjustable according to your body size and characteristics.

When you purchase a backpack, go to an outdoor store with salespeople who are knowledgeable in how to properly fit a pack. Once the pack is fitted for you, load the pack with the amount of weight you plan on taking on the trail. The weight of the pack should be distributed evenly, and you should be able to swing your arms and walk briskly without feeling out of balance. Another good technique for evaluating a pack is to walk up and down stairs and make quick turns to the right and to the left to be sure the pack doesn't feel out of balance. Other features that are nice to have on a backpack include a removable day pack or fanny pack, external pockets for extra water, and extra lash points to attach a jacket or other items.

**Sleeping bags and pads.** Sleeping bags are rated by temperature. You can purchase a bag made with synthetic insulation, or you can buy a goose down bag. Goose down bags are more expensive, but they have a higher insulating capacity by weight and will keep their loft longer. You'll want to purchase a bag with a temperature rating that fits the time of year and conditions you are most likely to camp in. One caveat: The techno-standard for temperature ratings is far from perfect. Ratings vary from manufacturer to manufacturer, so to protect yourself you should purchase a bag rated 10 to 15 degrees below the temperature you expect to be camping in. Synthetic bags are more resistant to water than down bags, but many down bags are now made with a Gore-Tex shell that helps to repel water. Down bags are also more compressible than synthetic bags and take up less room in your pack, which is an important consideration if you are planning a multiday backpack trip. Features to look for in a sleeping bag include a mummy-style bag, a hood you can cinch down around your head in cold weather, and draft tubes along the zippers that help keep heat in and drafts out.

You'll also want a sleeping pad to provide insulation and padding from the cold ground. There are different types of sleeping pads available, from the more expensive self-inflating air mattresses to the less expensive closed-cell foam pads. Self-inflating air mattresses are usually heavier than closed-cell foam mattresses and are prone to punctures.

**Tents.** The tent is your home away from home while on the trail. It provides protection from wind, rain, snow, and insects. A three-season tent is a good choice for backpacking and can range in price from 100 to 500 dollars. These lightweight and versatile tents provide protection in all types of weather, except heavy snowstorms or high winds, and range in weight from 4 to 8 pounds. Look for a tent that's easy to set up and will easily fit two people with gear. Dome type tents usually offer more headroom and places to store gear. Other handy tent features include a vestibule where you can store wet boots and backpacks. Some nice-to-have items in a tent include interior pockets to store small items and lashing points to hang a clothesline. Most three-season tents also come with stakes so you can secure the tent in high winds. Before you purchase a tent, set it up and take it down a few times to be sure it is easy to handle. Also, sit inside the tent and make sure it has enough room for you and your gear.

**Cell phones.** Many hikers are carrying their cell phones into the backcountry these days in case of emergency. That's fine and good, but please know that cell phone coverage is often poor to nonexistent in valleys, canyons, and thick forest. More important, people have started to call for help because they're tired or lost. Let's go back to being prepared. You are responsible for yourself in the backcountry. Use your brain to avoid problems, and if you do encounter one, first use your brain to try to correct the situation. Only use your cell phone, if it works, in true emergencies. If it doesn't work down low in a valley, try hiking to a high point where you might get reception.

## HIKING WITH CHILDREN

Hiking with children isn't a matter of how many miles you can cover or how much elevation gain you make in a day; it's about seeing and experiencing nature through their eyes.

Kids like to explore and have fun. They like to stop and point out bugs and plants, look under rocks, jump in puddles, and throw sticks. If you're taking a toddler or young child on a hike, start with a trail that you're familiar with. Trails that have interesting things for kids, like piles of leaves to play in or a small stream to wade through during the summer, will make the hike much more enjoyable for them and will keep them from getting bored.

You can keep your child's attention if you have a strategy before starting on the trail. Using games is not only an effective way to keep a child's attention, it's also a great way to teach him or her about nature. Quiz children on the names of plants and animals. Pick up a family-friendly outdoor hobby like Geocaching (www.geocaching.com) or Letterboxing (www.atlasquest.com; www.letterboxing.org), both of which combine the outdoors, clue solving, and treasure hunting. If your children are old enough, let them carry their own day pack filled with snacks and water. So that you are sure to go at their pace and not yours, let them lead the way. Playing follow the leader works particularly well when you have a group of children. Have each child take a turn at being the leader.

With children, a lot of clothing is key. The only thing predictable about weather is that it will change. Especially in mountainous areas, weather can change dramatically in a very short time. Always bring extra clothing for children, regardless of the season. In the winter, have your children wear wool socks and warm layers such as long underwear, a fleece jacket and hat, wool mittens, and good rain gear. It's not a bad idea to have these along in late fall and early spring as well. Good footwear is also important. A sturdy pair of high-top tennis shoes or lightweight hiking boots are the best bet for little ones. If you're hiking in the summer near a lake or stream, bring along a pair of old sneakers that your child can put on when he or she wants to go exploring in the water. Remember when you're near any type of water, always watch your child at all times. Also, keep a close eye on teething toddlers, who may decide a rock or leaf of poison oak is an interesting item to put in their mouth.

From spring through fall, you'll want your kids to wear a wide-brimmed hat to keep their face, head, and ears protected from the hot sun. Also, make sure your children wear sunscreen at all times. Choose a brand without Paba—children have sensitive skin and may have an allergic reaction to sunscreen that contains Paba. If you are hiking with a child younger than 6 months, don't use sunscreen or insect repellent. Instead, be sure that their head, face, neck, and ears are protected from the sun with a wide-brimmed hat and that all other exposed skin is protected from the sun with the appropriate clothing.

Remember that food is fun. Kids like snacks, so it's important to bring a lot of munchies for the trail. Stopping often for snack breaks is a fun way to keep the trail interesting. Raisins, apples, granola bars, crackers and cheese, cereal, and trail mix all make great snacks. Also, a few of their favorite candy treats can go a long way toward heading off a fit of fussing. If your child is old enough to carry his or her own backpack, let him or her fill it with some lightweight "comfort" items such as a doll, a small stuffed animal, or a little toy (you'll have to draw the line at bringing the 10-pound Tonka truck). If your kids don't like drinking water, you can bring some powdered drink mix or a juice box.

Avoid poorly designed child-carrying packs—you don't want to break your back carrying your child. Most child-carrying backpacks designed to hold a 40-pound child will contain a large carrying pocket to hold diapers and other items. Some have an optional rain/sun hood.

## HIKING WITH YOUR DOG

Bringing your furry friend with you is always more fun than leaving him behind. Our canine pals make great trail buddies because they never complain and always make good company. Hiking with your dog can be a rewarding experience, especially if you plan ahead.

**Getting your dog in shape.** Before you plan outdoor adventures with your dog, make sure he's in shape for the trail. Getting your dog into shape takes the same discipline as getting yourself into shape, but luckily, your dog can get in shape with you. Take your dog with you on your daily runs or walks. If there is a park near your house, hit a tennis ball or play Frisbee with your dog.

Swimming is also an excellent way to get your dog into shape. If there is a lake or river near where you live and your dog likes the water, have her retrieve a tennis ball or stick. Gradually build your dog's stamina up over a two- to three-month period. A good rule of thumb is to assume that your dog will travel twice as far as you will on the trail. If you plan on doing a 5-mile hike, be sure your dog is in shape for a 10-mile hike.

**Training your dog for the trail.** Before you go on your first hiking adventure with your dog, be sure he has a firm grasp on the basics of canine etiquette and behavior. Make sure he can sit, lie down, stay, and come. One of the most important commands you can teach your canine pal is to "come" under any situation. It's easy for your friend's nose to lead him astray or possibly get lost. Another helpful command is the "get behind" command. When you're on a hiking trail that's narrow, you can have your dog follow behind you when other trail users approach. Nothing is more bothersome than an enthusiastic dog that runs back and forth on the trail and disrupts the peace of the trail for others—or, worse, jumps up on other hikers and gets them muddy. When you see other trail users approaching you on the trail, give them the right of way by quietly stepping off the trail and making your dog lie down and stay until they pass.

**Equipment.** The most critical pieces of equipment you can invest in for your dog are proper identification and a sturdy leash. Flexi-leads work well for hiking because they give your dog more freedom to explore but still leave you in control. Make sure your dog has identification that includes your name and address and a number for your veterinarian. Other forms of identification for your dog include a tattoo or microchip. You should consult your veterinarian for more information on these last two options.

The next piece of equipment you'll want to consider is a pack for your dog. By no means should you hold all of your dog's essentials in your pack—let her carry her own gear! Dogs that are in good shape can carry 30 to 40 percent of their own weight.

Most packs are fitted by a dog's weight and girth measurement. Companies that make dog packs generally include guidelines to help you pick out the size that's right for your dog. Some characteristics to look for when purchasing a pack for your dog include a harness that contains two padded girth straps, a padded chest strap, leash attachments, removable saddlebags, internal water bladders, and external gear cords.

You can introduce your dog to the pack by first placing the empty pack on his back and letting him wear it around the yard. Keep an eye on him during this first introduction. He may decide to chew through the straps if you aren't watching him closely. Once he learns to treat the pack as an object of fun and not a foreign enemy, fill the pack evenly on both sides with a few ounces of dog food in resealable plastic bags. Have your dog wear his pack on your daily walks for a period of two to three weeks. Each week add a little more weight to the pack until your dog will accept carrying the maximum amount of weight he can carry.

You can also purchase collapsible water and dog food bowls for your dog. These bowls are lightweight and can easily be stashed into your pack or your dog's. If you are hiking on rocky terrain or in the snow, you can purchase footwear for your dog that will protect her feet from cuts and bruises.

Always carry plastic bags to remove feces from the trail. It is a courtesy to other trail users and helps protect local wildlife.

The following is a list of items to bring when you take your dog hiking: collapsible water bowls, a comb, a collar and a leash, dog food, plastic bags for feces, a dog pack, flea/tick powder, paw protection, water, and a first-aid kit that contains eye ointment, tweezers, scissors, stretchy foot wrap, gauze, antibacterial wash, sterile cotton-tip applicators, antibiotic ointment, and cotton wrap.

**First aid for your dog.** Your dog is just as prone—if not more prone—to getting in trouble on the trail as you are, so be prepared. Here's a rundown of the more likely misfortunes that might befall your little friend.

*Bees and wasps.* If a bee or wasp stings your dog, remove the stinger with a pair of tweezers and place a mudpack or a cloth dipped in cold water over the affected area.

*Porcupines.* One good reason to keep your dog on a leash is to prevent him from getting a nose full of porcupine quills. You may be able to remove the quills with pliers, but a veterinarian is the best person to do this nasty job, because most dogs need to be sedated.

*Heatstroke.* Avoid hiking with your dog in really hot weather. Dogs with heatstroke will pant excessively, lie down and refuse to get up, and become lethargic and disoriented. If your dog shows any of these signs on the trail, have her lie down in the shade. If you are near a stream, pour cool water over your dog's entire body to help bring her body temperature back to normal.

*Heartworm.* Dogs get heartworm from mosquitoes, which carry the disease in the prime mosquito months of July and August. Giving your dog a monthly pill prescribed by your veterinarian easily prevents this condition.

*Plant pitfalls.* One of the biggest plant hazards for dogs on the trail are foxtails. Foxtails are pointed grass seed heads that bury themselves in your friend's fur, between his toes, and even get in his ear canal. If left unattended, these nasty seeds can work their way under the skin and cause abscesses and other problems. If you have a long-haired dog, consider trimming the hair between his toes and giving him a summer haircut to help prevent foxtails from attaching to his fur. After every hike, always inspect your dog for these seeds—especially his ears and between his toes.

Other plant hazards include burrs, thorns, thistles, and poison oak. If you find any burrs or thistles on your dog, remove them as soon as possible before they become an unmanageable mat. Thorns can pierce a dog's foot and cause a great deal of pain. If you see that your dog is lame, stop and check her feet for thorns. Dogs are immune to poison oak, but they can pick up the sticky, oily substance from the plant and transfer it to you.

*Protect those paws.* Be sure to keep your dog's nails trimmed so he avoids getting soft tissue or joint injuries. If your dog slows and refuses to go on, check to see that his paws aren't torn or worn. You can protect your dog's paws from trail hazards such as sharp gravel, foxtails, lava scree, and thorns by purchasing and using dog boots.

*Sunburn.* If your dog has light skin, she is an easy target for sunburn on her nose and other exposed skin areas. You can apply a nontoxic sunscreen to exposed skin areas that will help protect her from overexposure to the sun.

*Ticks and fleas.* Ticks can easily give your dog Lyme disease, as well as other diseases. Before you hit the trail, ask your veterinarian about once-a-month treatments that repel fleas and ticks. There are also tick sprays and powders that you can apply just prior to hitting the trail.

*Mosquitoes and deerflies.* These little flying machines can do a job on your dog's snout and ears. Best bet is to spray your dog with fly repellent for horses to discourage both pests.

*Giardia.* Dogs can get giardia, which results in diarrhea. It is usually not debilitating, but it's definitely messy. A vaccine against giardia is available.

*Mushrooms.* Make sure your dog doesn't sample mushrooms along the trail. They could be poisonous to him, but he doesn't know that.

When you are finally ready to hit the trail with your dog, keep in mind that national parks and many wilderness areas do not allow dogs on trails. Your best bet is to hike in national forests, BLM lands, and state parks. Always call ahead to see what the restrictions are.

# Hike Index

# About the Authors

**John L. Young** was born and raised in Altoona, Pennsylvania. He has a degree in journalism and is a former newspaper reporter and columnist. His outdoor and travel articles have appeared in *Ohio* magazine, *Pennsylvania* magazine, and *Pursuits*, a publication of the Pennsylvania Tourism Office. His books include the career guide *Unemployed No More*; two historical, true-crime books, *Murder at the Airport Inn* and *Murder in the Courtroom*; and the true-life novel *From Pithole to Paradise*. He is also the author of two other FALCONGUIDES: *Hiking Pennsylvania* (fourth edition) and *Hiking the Poconos*. His love affair with the woods and mountains of Pennsylvania began at age 12, when he started deer hunting with his father and brother at their camp on Tussey Mountain in Huntington County.

**Debra Young** was also raised in Pennsylvania. She has a BS in education and an MA in counseling, as well as certificates in special education supervision and school administration from Edinboro University. She is a retired administrator from Warren County School District in Warren, Pennsylvania, and has worked as an adjunct at Jamestown Community College, Jamestown, New York. Her love for the outdoors began at an early age on the family farm and grew to include camping, biking, kayaking, hiking, and cross-country skiing in the Allegheny National Forest with her husband John.

Debra and John have hiked the Oak Creek Canyon Area of Sedona, Arizona, searching for the fabled vortexes, and the Presidential Range of the White Mountains in New Hampshire. They have biked the Great Allegheny Passage Rails-to-Trails bike path in western Pennsylvania, kayaked in the Gulf of Mexico, and have spent a brisk, rainy day hiking in Talkeetna, Alaska.

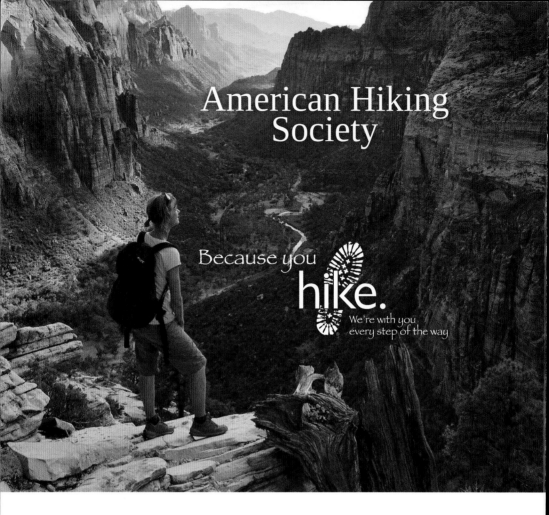

# American Hiking Society

Because you

hike.

We're with you
every step of the way